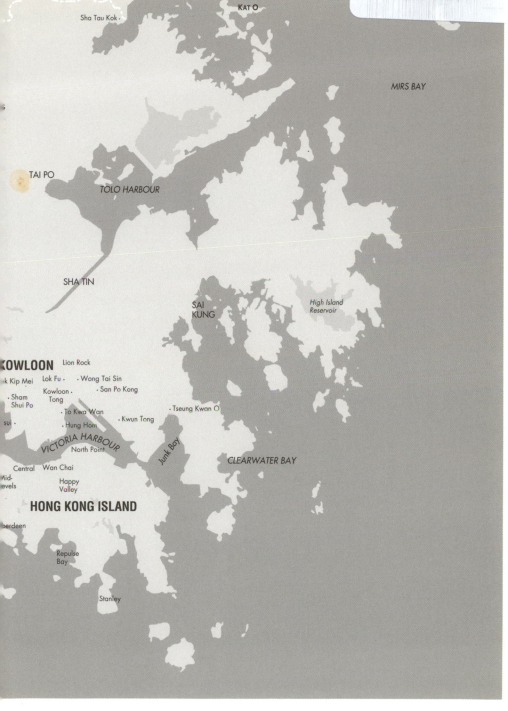

Sha Tau Kok

KAT O

MIRS BAY

TAI PO

TOLO HARBOUR

SHA TIN

SAI
KUNG

High Island
Reservoir

KOWLOON   Lion Rock

k Kip Mei   Lok Fu ·   · Wong Tai Sin

· Sham   Kowloon   · San Po Kong
Shui Po   Tong

· To Kwa Wan   · Tseung Kwan O

sui   · Hung Hom   · Kwun Tong

VICTORIA HARBOUR
North Point   Junk Bay   CLEARWATER BAY

Central   Wan Chai

Mid-   Happy
levels   Valley

HONG KONG ISLAND

berdeen

Repulse
Bay

Stanley

HONG KONG REMEMBERS

HONG KONG
REMEMBERS

With a Foreword by
the Rt. Hon. the Baroness Thatcher

Sally Blyth and Ian Wotherspoon

HONG KONG
OXFORD UNIVERSITY PRESS
OXFORD NEW YORK

Oxford University Press
Oxford New York
Athens Auckland Bangkok Bogota Bombay
Buenos Aires Calcutta Cape Town Dar es Salaam
Delhi Florence Hong Kong Istanbul Karachi
Kuala Lumpur Madras Madrid Melbourne
Mexico City Nairobi Paris Singapore
Taipei Tokyo Toronto
and associated companies in
Berlin Ibadan

Oxford is a trade mark of Oxford University Press

First published 1996
This impression (lowest digit)
5 7 9 10 8 6 4

Published in the United States
by Oxford University Press, New York

© Oxford University Press 1996

British Library Cataloguing in Publication Data
available

Library of Congress Cataloging-in-Publication Data
available

ISBN 0-19-587768-3

Printed in Hong Kong
Published by Oxford University Press (China) Ltd
18/F Warwick House, Taikoo Place, 979 King's Road,
Quarry Bay, Hong Kong

Acknowledgements

We owe a particular debt of gratitude to the people whose recollections appear in this book. All of them have given us a great deal of their time, and have spoken with candour and sincerity about their recollections of the past and hopes for the future.

Helpful editorial comments were made by Professor Joseph Cheng, Trevor Clark, and Neville Patterson, who each read all or parts of the manuscript.

We have profited greatly from the advice and suggestions of Cliff Bale, Patricia Blott, Alan Blyth, Elizabeth Bosher, Sir Jack and Lady Cater, Lindzay Chan, Mary Child, Sheri Dorfman, Cyrus Fung, Leo Goodstadt, Mike Hanson, Kent Kan, Edward Llewellyn, Rebecca Lloyd, David Mace, Richard Margolis, Kerry McGlynn, Peter Mok, Rebecca Ng, and others who would prefer to remain anonymous. A great number of other friends and colleagues have also readily offered advice and we are also extremely grateful to them.

We should like to make specific mention of Lucas Wun whose unrivalled knowledge of Hong Kong affairs, together with his linguistic skills, have played an important and vital part in the compiling and writing of this book.

Leisa and Ken Griggs, Wendy Larkin, Mandy Wong, and Louisa Kwok all worked on the preparation of the manuscript, and we gratefully acknowledge the assistance and support they have provided. Thanks should also go to Phil Smith for his technical assistance.

Finally, and we are aware of the form behind the words, we are grateful to our respective families without whose help and encouragement this book would never have been contemplated or completed.

The authors and publishers would like to thank the contributors to this book for providing photographs and illustrations, as well as the following for providing photographs: Trevor Clark, pp. 36, 111; Hong Kong Government Information Service, pp. 46, 55, 113, 130, 131; Peter Hookham, p. 227; The Maryknoll Sisters' School, p. 159; N.C.N. Ltd, p. 167; South China Morning Post Ltd, p. 108; John and Veronica Stericker, p. 1.

Foreword

By the Rt. Hon. the Baroness Thatcher, LG, OM, FRS

Fifty years ago, Hong Kong was impoverished by war and occupation. Today it is one of the most successful and thriving places on earth— a leading international financial centre, and an economic powerhouse in the booming Asia Pacific.

The Chinese people of Hong Kong are some of the most enterprising in the world. Their vigour has worked wonders within the fabric of a free economy, the rule of law, and the excellent administration that have been Britain's most important contributions to the Territory.

Hong Kong Remembers charts Hong Kong's history over the last six decades through the eyes of some of those who have made it. Their spirit—the essence of Hong Kong—shines through the pages; their resilience, determination, and irrepressible energy come alive. It is those qualities that give me great confidence that the Territory's future under Chinese sovereignty will continue on its successful path.

Margaret Thatcher

Contents

Introduction

Since the end of the Second World War, Hong Kong's largely Chinese refugee population has created a dynamic and cosmopolitan society which draws its strength and vision from both East and West, and stands on the frontier between them. This book provides a personalized and very human overview, by a cross-section of Hong Kong people, of some of the key events and issues which have combined over the past sixty years to create today's Hong Kong.

The celebrated and not so celebrated tell how they see their recent past, and give voice to the character and essence of Hong Kong, and to the perceptions and spirit of its people. Here are family stories and childhood memories; tales of revolution, war, and hardship, and of the opportunities that peace, hard work, and good luck can bring; recollections of hard graft and crime, and the triumph of the human spirit in the face of adversity; of frustrated ambition and the politics of yesterday; of democracy and freedom, and hope for the future.

These recollections are as diverse as the backgrounds and experiences of the interviewees. They range from communists to business people, émigrés to bankers, students to Hong Kong's governors, a newspaper editor and a rural community leader, a policeman and a cartoonist, a hairdresser and an industrialist, the leader of a political party and a nun. Together they provide a view of Hong Kong's recent past which is perceptive without being academic, authentic without being pedestrian, sharply drawn, highly individual, often affectionate and, in many cases, deeply religious. Though many political opinions are put forth—and Hong Kong's political life is by necessity a matter for discussion—this collection does not endorse one political viewpoint over another.

The book is divided into five sections each covering a decade since World War II. (The first chapter deals with a slightly longer period from before the war to the late 1950s). Although many of those interviewed could have provided recollections of many years, we have tried to restrict each interviewee to a particular decade when he or she (or a relative) was involved in key events at that time, or whose experiences typify that era in some way. Thus, although Sir Jack Cater's distinguished public service career in Hong Kong spanned nearly thirty years, he is interviewed about the 1960s, and reminisces about the 1967 disturbances. Similarly, Anna Sohmen, Sir Y. K. Pao's daughter, discusses her father's role in challenging the dominance of expatriate-owned and managed business enterprises in the 1980s. Tsang Yok Sing who, as leader of the pro-China party, was most influential in the 1990s, talks about the 1960s, describing his role in the 1967 riots, and his own conversion to Marxism at that time. While at pains to provide as broad a cross-section of the community as possible, we have also tried to interview people who remain in Hong Kong.

This book does not present a strict chronological approach to the events of each decade, nor does it provide a comprehensive history of Hong Kong since 1945. Some interviewees recall specific incidents: others range back in time—to Shanghai in the 1930s or to the 1960s in Guangdong—revealing the background to the events and people that made that decade memorable.

Where further explanation is needed this has been provided in square brackets; we have also shown pinyin romanizations in square brackets where appropriate. The views expressed in this book are the authors' own, and do not necessarily represent those of the individuals interviewed or of any other person or organization. A number of the interviews were conducted in Cantonese. We have endeavoured to ensure that individuals' recollections have been translated as clearly and accurately as possible.

A Hong Kong person is a complicated creature. Few recollections begin and end solely in the Territory, and few Chinese people discuss their roles and identities entirely separately from the context of their extended families. Whilst these recollections sometimes stray from a narrow discussion of public events in Hong Kong, the end result is a broader, richer, and more colourful picture of Hong Kong's recent past than a conventional history could provide.

Revolution and Refugees

1940s— 1950s

In 1945, British Prime Minister Winston Churchill declared that Hong Kong would be eliminated from the British Empire 'over my dead body'. But the British almost did lose Hong Kong before the end of that year. With the surrender of the Japanese in August, the Chinese Nationalist army, together with United States forces, were poised to sweep through Guangzhou (Canton) to liberate the Colony and restore it to Chinese sovereignty. An uneasy compromise was reached when the Commander of the British Far Eastern fleet, Rear Admiral Sir Cecil Harcourt entered Hong Kong Harbour on HMS *Swiftsure* on 30 August. He subsequently accepted the formal Japanese surrender, in a ceremony on 16 September, on behalf of China as well as Britain.

By 15 August, the Japanese had surrendered throughout Asia and the Pacific, but it was thanks to the pre-war Hong Kong Government Colonial Secretary, Franklin Gimson, that it was the British flag which was flown, metaphorically if not literally, during the intervening weeks until the arrival of the British forces. Franklin Gimson had arrived in Hong Kong to take up his post just three weeks before Hong Kong surrendered to the Japanese on Christmas Day 1941. With the capture and imprisonment in China of the pre-war Governor, Sir Mark Young, Gimson declared himself in August 1945 to be the highest voice of authority of the 'legitimate' government of Hong Kong. Following their release from the Stanley internment camp on Hong Kong Island, he and other government officials assumed their pre-war roles until the arrival of Sir Cecil Harcourt.

As the British Pacific Fleet lay at anchor off Victoria, one onlooker noted that now the people of Hong Kong would 'eat again'. Nobody really cared very much that the British had returned—only that the Japanese were going. Sullen and resentful, disarmed Japanese regulars awaited repatriation whilst their war-time civilian supporters melted into the shadows, fearful of a timely settling of scores in the unlit lanes and alleys off Hong Kong's bomb damaged waterfront.

The scars of those who had lived through the occupation were deep. For those civilians interned in Stanley, there had been the daily battle to maintain morale against a bleak existence of inadequate food and medical supplies, as well as all the vagaries of living in close confinement. In the military prisoner-of-war (POW) camps at Sham

Shui Po and Argyle Street, the regime had been much tougher. POWs were used for hard labour on a range of military projects with scant regard to their welfare or, indeed, their survival. The penalties for those who tried to escape from the POW camps were severe, but despite this, nearly a thousand did so successfully, aided in part by local volunteers, working for the British Army Aid Group (BAAG) based in Chungking (Chongqing)—China's wartime capital in Sichuan province—and the Communist guerrilla forces in Kowloon and the New Territories.

It was not only prisoners of war and the interned expatriates who had suffered, but the territory's Chinese population as well. There were chronic shortages of food, firewood, and medicine, compounded by arbitrary arrests and executions.

'Trouble in Hong Kong, go back to China; trouble in China, return to Hong Kong' was the old adage, and many took that advice despite the dangers and hardships involved. In 1940 Hong Kong's population stood at just over one and a half million; by 1945 it was a third of that number. But by the end of 1946 it was back to pre-war levels, and expanding rapidly. During the following decade a million people flooded over the border from China—an average of nearly three hundred people a day—bringing the total population in the mid-1950s to around two and a half million. As far as the Hong Kong Government was concerned, it was a population which was regarded (wrongly as it turned out), as largely transitory.

The embryo civilian administration faced daunting problems of reconstruction. Public facilities and private property had been looted, the Kowloon–Canton Railway was barely operating, and there was no petrol for other public transport. The people were malnourished and sick, and it was hard to maintain even basic supplies of electricity and gas.

Sir Mark Young, appointed Governor in 1941, returned to his post in 1946 after four miserable years of Japanese captivity. He was aided by the man who had headed the interim administration, Brigadier David MacDougall. Well liked and energetic, MacDougall was appointed as Colonial Secretary to Sir Mark, and has been credited for doing much to revitalize Hong Kong in the immediate post-war years. Sir Mark immediately set about initiating constitutional reforms aimed at introducing a limited form of democracy, which the Colonial Office enjoined on all its territories. But he was never able to see these through. Tired and ill from his war-time experiences, he made way in 1947 for Sir Alexander Grantham.

Sir Alexander's arrival coincided with the alarming realization that elections could become a focus for competing Nationalist (Kuomintang) and Communist rivalries. It was felt that measures intended to lead progressively to self-government did not accord with Hong Kong's relations with new China, nor with the Territory's transient population. The new Governor therefore deferred indefinitely all proposals for any form of constitutional change. It was almost thirty years before the question of political reform was looked at seriously again.

The British had returned to govern Hong Kong, but by the time Sir Alexander had become Governor, there was a recognition that pre-war Hong Kong values might not be sustained. The occupation had demonstrated both the vulnerability of the British and the key role played by the local population in resisting the Japanese. Whilst British political and business interests dominated, it was clear that the Chinese community was playing an increasingly important role in commerce and trade, if not in politics. The Communist victory in China reinforced this trend, as more and more refugees arrived from across the border.

Sir Alexander Grantham remained in office for ten and a half years— the second longest tenure of any of Hong Kong's governors. Many have paid tribute to the way he held the Territory together, through extremely troublesome times, and he is viewed by those who have worked with the majority of Hong Kong's post-war governors, as one of the best. By the time Sir Alexander retired at the end of 1957 trade with China had resumed, Hong Kong had re-established itself as one of the world's busiest entrepôt ports, and the Hong Kong economy had dramatically expanded into manufacturing.

Hong Kong's industrial revolution was propelled by the political revolution in China. The flood of refugees following the Communist victory in 1949, provided Hong Kong with the ready availability of a motivated, hard-working, labour force. Added to this was the combined capital, drive, and expertise of the hundreds of Shanghainese, who began arriving in large numbers in 1948.

Moreover, external circumstances also forced the Territory to look beyond its narrow economic base as a China trading centre. The United

Nations trade embargo on China, as a result of the Korean War (1950–53), had a disastrous effect on the Territory's entrepôt trade. Overnight exports to China of a wide range of goods were banned. Hong Kong's economic lifeline vanished, and it was feared that the remarkable post-war recovery would come to a halt. It was then, with the help of the Shanghainese, that Hong Kong's manufacturing base started to expand rapidly. Within two decades Hong Kong had become the world's leading textile manufacturer.

The large influx of dispossessed refugees gave rise to serious social problems—shortages of adequate housing, education, and medical care to treat the diseases which spread rapidly in the overcrowded conditions. By and large, the Government's attitude was that it saw no reason to provide for the new arrivals. It had neither the finances nor the will, since these workers were seen as a transitory population.

As a result, home for the majority of Hong Kong's population consisted of flimsy wooden, oil-cloth, and corrugated-iron squatter huts, which covered the foothills around the harbour, and below Lion Rock in Kowloon. These homes were always vulnerable to destruction from typhoons and natural disasters, but it took a major squatter camp fire at Shek Kip Mei on Christmas Day 1953 to shake the Government into action. Over fifty thousand people were made homeless, leaving the administration with little option but to initiate a programme of land clearance and basic construction to provide low cost housing. This was done under the auspices of a newly established Resettlement Department.

However, the parallel provision of publicly funded educational, health, and social facilities was slow. Dominated by a *laissez-faire* mentality, Government investment in new clinics and schools was minimal despite burgeoning demand. The newly reconstituted colonial Government relied on the services of churches, charities, and voluntary agencies to fulfil the need for basic health care and education for many Hong Kong families. Hong Kong received almost no financial support from Britain, which itself was suffering from the aftermath of war.

For most, the focus was on making a dollar rather than on politics, despite the underlying tensions between Nationalist (Kuomintang) and Communist supporters which occasionally flared up, as happened in 1956. Riots, which left a number of people dead, broke out between workers and trade unions representing the two ideological forces. The police were unable to quell the disturbances and the army was brought in.

In the New Territories, however, rural life continued largely unchanged—a quiet land of duck ponds, paddy fields, and vegetable gardens between Communist China and urbanizing, capitalist Hong Kong.

Against this background, economic development and social change in Hong Kong during the post-war years represented a triumph of hard work over adversity, the pursuit of competitive advantage in a hostile business environment, and hope over fear of the turmoil in China, as Mao drove his revolution to its historic conclusion.

Lady May Ride

Hong Kong Past

L ady May Ride has spent almost her entire life in Hong Kong, witnessing the Territory's transformation from its sleepy pre-war status as an outpost of the British Empire to an international financial centre. She was born Violet May Witchell in 1915, the fifth of six children. Her family had long been established in Hong Kong; both her grandfathers had come to the Territory in the nineteenth century to join the newly formed European Police Force, and both her mother and father were born in Hong Kong. Although her father was a Hong Kong Government civil servant, he volunteered to join the army during the First World War, just after May was born. He died in 1928, while the family was on leave in the UK, and her mother brought May and two of her three sisters back to Hong Kong where she brought them up single-handedly. May's mother finally left Hong Kong and retired to the UK just before the Japanese occupation.

At the outbreak of the Second World War, the majority of expatriate women and children were shipped out of Hong Kong, mainly to Australia. May Witchell, who had joined the Hong Kong Volunteer Defence Corps in 1935, stayed in the Territory. When the Japanese took Hong Kong she was imprisoned in the Stanley Internment Camp for expatriate civilians, along with up to 3,000 British, Americans, and other nationalities. The local Chinese population lived in fear of rape and brutal killings by the Japanese, while military personnel were all imprisoned in the barracks in Argyle Street and Sham Shui Po in urban Kowloon.

It was from Sham Shui Po that May Witchell's future husband, Sir (as he was to become) Lindsay Ride escaped, soon after being taken prisoner. He sought refuge in the interior of China, where he organized the British Army Aid Group (BAAG), which bravely assisted people to escape from Hong Kong, smuggled supplies and messages into the camps, and relayed out vital intelligence to the allied forces. BAAG, which operated from 1942 to 1945, in fact provided the only link Britain had with its subjects in the camps during the occupation. Lindsay Ride was awarded a CBE for his wartime exploits. In the years immediately following the occupation he devoted his

time to aiding the rehabilitation of the Territory, and, in 1949, was invited
to become Vice Chancellor of the University of Hong Kong. He succeeded
the pre-war incumbent, Dr Duncan Sloss, who had been interned in Stanley
with May Witchell.

Sir Lindsay's own connections with Hong Kong spanned almost fifty
years. He first came to the Territory in 1928, at the age of thirty, when he
was appointed Professor of Physiology at the university. Later he was made
Dean of the Faculty of Medicine, a position he held until the outbreak of
the war. May Witchell, who worked as secretary to Vice Chancellor Dr
Sloss before the war, became Sir Lindsay's second wife in 1954. Sir Lindsay,
knighted for his services to education, died in 1977 at the age of seventy-
nine.

Since the war May Ride's public service in Hong Kong has been varied
and extensive. She has been Chairman of the Heep Hong Society for
disabled children, Vice President of the Family Planning Association, and
Adviser to the Chinese Women's Association.

The ever-changing face of Hong Kong and the dramatic rise in the cost
of living eventually persuaded Lady Ride to leave the Territory after eighty-
one years. But St Stephen's College Chapel in Stanley, once part of the
internment camp, will, she says, 'always remain very close to my heart'.

She has refused to dwell on her past and has declined interviews about
her own life. This is a rare moment when she reflects on just that.

MY EARLIEST MEMORY is being in the Barker Road Hospital suffering
from meningitis. My mother's dearest friend, the headmistress of the
British School, was reading to me, and it is this that encouraged my love
of books. I am not sure how old I was, but I was a very sickly child and
I was not expected to live long. My mother was told that if I reached
eight years old it would be a miracle. In fact, out of the six children my
mother had, I am the only one now surviving.

My family has long had links with Hong Kong. My father was a Hong
Kong Government civil servant and he was born in the Territory. Both
my grandfathers had gone out to Hong Kong with the European police.
My father went to one of the best schools in Hong Kong during his day,
Queen's College. He certainly had many Chinese friends and was fluent

in Cantonese—we didn't bother with Mandarin then. As a result, our family was fortunate in having many Chinese friends and was able to visit their homes. In those days, expatriates were never invited into a Chinese home and were only entertained in restaurants. The wife rarely appeared, and it was usually only the husband who entertained. I remember friends of mine saying to me, 'How is it that you can go into these places and we can't?' Many of the well-known Chinese families today I have known since I was a small child.

I was born in Gloucestershire in the west of England while my mother was on leave from Hong Kong. I was only six months old when my courageous mother decided to bring her family back to the Territory. My father had already returned to Hong Kong, but communication was not very good in those days—not as it is today—and, by the time we eventually reached Hong Kong, Father was back in London, having volunteered to join the London Scottish regiment! That was in 1916.

We lived in Happy Valley where the British School was. I cannot remember when Father returned, but it was presumably after the Armistice, nor can I remember when we actually moved to Kowloon. We lived in Cox's Path in a row of terraced Victorian-style houses which are still standing. Ours was House 1, overlooking the Union Church in Kowloon.

I remember the first buses which were open like boxes. Before that, transport had been by rickshaw. Father's first car was an Austin, although when I went to school, we walked everywhere—there was none of this going by car! I went to Kowloon Junior School for a couple of years. I was sick most of the time, but I managed to win a scholarship to the Central British School [the main building is still in Nathan Road, Kowloon]. The British School had ceased to exist by that time, and had been replaced by the Central British because of the demand for a bigger school. I believe that Sir Robert Ho-tung had put up money for the school, and yet his daughters were not permitted to attend because they were Chinese [although in fact they were Eurasian]. They had to go to the Diocesan Girls' School.

My school days were plagued by illness. Due to my ill health I was never allowed to play sports, but I developed a great love of walking in the Kowloon hills and later in the New Territories. It was very safe to walk anywhere then.

The Compradore was the shop that supplied all our provisions. Dairy Farm had a butchery department which continued to exist after the Pacific War, right up until the advent of the supermarket. Vendors also used to come with fruit and vegetables to our back-door, and the cook would bargain with them. Our 'baby amah' [nanny] remained with us right up until she died in 1935. She had bound feet, and wore jade earrings and bracelets and an embroidered hat, which was really more of a band around her forehead.

After the outbreak of war in 1939, Hong Kong did all it could to raise funds for the war effort, and began producing tin hats, flashlights, and goodness knows what else. Chiap Wah was the company mainly responsible for the manufacture of these goods.

At the start of the war, I was Private Secretary to the Vice Chancellor of the University of Hong Kong, Dr D. J. Sloss, who was also Chairman of the War Supplies Board and Head of Censorship, so we had an extremely busy time. I never knew which office I was in! The university was still functioning, and, when Canton was occupied by the Japanese, Lingnan University came down to use rooms at night in the University of Hong Kong to teach their students. I was also a member of the nursing detachment of the Hong Kong Volunteer Defence Corps. I had joined in 1935 when it was inaugurated by the Commanding Officer of the Volunteers, Colonel Dowbiggin. Each year we did a stint of nursing at the Military Hospital in Bowen Road. After the war broke out in Europe we became part of the Essential Services.

After the outbreak of the Pacific War, there were two compulsory evacuations from Hong Kong for expatriate women and children. Only those women doing an 'essential service' job, in addition to their normal jobs, were permitted to stay. Alas, many women who did not like being refugees returned to Hong Kong with their children. They thought Hong Kong would be safe, but, unfortunately for them, they ended up in Stanley Internment Camp. That's why there were so many children there.

I was also appointed to the War Supplies Board, and I accompanied the members [The Vice Chancellor, the Head of the Whampoa Dock Company, the Head of Jardines, and the Attorney General] to Shanghai by boat to liaise with those also desiring to supply goods for the fighting services. Our meetings took place in a wonderful old Tudor-style building, and all the heads of the firms attended the meeting. Then we had to go to India to see what could be done there. I accompanied the Board to Delhi where I had the good fortune to be invited to dine with the Viceroy and the Vicereine at the Vice Regal Lodge—a beautiful place. For the first and only time in my life I ate off a gold plate! When Lady Linlithgow discovered my love of flowers she also invited me—not the Supply Board!—to tea to show me her lovely garden.

On 8 December 1941, I was on my way to Bowen Road Military Hospital to commence my fortnight's duty (as volunteer nurses, we had to work there two weeks a year) when the Japanese planes came over. I was walking along Pok Fu Lam Road to catch the bus, and, luckily for me, an army truck pulled up and took me to the hospital. I never went home again until 1945, when the war was over. When I did go home again I found everything had been looted. I had lost everything I treasured, which was of no value to anyone else.

To my knowledge, there was no panic in Hong Kong when the Japanese were on the border. I don't think we were altogether surprised when the attack came, nor were we surprised when we surrendered. We knew that Singapore, which was supposed to be sending reinforcements to our aid, had fallen, and we could not believe the foolish rumours that the Chinese Army was coming to our rescue: Chiang Kai Shek had withdrawn to Chungking [Chongqing] before the Japanese army had even attacked us. Once the Japanese had control of the water supply, we had no alternative. When we heard we had surrendered we just carried on caring for our patients. I was working in one of the surgical wards, and my older sister was in the operating theatres.

The first Japanese to come to the hospital were naval, and behaved decently. Remember, they had been trained by the British and were perfect gentlemen. The army was very different. When the Japanese soldiers came we had to line up outside the wards, and they took everything they could—watches, rings, pens. But again I was lucky. I only had a watch and pen, and I placed these on the floor in front of me. The Japanese would not bend down and pick them up! I still had these possessions in 1945. I told the others to do the same. I knew the Japanese very well from the time I had spent on holiday in Japan before the war, and I knew that they would not bend down in front of us. They were the conquerors and it was beneath their dignity!

I feel that too much has been made of our desperate ordeal in the Stanley Internment Camp. Mind you, I would not want to go through it again. After the war was over I did not return to Hong Kong until 1947, and, by that time, I had been made fully aware of conditions in the camps in Europe and in the Far East. The further south you went, the worse the treatment was. Going down to Australia after the war I met an Australian girl on the boat who had been interned in Java. The women there, for example, if they were considered to have done anything wrong—which in most cases was literally nothing—had their heads shaved and were made to work in the fields. They never did things like that to us: they did horrible things, but others really suffered a great deal more. Don't think, though, that Stanley was a picnic. I lost many friends, and learnt what it was to be hungry, as we were on starvation rations— not at all pleasant I can assure you! This is why I have always refused to be interviewed. A lot has been written about the occupation and life in the internment and POW camps, and a lot I don't agree with, so I just made up my mind not to write or talk about those years. It is an experience I would not want to go through again, so why relive it, especially when you know that many others also suffered, even more than I.

In the camp, those who refused to do any communal work were the ones who suffered. They were selfish and could only think of themselves. The majority of the interness were British and we organized ourselves in the camp [into what became the British Communal Council]. The work we did was voluntary—nobody could be made to do anything, except by the Japanese. It was wonderful to begin with as conditions were appalling and we had simply nothing. There was, for example, one man, a senior surgeon from the Nethersole Hospital, who took over the duties of sanitary officer, trying to clear up all the rubbish which others had not disposed of. Fancy a man of his position and stature doing those sorts of jobs! But it was necessary to be clean to prevent infections and disease, and we had to try and get that message through to everybody. We were, in that respect, lucky to be sent to Stanley.

It was the Chief Justice, Sir Athol MacGregor, who had suggested it, since the Japanese had not known where to put us. He told the

Japanese that there was a prison in Stanley we could go to, and they fell for it. There was a certain amount of chaos immediately after the surrender. There were so many people that the Japanese did not know what to do with us all. Some were put initially in brothels down in West Point where conditions were dreadful, with rats running all over the place. The fighting forces were in North Point to begin with, and then they were sent over to Kowloon to the old barracks in Sham Shui Po. They were made to walk all day, some from Mid-Levels on Hong Kong island, others from North Point, over to Kowloon side where they were marched up Nathan Road to the barracks.

Without hope we could not have survived. One just existed from day to day. My duties were twofold. First, I was 'wash amah' three times a week at the Tweed Bay Hospital in the grounds of the camp. We had to wash all the blankets and sheets from the patients' beds, but we had nothing to wash them with. At first we just put the unbleached calicos in water and jumped up and down on them! But we didn't feel up to it after a week or two—we just didn't have the strength—so we just trod on them instead! We were fortunate in that we could then spread the sheets across the hillside to dry in the sun. Later we were given lye to wash them with. This was wonderful stuff—we could even use it to clean our teeth. My other communal duty was to serve in the kitchen ladling out the 'stew'—goodness knows what was in it. There was one ladle for each person. I just couldn't look at the recipients; I couldn't bear that they were just getting one ladle of that muck. But I got to know all their hands: I could tell you anybody's hands in that camp; I recognized them all.

The food was all cooked up by people in the camps and, again, a team of us were rostered for this duty. The Japanese just came and dumped our rations in each section of the camp. There were three sections. I was in the slum in the Indian quarter, and then there was the married quarter, and then there was St Stephen's section. The rations were divided up amongst the three sections, and then we had to do what we could with them. The so-called rice was just the sweepings. It was full of bits of glass, broken porcelain, and cockroaches, and, by the time we all helped to get that out, there wasn't much left that we could actually eat. We cooked it in sea water to ensure that we had some salt. As the time passed we got very organized. Things became better, and demands were made for different types of food, some of which were met, some were not. But in the very early days I will never forget the taste of what we were given to eat. It was just appalling. It was some sort of meat with long hairs on it in just plain water. There was a senior matron from Kowloon who kept telling me that I had to eat it. She was right, but it just wouldn't stay down!

Lots of books were brought into the camp in the early days when the Japanese did not know what they were doing. This was a godsend. Relaxation was spent in the good weather in the Stanley cemetery. I have a deep love for that place, where so many of my dear friends are laid to rest.

When the Liberation came—of course we knew about the atomic bomb—planes came over and dropped parachutes of food and medicine into the camp. The parachutes were made of nylon which we had never seen before, and we had never seen a jeep either until the Navy arrived in Stanley. Rear Admiral Sir Cecil Harcourt [Commander of the British Far Eastern Fleet] came from Australia in answer to the broadcast from ZBW [the local radio station which became Radio Hong Kong in 1948]. Messengers working for my future husband's organization, the British Army Aid Group, brought word to the camp from London via Macau that the POWs should do what they could to take over Hong Kong. [On 19 August] the Colonial Secretary, Sir Franklin Gimson, the Vice Chancellor, Dr Sloss, and a group of men bravely went out of the camp, not knowing what they were going to meet, into Hong Kong to take control. The Postmaster General, Mr Gwynn-Jones, took over ZBW and sent out the message for help. Harcourt did not wait for any orders and steamed up here.

It was not easy to retake control. The Japanese had no orders other than to annihilate us all if Hong Kong was attacked, and the Chinese, understandably, were quite willing, if they were fit enough, to tear the Japanese to pieces, limb by limb. We were told to remain in the camp and not to try to leave until some order could be restored. Of course, before long, many of us were taken out to help. The actual ceremony in Stanley Camp was held when Admiral Harcourt came to visit us, and the flag was raised.

I was taken from the Stanley Camp to the Gloucester Hotel from where everyone had to be housed. I worked for the Naval Information Office and did not leave Hong Kong until October when I went to Australia. My sister, who had been in Stanley with me, went to England to visit our mother who had left Hong Kong some time before the war. My father had died in the 1920s, but mother had remained in Hong Kong for some years afterwards. Our younger sister and her husband were in Melbourne. They had been caught in Australia when the war broke out, and he had joined the Australian Navy.

My feelings after the Liberation were mixed. Joy at being released, but sadness at the terrible devastation. The police from Stanley were called upon to help the Navy restore order. Looting was going on right under our noses: the need for firewood caused our university registrar to see the whole of the staircase in the Vice Chancellor's house disappear!

There were major changes in Hong Kong after 1949. Many industries were started by the people from Shanghai, and this saw the beginning of Hong Kong's improved economy. I think the biggest change to Hong Kong life was when the airlines took over from passenger ships. It was no longer necessary then to take long leave of six months: shorter and more frequent breaks were possible. My last long leave was in 1951.

I met my husband long before we were married when he was Professor of Physiology at the University of Hong Kong before the war. He also conducted the Hong Kong Singers, of which I was a member. In fact, I worked for him at the university for a month when he was Dean of Medicine.

My husband, Lindsay, did not talk much about his work for the BAAG except to speak highly of his officers, and I know they thought the world of him. I knew he was in touch with Dr Sloss in Stanley Camp during our internment. I remember seeing him for the first time again in 1945 in the old Hong Kong Hotel, and thinking how enormous he seemed. Of course, we were used to our skeletal selves! We often used to laugh about it.

I can proudly say that, as Vice Chancellor, Lindsay put the University of Hong Kong on the map after the war. Never before had so many important academics come to Hong Kong from the UK and Australia. He also revived interest amongst the students in cricket, his favourite game, and in all sporting activities. He believed that university students should have interests outside their studies, in sport, in music, and an intelligent interest in community affairs. He would not have stood for the demonstrations and demands, which we have seen in the 1990s, to be allowed to take part in appointing the Vice Chancellor. Sadly, times have changed.

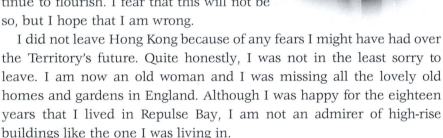

Like everyone who has spent a lifetime in Hong Kong, I hope and pray that the Territory will be allowed by Beijing to look after itself and thus continue to flourish. I fear that this will not be so, but I hope that I am wrong.

I did not leave Hong Kong because of any fears I might have had over the Territory's future. Quite honestly, I was not in the least sorry to leave. I am now an old woman and I was missing all the lovely old homes and gardens in England. Although I was happy for the eighteen years that I lived in Repulse Bay, I am not an admirer of high-rise buildings like the one I was living in.

Latterly Hong Kong has become so crowded. I just hated having to go to Central. Everyone now is in such a hurry, and one was lucky if one could walk along a pavement without being knocked over.

Hong Kong is no longer my Hong Kong, and I am not alone in feeling that.

Lau Kam Man

The East River Guerrillas

During the Second World War, many Hong Kong people, British and Chinese alike, risked their lives by actively and secretly resisting the Japanese occupation of the Territory. Lau Kam Man was just one of these people. He fought the Japanese as a Communist guerrilla.

The East River Guerrillas—named after the East River in Guangdong province near where their headquarters were based—was a Communist guerrilla organization. By operating from inside free China—those areas not effectively occupied by the Japanese—the guerrillas were able to set up an underground movement in Hong Kong. Lau Kam Man became the Secretary of the guerrilla column in Sai Kung in the New Territories.

The Japanese faced considerable problems controlling the Colony, despite the fact that the Battle for Hong Kong had only lasted eighteen days. Their forces had swept south through the New Territories and Kowloon, before taking Hong Kong Island. The British surrendered on Christmas Day 1941. Initially, the Japanese concentrated on controlling the urban areas. Their position was less secure in the rural parts of the New Territories, particularly in the rugged mountain areas of Sai Kung, where access was difficult and dangerous. This, however, allowed the guerrillas to establish a firm undercover network before the Japanese tightened their grip over the New Territories.

The resistance movement which operated in Hong Kong throughout the occupation, derived much of its support from the left-wing guerrilla forces who harassed Japanese operations and supply lines. Lau Kam Man and his comrades took enormous risks and faced torture and certain death if identified or captured by the Japanese. The people and information they spirited out of Hong Kong, and the supplies they brought in, were of vital importance to the war effort, and to sustaining morale.

The Hong Kong-based fighters formed an unusual, and mutually beneficial, relationship with the British Army Aid Group (BAAG) in China, established in 1942 by Sir Lindsay Ride, a British internee who had escaped from Hong Kong. BAAG helped escapees from Hong Kong reach free

China, and provided medicines and other support to those interned in the Territory. Much of the information supplied by the guerrillas helped BAAG with its work.

Lau Kam Man and many of the guerrillas remained committed Communists and he subsequently joined the Party to work for the Chinese Government after the Communists' 1949 victory. He is now retired, but his patriotism is still evident today.

THE EAST RIVER GUERRILLAS played an important and effective part in the war against the Japanese. Our underground network enabled some internees in the prisoner-of-war camps to escape; our spies were able to pass information over enemy lines on to our headquarters in unoccupied China, and we also made limited, but successful, attacks on Japanese positions in Hong Kong. Our headquarters also worked hand in hand with the British Army Aid Group, also based in China.

It was sheer fate that I even joined the Communist guerrillas, but I have remained a committed Communist ever since. New Territories villagers lived a very quiet existence before the war, with little involvement in politics. On the day the Japanese attacked Hong Kong in December 1941, I knew the peaceful life we had enjoyed had come to an end.

I was in my village, Sha Kok Mei, which overlooks Sai Kung Hoi. There was a prolonged bombardment of the surrounding area, and I saw an aircraft crash into the sea. I had no idea whether the aircraft was British or Japanese.

The Japanese invasion brought chaos to the New Territories. Once the British had retreated from the area, there was no formal government. Until 1943, the Japanese were based mainly in Hong Kong and Kowloon, since access to many rural areas was difficult. There were few roads in the Sai Kung area and the villages in the district were left in a vacuum, with no formal administration. A state of lawlessness prevailed.

Groups of armed bandits took advantage of this situation and compounded our problems. In the urban areas of Kowloon before the Japanese moved in, there was looting and robbing, mainly orchestrated by the triads. In the New Territories, we were hounded by armed gangs who came from China and made a great deal of trouble. They were not politically motivated—just bandits who saw the disruption caused by the Japanese invasion as an opportunity to roam freely, intimidating and robbing the villagers.

I was eighteen years old when my village was raided five times in one day by bandits. I fled, and set off to join the Chinese Nationalist army, the Kuomintang [KMT], to fight the Japanese. I thought this would help restore justice to China and bring peace to my home. New Territories villagers had generally always had a strong patriotic attachment to China, and, although we knew little about politics, we admired the Nationalist leader, Chiang Kai Shek, for leading the battle against the Japanese invasion of China in 1937. It was natural that I sought to join the KMT.

I set out with a friend for Shaoguan in northern Guangdong province where the KMT army had a base. But, since there were no roads in the area, after walking for a day we had only got as far as Long Ke village in the northern part of Sai Kung. There we met one of the leaders of the Communist guerrilla column, Gong Shui. He had been sent down by the head of the East River Guerrillas, Tsang Sang, from the group's headquarters in Waichow [Huizhou] in Guangdong province. He had come to drum up more recruits.

'Where are you going?', he asked.

'To join the KMT army to fight against the Japanese,' I replied.

'But the KMT always retreat,' he said. 'They have no fire in their bellies. If you want to fight the Japanese, you don't have to go all the way to Shaoguan. Join us!'

Shaoguan was a long way away and since both the KMT and the Communists shared the common goal of defeating the Japanese, I decided it would be simpler to join the guerrillas. There was also a sense of urgency, since the Japanese had already occupied Hong Kong. I promptly went back to my village to try and recruit others to join the Communist struggle against the Japanese.

Shortly afterwards Gong Shui came to Sai Kung town and called a meeting of youngsters in a bid to encourage them to join the East River Guerrillas. He helped us organize ourselves into militias which were based in each village. These were responsible for policing the area, and reporting on the Japanese.

The guerrilla militias were successful in driving out the bandits, and peace and order were restored for the two years that the guerrillas were able to govern the area. During that period, from 1942 to 1943, we were able to arrange to have oil and rice sent to us from China, and people began to trust us. This, in turn, enabled us to recruit many more youngsters. In 1943, after the opening of a road into Sai Kung town, the Japanese arrived, and our ability to move about was severely restricted. This made our operations more difficult, so we went underground.

The guerrillas developed an extensive undercover network, with a string of bases in Sai Kung, Sha Tau Kok, Yuen Long, and in the urban area. This gave us a very detailed knowledge of what was going on. I became Secretary of the East River Guerrilla group in Sai Kung. I was also employed by the Japanese in 1943 to work in the Sai Kung District Office. It was an ideal position to have, and the work tied in neatly with my undercover position. It helped to keep us well informed of Japanese plans, but I had to be careful not to compromise my position. The rewards were great, but so were the risks!

Our covert activities helped the war effort in three crucial ways. Immediately after the fall of Hong Kong we helped survivors of the fighting, and later escapees from the prisoner-of-war camps in Kowloon, to travel through Japanese lines to China. After the war, some of the men we had helped came back to say thank you. I remember a young American pilot travelling all the way to Guangzhou to meet the guerrilla who had saved his life. He asked him if he wanted to emigrate to the US but the former guerrilla said he preferred to stay on in China.

The second area of activity was our information-gathering network. We had messengers working for us throughout the occupation who carried information and messages back and forth between Hong Kong and China. It was a vertical undercover line of communication, stretching north from Hong Kong Island to the East River. BAAG and the East River Guerrillas were two separate organizations, but we cooperated closely and we each had our own network of messengers. The work of the messengers, who were mostly young boys, was extremely dangerous, and a few were captured, tortured, and killed. They never once betrayed us, and our network remained in operation throughout the war.

We were passing on details of Japanese military activities gathered by our spies. We were able to gather information on the strength and deployment of their forces, the number of ships in the harbour, and the positions of their aircraft at Kai Tak. We drew up maps detailing the information and smuggled them out.

The third area of our activity was simply to harass the enemy wherever we could. We could not afford to take any risks and the ambushes were always well calculated so we could be relatively sure of success. Uppermost in our minds was the protection of our own men. We did not want any of our operations to lead to the rounding up of people in the area whom the Japanese—rightly in many cases—suspected of helping us. We had adequate supplies of small arms and ammunition, much of which had either been left behind by the British or had come to us from China. Many of the skirmishes and ambushes were quite fierce, and a number of Japanese soldiers and collaborators were killed. But as far as I recall, we lost only one man in these military operations during the war years.

The main target of attack by the militia in our area were the Japanese who were stationed in Sai Kung. There was one particular soldier who was detested by the villagers. He manned the checkpoint in and out of the area. Once every three days, the villagers made the long trek into Kowloon City to collect their rice rations. This man treated the villagers very badly, threatening them and, on their return, often stole their limited supplies of food. He was killed after a successful guerrilla attack.

The Japanese had also forced many of our villagers to work on the construction of underground tunnels at Kwun Yam Shan [near Sha Tin]. We were able to launch an ambush on the construction site, killing three Japanese.

At the end of the war, the Japanese in Sai Kung were reluctant to surrender to us because they had been instructed to surrender only to regular soldiers from the KMT Government, which had its own bases in the New Territories. We saw no reason why they shouldn't surrender to the Communist guerrillas, and, to try and ensure this, we blew up the only bridge leading to Kowloon. The operation was only partially successful, and, after further days of negotiation with us, the Japanese suddenly departed Sai Kung one night by boat for Kowloon. I think they felt safer surrendering to the British than to us!

We took charge again of Sai Kung after the Japanese surrender. The local people were happy that the Communists were in control because they were grateful for our efforts during the war. They were pleased to see the back of the Japanese and they didn't really care whether the British came back or not. The British did reoccupy Sai Kung, but it was not until the end of 1946 that they physically moved into the area.

When the war was over, some 2,000 of my fellow fighters went to Shantung [Shandong] in North China to continue the fight against the KMT, whilst others resumed their pre-war civilian life. The British Army asked the guerrillas to help maintain law and order in the Sai Kung area. We were given $30 a month, and allowed to keep our weapons until the end of 1946.

Hong Kong was so poor and had suffered much under Japanese military rule. In the rural areas people had to live off the land, even during the occupation, and our produce was our main source of food. The people in the urban areas had faced much greater hardships during the occupation and there were serious problems after the liberation. There were food shortages and it was difficult to find a job. They were hard times.

In 1946, the KMT swept over Waichow, and many guerrillas were forced to come over to Sai Kung for refuge. Many of them were educated so we decided to try and start a school in each village using these men as teachers. We told the villagers they would have to pay $1.50 a month per child towards the teacher's salary. What is now Sai Kung Public School was started in 1946, and most of the other rural schools were established in 1947 and 1948.

In August 1949, when the KMT retreated, many cities in southern China were left vacant. I was recalled by my Party and asked to bring some forty educated young people to help fill the administrative vacuum. I lived and worked in China for thirty years. I finally retired as the Head of the Public Security Bureau in Waichow in 1979 to return to the village of my birth in Sai Kung.

I did not receive a warm welcome. On my arrival at the Lo Wu border crossing, I was interrogated by the Police Special Branch.

I also had to face up to the many changes which had taken place in Hong Kong. To begin with I couldn't even find my way to my village. People told me to take a Public Light Bus [minibus] to Sai Kung, but I didn't know what a Public Light Bus was! And when I got back to my own village, I couldn't even find my home as there were so many new buildings and roads. There was a great difference then between Hong Kong and the rest of South China, but not any more.

When I returned to Hong Kong, I had to obtain an identity card. The Immigration Officer asked me whether my nationality should be shown as British or Chinese. Why should I be British? I was born in Hong Kong: I am Chinese. So is Hong Kong.

Dorothy Lee
Release and Rehabilitation

Hong Kong people, native and immigrant alike, are renowned for their fortitude and resilience in the face of adversity. This quality enabled them not only to withstand the cruelty of the Japanese occupation, but, after Liberation, to work enthusiastically for rehabilitation, and aim for a better future. Dorothy Lee, Hong Kong-born and bred, is a shining example of this strength and spirit. Her early experience with voluntary social work during the war—which caused her to suffer torture by the Japanese—set her upon a lifetime career of improving social welfare in Hong Kong.

During the occupation, the local Chinese population, despite the fact that they were not interned, suffered enormous hardships. The chronic shortages of supplies and food meant that many starved. They lived in fear of the Kempeitai—the Japanese secret police—who made arbitrary arrests and executions. Dorothy Lee's retelling of her own experiences during her imprisonment by the Japanese is a moving testimony to the courage, loyalty, and deep religious faith, of some Hong Kong people during that horrifying period.

She was arrested, it is thought, for her association with the former government official, Dr Selwyn-Clarke, although she was not involved with his undercover work. He had shown enormous courage by smuggling medical supplies into the internment camps, aided by the British Army Aid Group (BAAG). Dr Selwyn-Clark was eventually arrested and severely tortured by the Japanese, but miraculously survived.

Following the Liberation, Dorothy Lee was at the centre of the relief efforts as Hong Kong tried to recover from the Japanese occupation. This movement was spearheaded by Bishop Ronald Hall, who for two decades after the war, devoted himself to community and welfare work. The Social Welfare Council, which he founded before the war, made way in 1948 for the Hong Kong Council of Social Service. Today the Council has around one hundred affiliated voluntary organizations.

While working for Bishop Hall, Dorothy Lee was awarded a two-year scholarship to train as a social worker at the University of London. The scholarships were created by the Labour Government of the day to train people in colonial territories to set up social welfare programmes in their countries. She returned to Hong Kong in 1948 to become one of the first four people in the Social Welfare Office—today one of the largest departments in the Government—and was responsible for helping to shape early social welfare policy. She served in the department until her retirement in the early 1970s.

According to Dorothy Lee, no accolades can do justice to the social workers who toiled with her during those early years: 'The workers first walked ahead of their charges, encouraging them to climb up the hilly path to see other possibilities and opportunities; later they walked beside them, helping them along the way; then they walked behind them, encouraging them to go through the many doors leading to further development.'

LIFE DURING THE pre-war years was very leisurely and peaceful. We were not affluent, but we lived extremely comfortably in a house on Robinson Road [Hong Kong Island] surrounded by servants. This was not unusual. We had about eight servants in all, one to look after each child, and others to do the household work.

It was also quite common for people to bring servant girls from China. They usually came because their parents didn't want girls, or couldn't afford to look after them. They weren't paid any wages but they were looked after and did little odd jobs to keep them occupied, such as sweeping the floor, fanning the older ladies of the house in the heat of the summer, giving them a massage—really all the extra things which the other servants did not have time to do. I think generally speaking they were well treated, and some never married, remaining with the family throughout their lives.

I had an amah who walked with me every day from Robinson Road to Central, so I could catch the Star Ferry to Kowloon to go to school where we were taught mostly by British missionaries. I liked when it rained because then we were allowed to take a sedan chair home. It cost 30 cents from the Star Ferry to Robinson Road. There were no motor cars at all when I first went to school but, later, when some friends started to go to the ferry by car, we could recognize which vehicle belonged to whom by the noise the car made.

Small things were special treats. There was the Lee Chim Kee ice-cream man, who came round the streets. He had a long bamboo pole and on one end carried ice-cream and on the other a bucket of water to wash the dirty cups. There was also the man carrying a makeshift stage and some puppets. He was more than willing to give all the children a half-hour show in the middle of the street, for 20 cents.

This quiet existence changed in 1941 with the Japanese occupation. I was twenty and working by then as a secretary. Everything was rather chaotic, and I spent most of the time during the war years doing voluntary work.

It was the pre-war Director of Medical Services, Dr Selwyn-Clarke, who approached me to help him. He was one of the few expatriates not interned because he was asked by the Japanese to remain in the Medical Department to help run certain essential services. He was able to get money from the British Consulate in Chungking [Chongqing] to provide financial assistance for the Chinese wives of expatriate soldiers, taken prisoner of war. I visited these women who had just been left on the streets and were by then squatting in vacant buildings. They were not well educated and found it very difficult to make ends meet. I looked after about forty of them and was able to visit them regularly.

These were difficult, uncertain days for everybody. There was no public transport because there was no petrol available and we had to walk everywhere. We had to try and survive on the rations we obtained from the Japanese, which amounted to about six ounces of rice a day for each person. How could we live off that without fat or protein? Butter and meat, even cooking oil, were out of the question because they were so expensive; even vegetables were a luxury, and many of us used to eat potato leaves. Sugar was expensive so we used brown sugar slabs, and whatever coffee we still had we used to brew five and six times because it was so precious—even the sixth brew was delicious! All basic necessities were very expensive and you had to be extremely careful because you never knew when you could draw money from the bank. When the bank did open from time to time, only very small withdrawals were allowed.

We also had to live with the fear of the 'midnight knock'. The Japanese might come to your door at any time to take over your house or flat and, in the early days, they came in to rape. Quite a few of my friends' sons worked secretly for the BAAG, which helped to filter information into the territory and aided some to escape from Hong Kong. Many of these young men were caught, and a few beheaded.

The Japanese gendarmes were very powerful, more so than the army officers. Even a corporal needed no authority to cut off your head. In fact, the more heads they chopped off, the quicker they were promoted. As I was working for Dr Selwyn-Clarke, I was always prepared that, one day, I would be a victim of an arrest and, sure enough, it happened. It was on the seventh day of the Lunar New Year in February 1943.

It was lunchtime and I was walking up and down Queen's Road Central waiting for the Hongkong Bank to open so that I could pass a message to one of the expatriate staff from Dr Selwyn-Clarke. Such staff were not interned, so they could serve non-Cantonese-speaking nationals. Suddenly I was conscious of two men in civilian clothes walking behind me. 'There she is, there she is,' they said. 'We want to interview you.'

I asked them on whose authority they were doing this. I was very clear-minded and, although I was young, I wasn't at all flustered because, psychologically, I had been prepared for this moment.

There was no answer. I was marched up Pottinger Street to Central Police Station and placed in a room to await interrogation. I knew it was 'the killer', who operated from Central Police Station.

Corporal Yishi appeared shortly afterwards and that's when the fun began. He was notorious for his ruthless and cold behaviour, which was why he was known as 'the killer'. Just a few weeks before, he had caught some people tearing down branches for firewood on the Peak. He collared twelve people, lined them up in a row, and chopped at them with his sword, one after the other, until the ninth, when the sword was too blunt to cut off another head. So he took the sword of one of his aides, and cut off the heads of the remaining three.

When Mr Yishi appeared he began to question me about Selwyn-Clarke, and I told him truthfully about my voluntary work. He was an unscrupulous and aggressive man. He didn't believe me, and from time to time beat me with something like a baton on very sensitive areas like my back, shoulders, and knees. Then as he beat me he would question me. All the time I would not accept that I had done anything wrong. He kept on repeating the same question in different ways trying to trap me and prove I was a spy. All the time I gave the same answer and he obviously became more convinced I was a trained spy.

The real torture started at about 2 o'clock. We had a brief break for him to take his supper at 6 o'clock, and he came back around 7 o'clock, and it started again.

He tied both my hands behind my back and slung me up so I dangled in mid-air without any support for my feet. In that way it was easier for him to hit me on my back because the height was really more suitable for him. The less he was satisfied with my answer, the more he beat me. The pain was so great that I couldn't even shed a tear—and the drier my face, the more violent he became.

By this stage I was in very poor condition with no water and nothing to eat. I believed though, that no matter how badly I was being treated, this was something that God had meant for me, and that He would get me out of this mess.

I don't know how much later it was, but eventually I was thrown into a small prison cell where I lay, tired, numb, and exhausted. The next morning was like a dream. I didn't know where I was, and when I looked at my kneecap it was completely black. I didn't know to what extent I was injured. The cell was only big enough for a small canvas stretcher—my bed—and I had been stripped of my coat, handbag, and spectacles. It was February. I just lay there shivering, hardly able to move.

On the second evening a colonel sent his aide to take me to see him. He apologized for Mr Yishi's treatment of me and sent me a glass of milk and a bun each day for the next two weeks, after which there was no contact. That was luxury compared with what I had later on: prison rice cooked in salt, wrapped in a newspaper, which was thrown under the prison cell door. The water was so dirty I couldn't drink it.

I was there for about five weeks. Mr Yishi would come at any time of the day or night for further interrogation. By day I wished for the night, and at night I wished for the day. There was nothing to occupy my time, except to wonder when the next encounter would be. Everything had been taken from me. I just stared at the ceiling blankly. Sometimes I remembered to pray. My faith kept me alive in that cell.

One day the sun was shining in through the single high window of the cell. The light on the window appeared like a cross. I felt that it was a message, a double-meaning, and I wondered whether I might be released. I had little idea of time, but I knew it was nearly Easter.

Late one night, shortly after that, I was released. My brother was waiting for me and cried with relief when he saw that at least I was able to walk. The Japanese usually released their prisoners at night so as few people as possible would be able to see any of the injuries the prisoners had suffered from torture. I went back to my parents where they had a hot bath waiting for me. I had a decent meal and we talked the whole night through.

During the next few months of the Japanese occupation I was called for further interviews by Mr Yashimoto who was stationed in the Supreme Court Building. But there were no beatings, no torture. He had by that stage already arrested Dr Selwyn-Clarke, who was badly tortured.

When the war ended, many of us were jubilant. Others had suffered so much, either through torture by the Japanese, illness, or loss of family members. My experiences were nothing in comparison. Many of these people were in a daze and did not really realize that the war was over.

Hong Kong was in many ways a shambles. There was so much damage through the bombing and by looters. Time was running out for many of us because we had no money left; others were in no physical condition to help in the rehabilitation of Hong Kong because of sickness and malnutrition. The expatriate civilians and prisoners of war were generally looked after by the British or Australian Red Cross, but the majority of local people really needed support and emergency relief because they had nothing. The immediate post-war years saw us desperately picking up the pieces from the trail of destruction left by the forty-four months of the Japanese occupation.

The Anglican Bishop, the late Bishop Ronald Hall, was not in Hong Kong when it fell, but, being the caring person he was, hurried back in October 1945. He immediately set about gathering a nucleus of staff to start large-scale relief operations. Bishop Hall's response to the immediate needs of the local population was most impressive, and he immediately re-established the pre-war Welfare Council which he headed. [He had set up the Council before the war to deal with the large influx of refugees who had come to Hong Kong as a result of the Sino-Japanese war.] The Council had the full support of the Military Administration and, soon after, of the Hong Kong Government when it was back in full control.

I joined Bishop Hall's team. We set up food kitchens, mobilized people to help clear sites which had been bombed, shelled, or vandalized, collected milk and milk powder from warships which were coming in with supplies, and distributed much-needed clothing to the general public, particularly as winter was approaching. We also helped provide financial assistance to individuals to set them on their own feet; for example, so that they could obtain a hawker's licence. Slowly, we were able to help people pick up the bits and pieces of their existence and get on with their lives.

Conditions gradually returned to normal and Bishop Hall was able to resuscitate many of the pre-war voluntary welfare organizations, which included the Boys' and Girls' Clubs Associations and the Hong Kong Society for the Protection of Children. He was an incredible man with tremendous leadership qualities and drive. He started many other welfare organizations which are still running today. The Welfare Council also set up a Child Welfare Committee to look into the needs of children and to help rehabilitate children's homes. One of the projects, was a temporary holiday house in an empty food storage godown in Stanley which gave some children the chance to have a week's holiday, some fresh air, and plenty of nutritious food.

Gradually the Welfare Council faded out and in its place the Hong Kong Social Welfare Council came into being.

There were also some very courageous war-time stories which began to emerge after the occupation. The Supervisor of the Tai Po Orphanage [now St Christopher's Home in the north-eastern New Territories], Miss Jennings, an elderly missionary, walked twenty miles each way to Kowloon and back, with some of the older children, to collect much needed rice rations every month. She pushed the heavy rice load through the streets of Kowloon back to the Home, so that all the children could at least have two not-so-full rice meals daily—what love and sacrifice!

By the time I came back to Hong Kong after studying in London, to join the Government in 1948, it was becoming increasingly apparent that a 'good heart' was no longer enough to tackle Hong Kong's welfare needs, and that professionals were required. I was one of only four in the newly established Social Welfare Office [SWO], and set about concentrating on youth work.

Many families were living in squatter areas, scattered all over Hong Kong and Kowloon. Squatter areas were very crowded and appeared like mushrooms on the hillsides. The huts were built on muddy ground with poor, flimsy materials, and, during wet weather, there was always the possibility of landslides, or huts would be blown down in summer typhoons. There was no water supply or electricity, and fires were frequent. Somehow the residents were very aware of the risks, so what little possessions they had were always tied in a bundle and, when an alarm went off, they picked up their bundles and ran for their lives.

There was a large number of squatter children living in these squalid conditions. Several voluntary organizations began to locate premises and established children's clubs, in a bid to keep them occupied. The Social Welfare Office backed this work and allocated part of the Feeding Centres to run such clubs.

This work was just getting underway when the Shek Kip Mei fire broke out on Christmas Day 1953. I remember being so impressed by many of the SWO Club children who did their share in trying to help during that emergency. For instance, they assisted with the distribution of milk to the children who had been injured in the fire.

Fifty thousand people were made homeless within a few hours as a result of the fire. At the same time, the number of squatter areas throughout the territory was escalating. It forced the Government to frame its first housing policy. This resulted, within a short time, in the birth of the six-storey resettlement blocks constructed on the fire sites.

Gradually more sites were identified to build many more housing blocks. The roofs of these H-shaped buildings were covered at both ends and used as playground areas. Space was at a premium and later the Government allowed voluntary organizations to operate children's clubs on the roof-tops.

The emphasis in all the Social Welfare Office Clubs was always on providing an education for living. The children attending the clubs could not afford to go to school. So, whilst the clubs were not there to replace a formal education, the children did have an opportunity to learn 'The Three Rs'. More importantly, they learnt to work hard, play together, share their time, and act responsibly. We tried to make them more aware of what was going on around them and gradually to develop a sense of responsibility to the community.

Later on 'Youth Groups' were set up for older teenage children. There were many evening activities. Most of them were given a basic practical training, be it woodwork, weaving, or sewing. However, as the Youth Groups developed, the social workers branched out and tried to identify children who were in the clutches of the triads. This was a difficult task, trying to detach the kids from the 'big brother', whose hold over the children was great, but we did have a few rare successes.

The Government was constantly trying to think of ways to keep some of the youngsters gainfully occupied. It endorsed a proposal put forward by the Jesuits in the early post-war period to issue shoe-shine licences. These were granted to boys, at certain designated sites, to enable them to help supplement their family's income. They charged 20 cents to shine a pair of shoes. I had my own 'shoe-shine boy' who came to my office early each morning to shine my shoes before he set off to start work at Theatre Lane, Central. This daily contact gave me the chance to have a little chat with him and to get to know him and help him with any problems. Today Ah Sui owns a flat in Wan Chai, a printing business in Aberdeen, and he has invited me to join him and his family in their house in Guangzhou! We still meet occasionally for *yam cha*, and he insists on being the host!

As the population grew in the fifties, attention began to be focused on community building to try and help residents to understand their responsibilities and to work together. People were living so closely together, particularly in the new resettlement estates, it was necessary to promote a community atmosphere. This was not always easy since many of the residents were new arrivals and spoke different dialects, and, even if it was possible for them to communicate, many were too inward-looking, with no time for anything except their own daily existence. The first Community Centre was set up in Wong Tai Sin, where fifty thousand people were living in one resettlement estate.

I have often reflected on my work and experiences of the early post-war years and I realize I was very fortunate to have been involved at the grass-roots level, helping to shape a welfare policy for the years to come. Social workers then were so dedicated, and I think we were able to help people face up to and adapt to new situations, and give them some hope and confidence for the future. This was not easy when so many were struggling to earn enough for one square meal a day.

Cheung Yan Lung
Rural Politics

Hong Kong has been singled out among other past colonial territories as a rare example of a relatively peaceful and cooperative marriage of interests between the Government and the local people. This could not have been possible over the years without those local people who have served as critical, political mediums between the two. Cheung Yan Lung fulfilled this role in the rural New Territories, where for more than forty years he has helped to represent and protect the interests and traditional rights of the indigenous people.

The New Territories comprises the part of Hong Kong north of Kowloon beyond today's Boundary Street, as well as a number of outlying islands. It was leased by China to Britain on 9 June 1898 for ninety-nine years. The then Colonial Secretary, Stewart Lockhart, noted in a report that the area acquired was almost entirely rural with no proper means of communication, other than irregularly paved paths which wound around mountains and paddy fields to small towns and villages. As a result of this land lease, Hong Kong gained a new segment of the Chinese population— land-based, traditional rural and village people whose lives had been much the same for centuries.

A consultation process gradually evolved between resident government representatives—the District Officers—and village and clan leaders, enabling the Government to administer the area and, by and large, to cooperate politically with the people of the New Territories. This allowed the administration, in turn, to foster the support of local residents on a number of wider policy issues over the years, mainly related to the environment and natural resources, such as forestry and fisheries development, and the provision of water supplies.

Various informal consultation channels have always exisited, but the main body advising the Government on rural affairs has been a council of New Territories notables called the Heung Yee Kuk. Representatives to this council are elected on a very restricted franchise, and the body has wielded a great deal of influence, both with the Government and the local population. Cheung Yan Lung became a member of the Kuk in 1947 and went on to become its Chairman, during the 1960s.

Cheung Yan Lung was appointed to the Legislative Council to represent New Territories' interests, and helped with the establishment of the District Boards. These were partially elected consultative bodies, set up in the early 1980s, to advise the Government on local issues which affected the well-being of residents of the district. Mr Cheung became Chairman of a new local authority, the Regional Council, which was formally established in 1986. The new body assumed responsibility for environmental services, cultural affairs, and sporting activities throughout the New Territories. He retired in 1995.

Cheung Yan Lung represents a small, but politically powerful and extremely influential group of New Territories leaders. Though he has retired from politics, and spends some of his time with his family in Britain and America, he remains an influential voice. He has witnessed the transformation of his homeland over the past seventy years, and well remembers the 1950s and the beginnings of the great change to simple, traditional village life.

I FIRST WENT to Kowloon when I was aged eleven, and it really was like going nowadays to study overseas. Everything was so different. There were many large and elegant buildings, lots of people, and constant hustle and bustle. It was a very different world from where I'd been brought up in Shek Wu Hui [just north of Fanling] in the north-eastern New Territories.

I seemed to spend a lot of my childhood travelling to school. First, to Tai Po market where I went to the government primary school and then to Kowloon, where I attended La Salle College. We were fortunate living in the eastern part of the New Territories, because we had access to the Kowloon–Canton Railway which snaked its way through the rural areas of the New Territories, linking Hong Kong and Canton. It took an hour each way to travel to school in Kowloon from where I lived, on what was a rather dirty, bumpy, steam-driven train.

I was born in 1922 in Shek Wu Hui, where my father had a small retail business. [He later obtained the licence for the distribution of petrol

throughout the New Terri-
tories for one of the
leading American
oil companies.]
In those
days there
was only
one street
in Shek Wu
Hui and one
weaving factory.
Later, as the town
began to develop, other
shops and small factories began
to appear. We didn't feel at all remote despite
the fact that we lived in the midst of paddy fields in a largely agricultural
area. We had the South China Bus Company which provided a once-a-
day service to take people to Yuen Long in the western New Territories,
giving us access to what was then a big market town.

Markets were a very important part of our lives. They were great
social gatherings, and were very colourful and noisy occasions in
comparison with the more staid, regulated markets of today! In addition
to all the normal produce, there were people selling special Chinese
cures and remedies, letter-writers, and even acrobats to provide some
entertainment. The markets at Shek Wu Hui, Tai Po, and Yuen Long
were each held on fixed days of the Lunar month. This tied in neatly
with the main market in the area, at Shenzhen, just over the border,
which was held on different days again. The market days never
changed, so people knew exactly where and when to go to sell their
produce.

Shortly before the Japanese occupation I, like many other people, left
Hong Kong and went to live in China, where I studied at Chung Shan
[Zhongshan] University in Guangzhou.

Life in the New Territories during the dark days of the occupation was
extremely difficult. People didn't have enough food to eat because the
Japanese had taken much of it away. They often had to eat the bark

from the trees growing along the sides of the roads. The indigenous villagers who owned land were a little better off because they could still grow their own rice and yams, but that was the basic diet with little else. People generally detested the Japanese because they were overbearing and very fierce, and tried to keep out of their way. However, the villagers did play their part in collaborating to help British soldiers and civilians escape to safety through the New Territories and on into China.

I came back to Hong Kong in 1945 so that I could help my father with his business. In 1946 I became the Chairman of the Shek Wu Hui Chamber of Commerce, which saw my first involvement in public life. I was the Chairman of the Chamber for sixteen consecutive terms.

In 1947 I became a member of the Heung Yee Kuk. This council of rural leaders had been set up in the 1920s, as a forum for New Territories leaders to exchange their views. The Kuk was not formally constituted until 1959, and had very limited official powers, but it always commanded and retained the support of the indigenous people in the New Territories, largely because it was the only body which could reflect their views. Later, when the New Towns were developed in the New Territories, the Heung Yee Kuk was responsible for negotiating with the Government levels of financial compensation for land on behalf of the villagers, and this reinforced its position in the rural community.

In the 1950s and 1960s, the resident government representative, the District Officer was responsible for implementing government policies in his local area, but he also acted as the Land Officer and Magistrate. Maybe these District Officers were very efficient, or perhaps our needs were simple, but I remember being very impressed by the District Officer system which seemed to work effectively. It was certainly much easier then to get decisions about matters affecting people's lives. You didn't have to go through so much formality in various departments and there was no bureaucracy—there wasn't even a file! All you had to do was contact the departments concerned, and that was it.

These administrative arrangements seemed to benefit us, and the British seemed to treat the New Territories differently from the urban areas. A lot more was done to help the local population. What is now the Agriculture and Fisheries Department provided support to farmers to help them improve their crops, and there was a major tree-replanting programme. Many trees in the New Territories had been destroyed during the war, mostly for use as firewood for cooking. A great deal of effort was also given to help quickly re-establish the fishing industry after the war as well. The Department assumed the responsibility for managing and marketing the catch from Hong Kong's growing fishing fleet.

I think the differing government attitude towards the rural and urban areas came about for various reasons. It was partly because the urban areas were overwhelmed with refugees that the administration found it difficult to cope with just trying to house the growing population.

It was also largely because the New Territories was always perceived to be leased land, so there was a different attitude. In the 1950s, the Government's objective in the New Territories appeared to be to maintain the status quo. There were no plans for redevelopment, and certainly no thoughts then of building new towns. The New Territories was simply a large farming area which was used to provide food for the urban area, and also, of course, water which was stored in the major reservoirs such as Tai Lam Chung and High Island.

The people of the New Territories benefited greatly when the Korean War broke out in 1950, and many became very rich. The trade embargo against China gave many the opportunity to smuggle illegal goods into China. This was quite simple since there was only a small, symbolic fence marking the Sino-Hong Kong border, so it was easy to get back and forth. It wasn't until after the great influx of illegal immigrants in 1962 that the fence was strengthened.

Smuggling took place all along the border from Kat O in Mirs Bay, to Lok Ma Chau and on to Yuen Long. Everything that was needed in China was smuggled—tyres, petrol, medicine, even engines for aircraft! Whatever could be sold in China was smuggled by truck or ship. On a dark, moonless night the beach at Kat O often resembled how I imagine a smugglers' cove in eighteenth-century England would have looked, with small boats, men with lanterns, and piles of goods! The length of the border meant it was almost impossible to police it effectively. In fact, I am not even sure there was the will: it's said that the most prosperous people at that time were the police staff sergeants at police posts along the border!

Village life in these days was really quite simple. There was no tap water so everyone was dependent on well water. Most of the towns had electricity, but the majority of the villages did not, and if you had a telephone, you really were somebody then! Medical facilities were fairly primitive; the nearest clinic was in the market towns, such as at Tai Po, where a doctor would visit only once or twice a week. Most of us used to look to Chinese herbs and the Chinese herbalist if we were ill.

There were few schools. The richer people were able to afford to send their children to a decent school, but the parents of many village children were either unwilling or unable to pay for that type of education. Normally the village itself would invite a teacher to stay in the Chi Tong [ancestral memorial hall] where the young ones would learn at least elementary Chinese and some mathematics.

The seasons of the year set a rhythm to life then as most people were involved in farming. The main focus each year was the Lunar Year festivities when villages celebrated the New Year. There were also other festivals such as Ching Ming [in the spring] and Chung Yeung [in the autumn] when the graves of the ancestors were swept, and the Mid-Autumn Festival.

The development of cottage-type industrial enterprises led to the rapid expansion of many villages and small towns in the New Territories in the 1950s. Most of the simple, wooden factories were put up quickly, and posed a great fire hazard. I spent a lot of time and effort in arranging for people to rebuild Shek Wu Hui after major fires there in 1955 and 1956.

By the end of the 1950s, the quiet settled rural life of the New Territories was changing. New textile factories had opened up in Tsuen Wan some years before, and the area was becoming progressively urbanized; many young people from villages in the New Territories were going overseas to work in search of a better future—an old tradition for people in South China; and for the first time there was talk of developing New Towns to provide homes for Hong Kong's expanding population.

The farmers and fishermen of the New Territories are tough and resilient. They have been able to adapt to the vagaries of war and peace, and have made a greater contribution to Hong Kong's economic development and social stability than is often recognized. I am quite certain that a New Territories' identity will survive after 1997 as I believe the Special Administrative Region Government will respect the commitments that have been made in the Joint Declaration.

One thing is sure. The New Territories has changed a great deal from when the British took over in 1898. I don't know who got the better bargain, but New Territories people like me are conscious of something we have lost—and our younger people, perhaps, of something they have never known.

Mary Bloch

South from Tianjin

When the Civil War broke out in China, the refugees who began streaming into Hong Kong were, by and large, ethnic Chinese. They came from over the border in Guangdong, or from Shanghai, and many other parts of China. However, non-Chinese immigrants, including people of European descent also sought refuge in Hong Kong, and they, too, brought with them their own experiences of Chinese life—mainly from the Western enclaves of Beijing, Tianjin (Tientsin), and Shanghai.

Among the 1950s exodus were many Russians from northern China. They were not immediately denounced by the new Communist regime in 1949, but were gradually squeezed out when it became apparent that they would become stateless if they remained. Those who came to Hong Kong represented a cross-section of the Russian communities in China. Many were workers from Manchuria based in Harbin, but some were wealthier merchants and traders. The majority who came were genuine refugees, who had been born and brought up in China, and arrived in the Territory with little money. For them, Hong Kong was only a transit point on the way to other countries.

But some never left, and Hong Kong became their home. Among those who eventually moved south was Mary Bloch, who was brought up in the treaty port of Tianjin, the 'Shanghai of the North'. Her father, a trader, had been born in Russia, but both her mother and her grandmother, although of Russian descent, had, like Mary herself, been born in China. It was therefore an enormous upheaval for them when, after the Communist revolution, the family left China for Japan. Mary then moved to Hong Kong with her first husband in the 1950s, and has remained in the Territory ever since.

Together with her second husband, George Bloch, she has made a significant contribution over the years to the arts in Hong Kong. Their collections of sculpture and paintings—post-impressionist, modern, and contemporary, as well as Chinese—have been exhibited at numerous cultural venues in the Territory, while their collection of Chinese snuff bottles has been displayed in Paris, Vienna, and London, as well as in Hong Kong. Despite their travels, however, Mary Bloch still lives in the Territory and maintains that her links with China will always remain strong.

WHEN I CAME to Hong Kong in 1956, I was absolutely delighted because, in my mind, it was like going back to China. I had been brought up there and when we were forced to leave during the Civil War, I missed China enormously.

I was born in Harbin in Manchuria, in what is today north-eastern China. My father was born in Russia, but his family had moved when he was seven years old to Manchuria, so he had really spent most of his life there, as had my mother. There was a very large Russian-speaking community in Harbin, with Russian schools, universities, Russian theatre, and Russian food and restaurants. It was a close-knit, self-contained community, which very much kept to itself.

Most of the Russians there were traders, and my impression was of a community leading a very comfortable existence. There certainly never seemed to be a shortage of things to buy. My mother used to tell me how the Trans-Siberian Railway from Paris brought French perfumes, clothes from all over Europe, and many items from Russia. There were touring artists as well, so there was also quite a cultural life.

My father was a fur trader, and when I was three my parents moved to what is today Tianjin which was then a Treaty Port. I lived there until I was eighteen, so it was very much my home. I have extremely happy memories of my years there and we had a wonderful life. I don't think my parents found it too hard to move there from Harbin. It was very cosmopolitan, with a large Russian community, as well as many other nationalities living there. Tianjin was divided into concessions. There were the British, French, German, Italian, and Russian concessions, but for some reason none of the Russians I knew lived in the Russian quarter. We all lived in the British concession, which was the centre of European life in Tianjin. The European communities mixed quite a lot, although the Russians kept more to themselves.

My parents must have been more internationally minded. I was sent to an English school, which wasn't a bad idea, but it was pretty frightening. I had never heard a word of English before; my parents hadn't even had any English friends. We spoke Russian, obviously, at home, and Mandarin, because the amah looking after me was Chinese. Anyway, at the age of five I started at Tianjin Grammar School.

The climate in Tianjin was very extreme. The winters were bitterly cold and we could ice skate on the ponds, while the summers were oppressively hot. Most of the international community used to escape to the beach resort at Pei Tai Ho [Beidaihe], where it was beautiful, cooler, and very unspoilt. There were few hotels and many of the Tianjin families took a villa. My mother and her friends would go in January to make all the arrangements for the summer. We never considered buying a place there, although we rented the same house almost every year. The day after school finished for the summer, we took a six and a half hour train journey, along with the amahs, the dogs, and whatever to Pei Tai Ho. Everything went and there we remained for the season, until the day before school started in the autumn.

There were many colonial buildings in Tianjin because of the strong British influence in the city. It was a very charmed existence and many people were very comfortably off although not extravagantly rich. My mother used to go to the café and meet her friends at eleven every morning, and she played mahjong in the afternoon. For the British, life tended to revolve around the Tianjin Club, which had an equivalent atmosphere to the Hong Kong Club. My family were not members, but when I was around sixteen I was able to join, as a junior member, the beautifully situated Tianjin Country Club. The other two places to go were the Victoria Café, in the British concession, which was the place for coffee or lunch, and Kieslings, in the German concession, which was where you met your friends for evening drinks. I had lots of friends, and many of them later came to Hong Kong as wives of Hongkong and Shanghai Bank employees, or of businessmen with shipping and trading companies.

I didn't envisage living anywhere else except Tianjin as I was growing up. I didn't travel very much. My first trip was when I was about thirteen, when I went to Beijing to stay with some Russian friends of my parents.

We never even considered moving during the Japanese occupation because there wasn't really anywhere else to go. The Japanese sent all the English and American families to a camp at Wei Shan [Wei Xian in Shandong province]. This meant we were left pretty much with our Russian friends. There were not too many hardships, and life was not bad. Many shops and businesses closed down, and there were enormous shortages: there was no white bread, for instance, or butter, or chocolate, but there was enough food to live on.

People started to consider moving elsewhere in 1949, when the Communists came to power. I am sure that if none of the international community had left, probably nothing would have happened. It seemed as if people were following a trend. Suddenly, everyone in the Western community wanted visas for different foreign countries, and there was a mass exodus. It was really the fear of the unknown. Nobody knew what it would be like under Communist rule.

Naturally, for me it was an enormous upheaval. My whole family moved to Tokyo to join my two uncles who were already living there. I spent a year there on my own, before my parents were able to join me, because at eighteen it was easier to obtain a visa. I stayed in Japan for seven years and by the time I arrived in Hong Kong, I was married with two children.

I had imagined it would be like going back to Tianjin, but Hong Kong was different from China. It was a British colony and a great deal more sophisticated. I had also grown up, so my lifestyle had changed. It helped having so many old friends, many of whom had come directly to Hong Kong from Tianjin after 1949.

There were quite a number of Russians in Hong Kong in the fifties and certainly enough to have vodka parties. Many were refugees just in transit in Hong Kong, on their way to Australia, New Zealand, America—to wherever people were emigrating. We were able to have Russian food and vodka, and some gypsy singing. So there was a large enough Russian community to make us feel at home.

I'd always been used to a cosmopolitan existence and quickly settled into the lifestyle in Hong Kong. We lived on Old Peak Road, in the Mid-Levels, I became a member of the Ladies' Recreation Club and my boys went to school in Glenealy. We often went to any one of the number of beaches around Hong Kong Island, and there was never a problem with pollution. Most of the time was spent chauffeuring our children to various activities.

Almost everyone in the expatriate community during the fifties and sixties had heard of Billy Tingle. He was extremely popular, and organized a number of extra-curricular activities for the expatriate children. They went to him for swimming lessons at the LRC, and cricket at the Cricket Club on the green in the heart of Central. There were many other activities for the children as well, such as piano, judo, and boxing lessons.

The expatriate community was relatively small compared with today, and was much more closely knit. Everybody knew everyone, and you could go, as my husband used to say, 'from one cocktail party to another and see the same faces'. We all considered Hong Kong a wonderful place to live, with lovely homes, domestic help, perfectly good schools for the children, and a lively social life.

When I arrived in 1956, the Territory was a little more primitive than it is now, and I missed enormously the many cultural events which had been part of our lives in Tianjin and Tokyo. In the fifties, the only concerts were those held in the old Loke Yew Hall at the University of Hong Kong. It was a momentous occasion when the City Hall opened later, in 1962. It was a big event, highlighted with a concert given by the London Symphony Orchestra conducted by Sir Malcolm Sargent. That really marked the beginning of Hong Kong's musical and cultural development. Enormous strides in the arts have been made since then with the construction now of the Cultural Centre, the Academy for the Performing Arts, museums, and the Arts Centre.

Hong Kong physically was very different in the fifties. There were, of course, none of the enormous buildings, like Exchange Square, nor were there the large hotels. When the Hilton and the Mandarin were built it was a great event. Suddenly there were two extremely comfortable hotels in the middle of the city, which became a meeting place for a lot of people. In those days the two restaurants were Jimmy's Kitchen, and the Parisian Grill on Queen's Road, which was, coincidentally, managed

The new City Hall is in the foreground with the Mandarin Hotel (under construction) on the right and the former Hilton Hotel (under construction) top left.

by a Russian.

People were attracted to Hong Kong because of the favourable business environment. By the mid-fifties, Hong Kong was back on its feet. Many of the people who came here were refugees, but they managed to maintain a very positive attitude, which I admired, and, in no time at all, had built up businesses and started factories. Hong Kong is considered a materialistic society but there were many who were doing a great deal of charity work, even in those early days. I became very involved with the Society for the Protection of Children (SPC), an organization close to my heart. It was involved in those days mainly with running day and residential centres for children who came from very poor backgrounds. Many of the day centres were used by working mothers, who had no one to look after their children while they were out all day. Hong Kong was not as prosperous as it is today so fund-raising was not such an easy task; we certainly weren't able to raise the sums of the money that many charitable organizations are able to do today.

It is easy to reflect fondly on the 'good old days', but it would be unrealistic to think that life remains the same forever.

Sir S. Y. Chung
Industrial Revolution

'**B**lunt', 'hawkish', 'stubborn', 'tireless', 'turncoat': these are but a few of the words used to describe Hong Kong's elder statesman, Sir Sze Yuen Chung.

Sir S. Y. has devoted thirty years to public service. He emerged as an important political leader during the 1980s, when, as the Senior Executive Councillor, he took a tough position with both Britain and China to argue for a better deal for Hong Kong during the Sino-British negotiations on Hong Kong's future.

He first brought into the open public concern about the question of Hong Kong's post-1997 future during his welcoming address to the new Governor, Sir Edward Youde, in 1982. He shuttled backwards and forwards with his Executive Council colleagues between London and Hong Kong during the Sino-British negotiations on the future of Hong Kong, arguing initially for continued British administration, and then for a 'detailed and legally binding treaty, acceptable to the people of Hong Kong'.

The Executive Council members also showed they were prepared to be just as frank with China. In 1984, Sir S. Y. Chung led an historic delegation to Beijing, where he was admonished by China's paramount leader, Deng Xiaoping, for casting doubts over China's ability to stick to the 'one country, two systems' concept.

Eight years later, Sir S. Y. was appointed as a Hong Kong Affairs adviser to China. He served on the two Beijing-appointed committees set up to oversee the transition: the Preliminary Working Committee, and the Preparatory Committee.

Having served the British colonial government in Hong Kong and received two knighthoods, Sir S. Y. has been accused of changing political horses to ensure his own future. He argues he has never held back from telling either the British or the Chinese Governments what he feels, and, whether as an adviser to Britain or China, he is fighting solely for Hong Kong's best interests.

Sir S. Y. Chung comes from an old established Hong Kong Cantonese family. His parents emigrated to Hong Kong as merchants just before the turn of the century and he was born and brought up in the Territory. He is an engineer by training and played a key role in the development of Hong Kong's manufacturing industry in the 1950s.

While he might be better known for his more recent political role, he has been lobbying Britain on behalf of Hong Kong since the late 1950s. He was one of the prime movers behind the formation of the Federation of Hong Kong Industries, which came into being in 1960. Six years later, just before the age of fifty, Sir S. Y. gave up his private sector career, and became the Federation's Chairman, marking the start of his long public service career.

HONG KONG before the Pacific War was a very peaceful city, and in fact when I returned to Hong Kong from China at the end of 1946, social conditions hadn't changed very much. There was a tremendous difference in lifestyle between the Chinese and the foreigners and this didn't change much until after the war. There were very few Chinese living on the Peak before the war, for instance, but there was little resentment. Hong Kong was a British colony and we just accepted these differences.

I had been educated in the pre-war years in China and Hong Kong. My main memory of my year at St John's in Shanghai, was of the magnificent processions in the streets of the International Settlement, celebrating the British coronation [of George VI] in 1937. My time in Shanghai was cut short with the start of the Sino-Japanese War that same year, and I continued my studies at the University of Hong Kong.

It was then that I became the proud owner of an open-topped Austin 7, and, since I was reading engineering, I used it for pleasure and study. That meant I would take the whole engine apart and then reassemble it! I drove the car everywhere. Traffic was no problem, and you could park on any of the main streets in Central; in Pedder Street, cars were double parked in the middle of the road, herring-bone style!

I had to escape from Hong Kong in early 1942 during the Japanese occupation. As an engineer in the Whampoa dockyard, I heard that I had to report for work there. I did not wish to work for the Japanese, so I told my family to tell anyone who came looking for me, that I had gone missing during the hostilities. I crossed to Macau where I made contact with one of my former university teachers who invited me to go and work with the Nationalist Government in China. I went as a chief designer to a machine factory in Jiangxi province, but, when I got there, I discovered there were no technical books available.

I returned to Hong Kong undercover during the occupation, disguised as a fisherman, to pick up all my engineering books. The Japanese were refusing to allow people to return to Hong Kong, so I paid a fisherman to smuggle me back. He told me I didn't look anything like a fisherman and I had to 'blacken' my face, and my arms and legs, before he would take me, or else we would arouse too many suspicions if we were stopped. I lay outside for about ten days to get sunburnt and made my hands rough and weathered-looking with sand. We sailed into Aberdeen one evening, and I sneaked back to my home near the University of Hong Kong. I collected two trunks of books, and had a lucky escape trying to return to Macau, dodging a Japanese sentry on the way, who had been on the verge of inspecting my cases. From Macau, I made my way back to China.

I spent the remainder of the war years in China, where I lived quite a good life. After the war I was offered a vice-minister's post in one of the provinces in Manchuria. I had already arranged to further my studies abroad, and, although it was very tempting, I turned down the offer. We returned to Hong Kong, and I'm glad I made that decision. Manchuria was later completely cut off by the Communists, so who knows what the outcome might have been?

I was surprised how active Hong Kong was when I returned at the end of 1946. Hong Kong had revived as a trading port after the war, and business was already thriving. People were making very easy money and I was really tempted to go into business. But I had won a British Council research scholarship to do my post-graduate study in metallurgy, so I left for Britain in 1948.

In 1951, when I had finished my studies, China was attempting to attract overseas Chinese scholars to return to the Motherland to work as experts. Eight out of ten of my Chinese colleagues at Sheffield University went to China after completing their post-doctorate research. I never saw or heard from them again until after 1979. By then, some had passed away and others were high ranking officials. I turned down that opportunity and went back to Hong Kong.

When I returned to Hong Kong in October 1951, I was very distressed. Things had taken a turn for the worse and these were extremely dark days for Hong Kong. First, there were the US and UN trade embargoes against China [due to the Korean War] and Hong Kong's entrepôt trade with China was greatly diminished. There was also the dramatic increase in the population of the Territory because of the influx of refugees from China, and that happened just as our own economy was suffering. Third, no one wanted to invest in Hong Kong because there were worries that China would demand the return of the Territory. The situation gradually improved when there were indications from China that the 'matter of history', in other words the question of the sovereignty of Hong Kong, would be resolved when the time was right ,and, until then, Hong Kong should remain a British colony. It is interesting to note that China was giving that message even then.

I started working in Hong Kong, then, just at a time when the Government was trying to encourage investment in industry. I was a consulting engineer, advising and helping investors to set up factories. Normally I would start one factory a year, mainly in the urban areas of Kowloon around Tai Kok Tsui and Hung Hom.

There are a number of reasons behind Hong Kong's phenomenal industrial success after those gloomy days in the early fifties.

The first was the influence of the Shanghainese, who kick-started Hong Kong's industrial revolution by providing much of the capital for the new ventures. Shanghai had been a centre for light industry before the war, producing textiles and metal products. Hong Kong was fortunate because just after the war, the Shanghainese entrepreneurs had ordered a lot of new machinery for their textile mills in Shanghai. The Civil War, and the Communist revolution interrupted these plans, and, instead of shipping their equipment to Shanghai, they had it sent to Hong Kong, where it had been stored. So when the Shanghainese came to the Territory, they just opened up the boxes! That's why the first major industry developed here was the cotton textile industry. All the spinning and weaving was done on new machines originally destined for Shanghai.

The Shanghainese were also aided by the helpful attitude of the banks at the time, which were willing to lend money to industry. However, Hong Kong's industrial revolution cannot just be credited to the Shanghainese.

Rising land prices in the urban areas was another major contributing factor behind the rapid twenty-year growth in Hong Kong's manufacturing industry. This encouraged entrepreneurs to relocate to cheaper suburban areas such as San Po Kong and Kwun Tong. With the large capital gain from the sale of the old factory in the urban area, owners were able to build larger new factories, with modern equipment. In the 1950s land was quite inexpensive in the urban area. Ten years later, prices were rising very fast. I can cite my own case. We constructed a two-storey factory on a 10,000-square-foot plot of land in To Kwa Wan: the total cost was around HK$750,000. In the early sixties we bought a 35,000-square-foot plot of land in San Po Kong for less than half a million, while our old factory was sold for more than three million, which was used to finance the new plant.

The other important contributing factor in the development of Hong Kong's manufacturing industry, especially the textile industry, was the quota system. When Hong Kong faced the imposition of quotas from the UK and America [during the late 1950s and early 1960s], we thought that was the end of the textile industry, but actually the reverse happened, and it was a blessing in disguise.

The quotas were designed in three ways which, with hindsight, benefited Hong Kong. First, the quota was fixed in quantity, not in value. This encouraged Hong Kong manufacturers to trade up, and it improved the quality and value of their products. Second, the quota was controlled by the exporting country, that is the seller, not the buyers. This meant manufacturers could choose the buyer, and obviously could sell to the person offering the highest price. Third and most important, the level or amount of the quota was based on past performance. Hong Kong was one of the first in the world to export clothing, and was the world's leading exporter of some textiles. We therefore had a quota much higher than any other country—even India, with a population a hundred times that of Hong Kong!

Hong Kong industry actually prospered under the quota system and without it Hong Kong would never have been able to achieve the same standard of development. At the time we thought that quotas would restrict the growth of the industry and it was the fight against the imposition of quotas which saw the establishment of the Federation of Hong Kong Industries. It also triggered my first involvement in public service.

The Hong Kong Government, as a colonial administration, was powerless to argue against the British Government's decision to impose quotas, since it was effectively under British control. However, it encouraged the private sector to lobby against the decision. The Hong Kong Government established a working party in 1958 with the aim of setting up an umbrella organization representing all Hong Kong manufacturers, and I was appointed to that committee. This led to the establishment of the Federation of Hong Kong Industries in 1960. I was an active member on the Executive Committee, and eventually I became Chairman in 1966.

In the fifties, factory conditions in Hong Kong were similar to those of 1980s China. They have been described as deplorable, and indeed they were. Conditions did improve significantly in the late fifties and sixties, when factories started to install air-conditioners. The objective was not really to improve the welfare of the workers, though, but to enhance productivity. People were willing to work a bit faster, especially in the summer, if they were not sweating. Factories might have been described as sweat shops but I remember when I was in England in the late forties, seeing young female workers coming out from the cutlery factories in Sheffield, covered in black dust: Hong Kong wasn't that bad in comparison.

The Hong Kong Federation of Industries worked hard to improve industrial safety during the sixties, but it didn't work. It couldn't work: people were just not interested. The focus then was on getting factories into production—and making money. Factory workers were only interested then in three questions: How much will you pay me?; Do we have overtime?; and Is the overtime regular or irregular? They wanted high pay and regular overtime. In the affluent eighties they asked the same three questions: they still wanted high pay, but little or no overtime so that they could spend more time with their families on Sundays and in the evenings. In the early days when Hong Kong was poor, people were only interested in making money, and life was cheap. There was no interest in industrial safety even if the employer tried to encourage it. Today, more affluent workers see things differently and they do take note of industrial safety. That's progress.

Hong Kong has benefited over the years from the lack of democracy. The irony is that, in the late fifties and sixties, I was supporting the manufacturers' demands that the Government do more to protect industry by imposing an import duty on some products, and providing incentives for local factories. There were also calls on the administration to introduce a minimum wage for workers. If there had been any form of democracy then, the Government would have been under pressure to meet these demands, and it would have been the end of Hong Kong as a free port and a territory with low taxation. I have always said that if Hong Kong had had democracy then, it would never have been able to maintain its free port status.

There had been a proposal to introduce limited electoral reforms with the 'Young Plan' in 1947. Later a revised proposal was put forward by the prominent legislator Man Kam Lo, who suggested partial elections to the Legislative Council over a number of years. These had been approved by all the councillors and the then Governor, Alexander Grantham. At the last minute the unofficial legislators saw the troubles and threat from over the border and asked the Governor to drop any idea of electoral reform. With hindsight, if they had gone ahead it could have been a disaster for Hong Kong. Apart from the threat to Hong Kong's trading status, it would also have given China a chance to interfere in Hong Kong.

I took the same view during the debate on democratic reforms in the 1980s. Strong Government has always been a major factor behind Hong

Kong's success, and has enabled successive administrations to take a long term overall view on policy changes. Once you lose that, issues are looked at more for short-term gains. I still argue that any electoral changes should be gradual and step by step.

Hong Kong is very fortunate in that its geographical position and British administration has enabled the territory to benefit in the past from the turmoil in China. In the future, however, we will only benefit from peaceful developments on the Mainland. Previously, the Western world needed a window to look into China, and China, which was isolated, also wanted a window to look outside. Hong Kong provided that window. Since the signing of the Joint Declaration we can no longer isolate ourselves from China. The world will look at Hong Kong as part of China. If there is any turmoil in China, any isolation of China, Hong Kong will be included.

But one thing must remain unchanged: Hong Kong's political neutrality. The neutrality of the Hong Kong Government and the people towards domestic politics in China has been another major contributing factor to Hong Kong's prosperity and stability since 1950. My view has been that this situation should not change as a result of the Sino-British Joint Declaration. We came dangerously close to compromising this position in 1989, and some people over-stepped the mark. Our main objective must be to maintain our usefulness to China, not be a burden or a threat. Neutrality is the only way that we can survive.

I have always given advice with the best interests of Hong Kong in mind. I came back here in 1951 to serve Hong Kong, and today, whether I am speaking to the British or Chinese Governments, I am still doing the same thing: fighting for Hong Kong.

Hearts and Minds

the 1960s

Post-war Hong Kong came of age in the 1960s, following a period of considerable economic progress and political *status quo* under the governorship of Sir Robert Black. The rite of passage occurred in 1967, when civil disturbances challenged the legitimacy of the colonial administration.

The extended civil disorder, which had been stimulated by the Cultural Revolution in China, included anti-government street protests, strike action, death threats, and a bombing campaign. A mixture of pro-China and anti-British sentiments fuelled the unrest. Socialist and long-repressed anti-colonial attitudes were openly expressed. These served to highlight the large and growing gap in living standards between the working class and the governing and industry élite. While on the one hand Hong Kong's industrialization grew rapidly for the greater part of the decade and benefited many, the influx of rural peasant farmers from China outpaced the Government's ability to keep up with the needs and expectations of the Hong Kong people.

Between 1960 and 1970, Hong Kong's population increased by nearly 25 per cent; almost one million people flooded into the Territory, bringing the total population to around four million. The vast majority arrived in the early 1960s, and it was Sir Robert Black, Governor for six years until 1964, who had to cope with the crisis. The main reason for the sudden surge in illegal immigrants from China was the failure of Mao's Great Leap Forward (1958–61), and the ensuing 'Three Years of Natural Disasters' (the three-year famine). Many of the immigrants were starving, and all were desperate for work, which was readily available in Hong Kong's burgeoning mass production industries, and which did not require skilled labour.

This influx of refugees, in fact, provided the manpower which helped Hong Kong become one of the world's leading manufacturing centres in the 1960s. During the first half of the decade, the number of factories nearly doubled, and the number of people they employed trebled, to over 600,000 people. By the end of the 1960s, Hong Kong was the world's leading textile exporter, with textiles representing 70 per cent of the Territory's total exports. But labour conditions were mostly Dickensian, and hours of work invariably long. It was only after the civil disturbances in 1967 that improvements—a statutory day off each week, for instance—were brought about.

Hong Kong's economic growth in the 1960s benefited from the free trade policies pursued by Sir John Cowperthwaite, Financial Secretary from 1961 to 1971. Since the war period, Hong Kong had received no financial aid from Britain, and, by 1970, it had no need to look to Britain for help. Sir John successfully established Hong Kong's financial independence, whilst strengthening the Colony's fiscal reserves. However, despite a prolonged period of economic growth, the economic downturn in 1967 resulted in the collapse of many local banks. The largest of these was the Hang Seng Bank, which was taken over by the British hong, the Hongkong and Shanghai Bank. The devaluation of the British pound, to which the Hong Kong currency was linked, brought about the financial crisis. The Hong Kong dollar was eventually delinked, and, as a result of the growth in Hong Kong's exports, the economy recovered, and by the end of the decade was buoyant again.

Sir John's fiscal policy spurned the idea of a welfare state, and public expenditure was strictly controlled, restricted to helping only those most in need. The already swamped social services, together with long working hours and bleak living conditions, engendered a sense of frustration and alienation which was easily exploited by those who sought to export the Cultural Revolution from China to Hong Kong.

The Governor who presided over this dramatic period was Sir David Trench, Hong Kong's last viceroy from the old Colonial Service, and Sir Robert's successor. He arrived in April 1964, and, some believe, nearly cracked under the strain in the ensuing years.

1966 saw the start of Mao's Cultural Revolution, which spilled over into Macau that year, and to Hong Kong in 1967. Sir David had a tricky balancing act to perform between the old guard, official and commercial, and the growing influence of those in the civil service, voluntary agencies, and tertiary institutions who believed the *status quo* to be untenable. The civil disturbances which continued through much of 1967, but which reached their height during the hot summer months, resulted in more than fifty dead and 800 injured. With a mixture of bluff and brawn, the British colonial administration managed to contain the civil disorder, but only just.

The violent confrontations were a watershed in Hong Kong's development. Senior officials in Hong Kong and London began to accept that, if the colonial administration was to continue to govern Hong Kong with any claim to legitimacy, social conditons would have to improve, and more Hong Kong people would have to be, or perceive themselves to be, associated with the governmental process.

The Government, which had not considered political reforms since shelving the 'Young Plan' in the early 1950s, set out to enhance consultation and feedback through the creation and expansion of advisory committees. A City District Officer system, modelled on long-standing practices in the New Territories, was set up to handle local complaints, provide a sounding-board for public opinion, and marshal support for government policies and programmes. But power would not be diluted. In deference to the wishes of China, and the Territory's powerful business élite, the Legislative Council would remain a reliable rubber stamp for executive formulated policy and legislation.

Maintenance of the political *status quo* was tacitly endorsed by a community weary of demonstrations, strikes, and propaganda. People wanted a return to normality, and the chance to get on with their lives, rather than debates about political structures and representation. Moreover, other more pressing and practical problems, such as social conditions, housing, education, and health care, had to be immediately addressed if the fragile stability of the Territory was to be sustained.

The vast improvements in living conditions, which were the hallmark of the next decade, were initiated in the late 1960s, as a result of the lessons learnt in 1967. Sir John Cowperthwaite's fiscal policies simply had not allowed the social programmes to progress fast enough to meet the needs of the community.

The housing programme, initiated in 1954, and given unswerving support by Sir Robert Black, was well underway. By then the Government recognized that Hong Kong's refugee population had come to stay and had to be supported, if only minimally. Conditions in the early resettlement estates of the late 1950s and early 1960s, were far from ideal. The so-called 'H' (shaped) blocks were stark, concrete structures with communal cooking and lavatory facilities, and with an original design specification of 24 square feet (2.23 square metres) per adult. Although the Government had considerable success in clearing many of the larger squatter settlements in the urban area, new squatter areas continued to appear, and basic housing conditions remained appalling. New immigrants usually lived in cramped, unsanitary accommodation little different from what they had left in China. This situation was to continue into the next decade until new initatives were launched.

During the 1960s, the Government mounted a series of public health programmes, including immunization and child health care, to meet the demands posed by a young, expanding population. At the same time, there was a steady expansion in the number of clinics and hospitals, many funded by local charitable or religious groups. However, although Queen Elizabeth Hospital, opened in 1963, was the largest in the Commonwealth, all hospitals and clinics remained overcrowded, and patients frequently had to share the same bed.

Providing even basic primary education remained a challenge throughout the decade as the number of school-age children increased dramatically. Many children had little or no formal education, despite the stout efforts of so many voluntary agencies, and much of what was available was expensive for the majority of the population. Compulsory free primary education was not introduced until 1971, and 1978 for the secondary level. At the tertiary level, Hong Kong's only university was upgraded in 1963, and the Chinese University opened the same year in Sha Tin.

A significant feature of the 1960s was the vocal debate about corruption, particularly in relation to government services. The police were singled out for particular criticism, because of their high public profile and close dealing with triad and other racketeer organizations. People came to see institutionalized corruption as detrimental to Hong Kong's growth as a modern international trading centre.

This syndicated corruption caused the resentment that was one of the underlying causes of the 1966 Star Ferry Riots. The riots sparked off by a minimum increase in ferry fares, quickly escalated to sit-ins, hunger strikes, more riots, and looting in urban Kowloon. The disturbances were seen at the time as a spontaneous outburst by a minority of troublemakers against increased travel costs. With hindsight, it was evidence of the general feeling of discontent brought about by economic and social conditions.

However, by the end of the decade, in line with the growth of the economy, more Hong Kong people were able to edge themselves away from a subsistence existence to a more consumer-based lifestyle.

Although for most people, life continued to be focused on finding somewhere to live, getting a job, and raising a family, Hong Kong provided other interests.

There was horse-racing at Happy Valley in the cooler months, and there was the entertainment industry led by Shanghainese movie mogul, Sir Run Run Shaw. The prolific number of films produced by the Shaw brothers provided a heady mixture of Kung Fu, violence, romance, and popular versions of tales from China's imperial past. The late 1960s saw the return to Hong Kong from the United States of Kung Fu legend, Bruce Lee, whose films blended Western and traditional Chinese cultural tastes. 1967 was a watershed in one other respect: the start of commerical television launched by Sir Run Run Shaw. Before then, only expensive cable television had been available to a limited audience. By the end of the decade, Television Broadcasts' (TVB) audience ratings were estimated at two million—nearly half of the total population.

By the end of the 1960s, Hong Kong was a rich amalgam of Chinese regional cultures—Shanghainese, Fujianese, Hakka—with Cantonese as the dominant overlay. Despite the many divergent interests and disparities which existed in Hong Kong society, a sense of belonging was slowly beginning to emerge. This was actively reinforced by the Hong Kong Government as it sought to brighten its tarnished image, and win the hearts and minds of the population in support of maintaining Hong Kong's economic and social freedom within a traditional British legal framework.

Hong Kong was no longer a first generation refugee transit stop, but was becoming a place which a new Hong Kong generation would identify as home.

Don Watson

The People from 'China Mountain'

Don Watson arrived in Hong Kong in 1960 to join the Royal Hong Kong Police as a sub-inspector. New recruits spent six months in the Police Training School learning the rudiments of policing and legal procedure, and basic spoken Cantonese. Don Watson came initially for three years, but, attracted by the excitement and demands of the job, he stayed for almost forty.

In the 1960s, the Hong Kong Police, quasi-military in ethos and command structure, was organized along traditional colonial lines. The majority of its officers were expatriate, many having seen service in Africa, Malaya, and Palestine, while junior personnel were Hong Kong Chinese. However, reflecting the Territory's imperial past, the force also included personnel recruited from other British colonies. The Sikhs, who had largely sided with the Japanese during the occupation of Hong Kong, were no longer recruited after the war, but, following the partition of the Indian subcontinent in 1947, the force began to recruit from Pakistan. These officers were usually deployed in the New Territories. The force also recruited from the former British enclave of Wei Hai Wei (Wei Hai) in Shantung (Shandong) province in northern China, and these people were traditionally based in the urban areas.

Part of the police force's responsibility was illegal immigration control along Hong Kong's 35-kilometre land border with China—no easy task in the marshy, rugged terrain with few roads. One of the main reasons for the flood of immigrants during the early 1960s was the failure of Mao's Great Leap Forward. This campaign, launched in 1958 to push forward China's industrial revolution, resulted in a three-year famine. The massive influx of starving refugees from China reached its height in 1962, when it was estimated that nearly 150,000 immigrants flooded over the border into Hong Kong during that year alone. When a month-long mass influx occurred, Don Watson was sent to the New Territories to help deal with this problem.

The Foreign Office in London made representations to China to persuade officials to do more to stop the stream of immigrants, and, in a

bid to contain the problem, a new border fence was constructed.

In sharp contrast to his experiences in the New Territories, Don Watson later served as an aide-de-camp to the then Governor, Sir Robert Black. Many young officers in Hong Kong, like Don Watson, led long and varied careers, and were often given opportunities and responsibilities far greater than their counterparts in Britain. In 1993 Don Watson was transferred from the police to become Commissioner of Customs and Excise. By the time he retired in 1996, after more than thirty-six years of government service, the Hong Kong border, which he had patrolled when he first arrived, had long ceased to symbolize the divide with Communist China.

ALL DAY LONG we had watched thousands of people make their way like huge snakes down 'China Mountain' [Wu Tong Shan] towards Hong Kong's border with China. By dusk a huge mass had assembled and were organizing themselves into a procession, four or five abreast. Then, marshalled by the local Chinese militia, they were escorted over a small stream to the border; they pushed down the fence, and in they came.

We were lying in ambush but were by no means strong enough to hold them all, so quite a few got through our lines. I told those we rounded up to sit down, but several of them went for me. Just as I thought my last day had come, a black apparition materialized out of nowhere. It was a platoon of Pakistani police officers who, with their black raincoats and dark hats, had merged into the shadows. They stood up, a wall of black. A sharp command was given and instantly obeyed. 'Stop! You must not hit the sahib.' Thanks to them I got away relatively unscathed.

Illegal immigration was not unusual in Hong Kong, but the mass influx of 1962 was. I was sent up to the border with a platoon of police officers from Central. The newspapers had been full of what was going on, but I had absolutely no idea of the magnitude of the problem until we arrived at the frontier. It had by then reached crisis proportions. The number of police deployed on the border had been insufficient to handle the situation. All the police divisions from the urban areas had then been mobilized and were despatched to the border, and that was when I went up with my platoon. The problem was compounded by thousands of Hong Kong people coming up to scour the hillsides for their relatives.

Nobody knew at the time exactly what had triggered off the exodus, but for nearly four weeks, the Chinese authorities made no attempt to try and stop it. There were even rumours that the authorities in Canton [Guangzhou] had opened the jails, and told the inmates to make use of the chance and go as quickly as they could to Hong Kong. Once the exodus had started, it was then a question of everyone jumping on the bandwagon, trying to escape over the border and make their way into the urban area, where they hoped they would not be detected and sent back. We repatriated around 100,000 people to China, but I suspect just as many made it through to the urban area where they could find work and, for some, their families.

Most of the people who crossed the border into Hong Kong were peasant farmers. The majority were in their twenties and thirties, but there were babies and grandmothers as well. All of them were very poorly dressed, tired and dejected, and most were starving. There were no indications that they were coming for political reasons. Nobody ever mentioned human rights at that time, or requested asylum. And, as far as I was aware, for those who were repatriated there were few, if any, penalties.

Once the refugees had been intercepted, we took them to the Police Training base near Fanling where we made a note of their personal details. We gave them a meal which they usually devoured immediately. I don't recall there being much animosity after the illegal immigrants had been taken into custody. Of course, if they had a chance, they would try to run away, but mostly they just accepted they would have to go back.

They were transported by truck to the Lo Wu Railway Bridge, where they walked back into China. [At that time the only road link between Hong Kong and China was a small temporary bridge at Man Kam To. All immigration procedures, including the repatriation of illegal immigrants, were carried out at the Kowloon–Canton Railway Bridge at Lo Wu.] Many then just made their way further down the border, to look for somewhere else to cross back into Hong Kong. I remember one illegal immigrant we intercepted and sent back several times. Perhaps he eventually got through to the urban area—he deserved to!

The fact that so many kept returning to Hong Kong highlighted one of the major problems we faced at that time in stemming the flow of illegal immigrants. The border fence running along the hillside was totally inadequate. It certainly was not strong enough to deter determined, hungry people, desperate to come to Hong Kong. It was easy to cut, scale, or simply push over. As a result, we had to construct a new, stronger fence, and, because of the urgency, it was done in a very short period of time. However, constant vigilance was required to ensure it remained intact.

My first posting as an inspector had been to Central Division, in the heart of the urban area of Hong Kong Island. We lived in the police station which hadn't changed much since it was first built in 1864. It was rumoured that the building had been condemned in 1929, so accommodation was pretty basic. Back then, every police station had an Inspector-on-Duty, or, as we know it today, a Duty Officer, and we initially spent a lot of time as Duty Officers.

Our job was to deal with arrests brought in by the constables on beat duty, and attend to people coming to the police station to make a wide variety of reports, many of which were not police-related at all. Disputes with neighbours, domestic upsets, difficult children all seemed to end up eventually in the Report Room.

In those days, there was a very colonial atmosphere to the police station. The reception desk in the Report Room was extremely high, and, as Duty Officer, you sat perched up on a tall stool, a bit like a tennis umpire, with a corporal on either side, each of whom ran a different miscellaneous report book, one dealing with arrests and charge cases, and the other with miscellaneous reports. The Duty Officer's job was to take the reports, and make sure that action was taken.

Going through the standing orders for Central Division, one thing which amused me was an order from the Sub-Divisional Inspector that we were not allowed to use Greener guns to shoot monkeys on the Peak. In those days there were quite a few monkeys there, and the Greener gun, although a shotgun, was a specific anti-riot weapon. But it didn't have any real effect beyond thirty yards, so there was not much point going up to the Peak and firing off these massive great shotguns at monkeys because it wouldn't have done any good anyway!

A great asset to the force then were the Shantungs, all very large northern Chinese. If you were ever on patrol in Wan Chai, for example, and there was a spot of bother in a bar, you were very lucky if you had the Shantungs with you because they would physically move the young gweilo [expatriate] police officer to the back of the entry party, and you didn't get into the place until everything had been subdued!

Hong Kong was a far less sophisticated place then, and the policing was much more straightforward. I think as a young inspector you were allowed to use your own initiative much more than young men who join the Force today.

At the end of 1962, I was posted as aide-de-camp [ADC] to the Governor, Sir Robert Black. Government House then was a much smaller organization. The team consisted of the Governor's Personal Secretary, two full time ADCs—one from the Police and one from the Army—and the housekeeper. The Governor didn't have the workload his successors have had, but at the time, Sir Robert's responsibilities were considerable, and, being the conscientious person he was, he worked long hours.

We also played the role of the Governor's social secretary, in addition to our other duties, as there was a great deal of socializing at Government House! Our job would be to arrange the guest list, confirm the menus with Lady Black, organize the seating plan, greet the guests, and provide idle conversation at the end of the table during the meal.

It was the custom then for people to sign the Visitors' Book at Government House when they arrived or departed Hong Kong. We would check the Visitors' Book frequently, to see who was in town so that the Governor could decide whether or not he would invite them for lunch or dinner. For those of some international standing or interest, there would be a special dinner or luncheon party.

Sir Robert Black was not one for spending money on himself or on Government House. In fact, he was extremely frugal, and very cost conscious. That ran through every aspect of his life, including meals, whether he was entertaining or not. There was one legendary example of a very embarrassing situtation during a lunch he was hosting, when there hadn't been enough food to go round. Twelve lamb cutlets had been prepared—one for each of the twelve guests. By the time the last guest came to be served, the silver platter was empty. In serving himself an imaginary cutlet, the unfortunate man glanced over to the guest opposite who had taken two, and was by then bright red!

There had also been plans in the pipeline to move Government House to a more prestigious location, on the Peak. A site in Mansfield Road had even been allocated for the new premises. However, Sir Robert said categorically 'No!' He felt the move was unnecessary and too expensive! In fact, in his day, Government House was not the luxurious residence one might have imagined it to be: the decor was very basic, and there was no air-conditioning. He argued that money which could have been spent on his own accommodation, should be put to better use.

During a major water shortage crisis in 1963, Sir Robert insisted that Government House be subject to the same restrictions as the general public, which meant four hours supply every fourth day. There had been some suggestion that Government House might be exempted, but Sir Robert had disagreed. I think this was the measure of the man. He put the people before himself and treated everybody fairly.

Perhaps his wish not to be ostentatious stemmed from his Colonial Service background and career which must have affected his thinking and attitudes. He was schooled in a hands-on tradition, which hated pomp and pomposity, preferring to go out and understand, from first-hand experience, how things were on the ground. He frequently made unannounced trips to major housing and community projects to see exactly what progress was being made, and whether there were any problems. I think this helped him keep in touch with the pulse of the community, and with the needs of the population.

One of his major priorities was to ensure that programmes like the housing resettlement programme, which had begun in the mid-1950s, went ahead quickly and effectively. He was very keen to get everyone out of squatter areas where they were at risk, not just from fires—like the one which precipitated the housing programme—but typhoons and mudslips as well. He was also instrumental in expanding the hospitals and medical services. During his term of office Queen Elizabeth Hospital was opened. At that time, it was the largest hospital in the Commonwealth.

Looking back over the governors of Hong Kong, most of them had some major crisis during their term in office. Prior to Sir Robert, there had been the immediate post-war problems; following him, Sir David Trench had the riots and confrontations in 1967 to deal with; Sir Murray MacLehose had the corruption problems; and then Hong Kong went through the transition and the difficulties arising from that. Sir Robert had to deal with the sudden and enormous influx of refugees, but, aside from that, I think he had five years when he was able to concentrate on getting Hong Kong society further up the ladder.

He was a 'nuts and bolts' governor, and not one to go for any grandiose schemes. His aim was to make sure that the average man in the street had somewhere to live, that he could be reasonably certain that his children could be educated, and, when he was sick, could receive a reasonably high standard of medical treatment.

As regards the future, I am optimistic. Hong Kong's prosperity has been built by that man in the street, and he is not going to lie down, curl up, and die just because there is a change of sovereignty. If there's money to be made, then the average Hong Kong person is going to find a way of making it. I think Hong Kong will continue to prosper. I just cannot see people throwing away what they've worked one generation, two generations, to make—a decent life in Hong Kong far away from China Mountain.

Lau Chin Shek

From Refugee to Trade Union Leader

Lau Chin Shek was one of the many thousands of refugees who came pouring down 'China Mountain' at the height of the influx in the early sixties.

His reasons, like most, were two-fold: economic and political. Guangdong, his home province, had suffered enormously from the droughts, famine, and starvation which followed Mao's Great Leap Forward. Soon after Lau arrived from Guangzhou in 1963, he, like so many others, found himself on the factory floor.

Unlike many though, his is not a rags to riches story. He has remained on the factory floor but as a defender of labour interests as a trade union leader. His involvement began with the Christian Industrial Committee (CIC), a pressure group set up in the early 1970s to represent the interests of the differing unions which existed in Hong Kong. It acted as a research organization, and has concentrated on specific issues, such as industrial safety. In 1980 Lau Chin Shek became the Director of the CIC.

Through his involvement in the Committee, Lau Chin Shek has been a prime mover in the growth of the trade union movement in Hong Kong, playing a key role in bringing the independent unions together as a powerful agent in the development of Hong Kong democracy. He represented the Confederation of Trade Unions in the Legislative Council, when he was directly elected to the Legislative Council in both the 1991 and 1995 elections.

He is a core member of Martin Lee's Democratic Party, and was a leading light in the Hong Kong Alliance in Support of the Patriotic Democratic Movement in China, set up in 1989 after the student protests in Tiananmen Square. It is an organization which Beijing has labelled as 'subversive', and has been used as an excuse to bar many of the pro-democracy forces from the consultative organs set up by China during the transition. Allegiance to the Alliance has almost certainly meant political exile after 1997.

However, grass-roots representatives like Lau Chin Shek have managed to maintain a loyal and large following, and it is hard to envisage that they will cease to defend vociferously workers' interests or democracy in the future. Lau Chin Shek has refused to learn English, as a demonstration of support for the workers, the majority of whom speak only Chinese. English was for many years the only means to secure a say in the government of the day. Despite this, Lau Chin Shek has successfully made sure that his voice has always been heard.

RECENTLY I HAD trouble with my back and went to consult a chiropractor. After he had seen the X-rays of my spine, he asked me whether I had had an accident when I was a child and had damaged my back. He said that, even though I was only having problems now, my back had suffered from a sudden impact a long time ago. I couldn't remember ever having been in an accident or injuring my back. But later on it dawned on me. When I was around ten or eleven years old I had to do some 'voluntary work', meaning I had to carry coal. I only weighed about a hundred pounds, but the weight of the coal I had to carry was more than my body weight. That was why my spine did not develop properly, and, of course, it was not voluntary work, it was forced labour.

I was brought up in a village near Guangzhou and was at secondary school during the late 1950s and early 1960s. After I left school, I was jobless and my mother had almost no money. She was illiterate, and my father had died when I was ten. I knew I couldn't live any longer under the kind of political pressure which existed in our daily lives. I couldn't even talk to my own mother or my friends about the way I looked at life because we didn't trust each other.

I was never happy during my childhood. My father had been an apprentice mechanic when he was young, but later went into a small metal-welding business. We were not directly affected by the political upheavals in China, but he suffered seeing his friends persecuted. Every time he went to work I was afraid it might be our turn, and that he would never return. My father wasn't really able to communicate with my mother because she had had a very simple upbringing, and that put extra strain on him. From the time that I was about seven years old, he used to ask me for advice about how to deal with problems. I was so young that I don't think he was expecting any particular sort of an answer from me, but he just wanted someone to talk with.

There are two memories from my school days, which stand out in my mind. The first is the sound of the telephone ringing at school, and the fear which gripped me each time it did. I was always worried that the teachers might call out my name and, if they did, I knew that someone in my family would have died. The news of the death of my relatives was always sudden and very traumatic. I lost an uncle who was in his early forties, and my cousin died in his thirties. Ostensibly they died of cancer, but the real cause was the strain on their daily lives. They always felt they were treated unfairly. They were not capitalists, they were self-made men, like my father, who had started from scratch, and had become their own bosses. They worked very hard, but they were treated as capitalists by others, and were ostracized by their friends.

The second memory, and the one which shocks me most, was watching the persecution of some of my teachers, who were tied up and denounced in front of us because they were considered intellectuals, and were, therefore, politically unacceptable. Whenever there was an anti-rightist campaign, they were always easy targets. A watchful eye was also kept on those of us whose family backgrounds fell under the 'Five Black Categories'. [The categories were landlords, rich peasants, counter-revolutionaries, rightists, and bad elements.] Nearly all my classmates and I were classified as counter-revolutionary, along with our teachers, because many of our parents ran small businesses, and were considered capitalists. We were all collected together in a so-called school, formerly a restaurant, and educated separately from the other children.

I escaped to Hong Kong in 1963, when I was sixteen years old, smuggled in the bottom of a fishing boat. I decided to leave China for two reasons. First, after I left school, I was jobless, and, after a great deal of effort, I realized that it was impossible for me to get work. My mother, who by that stage was on her own, did not have any money, and I couldn't ask her to support me any longer. Second, the political pressures were such that I had no wish to stay in China any longer. I had heard of many illiterate people who had left China and were making a living in Hong Kong. Many of them were domestic workers, but I thought, 'Okay, if these people, who can't even read or write have been able to find jobs, why can't I?'

My first impression of Hong Kong the night I crept ashore was of the lights: they just seemed so much brighter. I also felt incredibly helpless. Initially, I went to stay with my cousins, who had started a small barbecued pork cooked-food stall in Central, and then I went to live with my other cousin, who was staying in Tsuen Wan. She lived with her family, in one small room in a tenement building which had been divided into eight rooms. The room was the size of their bunk-bed: my cousin's two daughters slept on the top bunk, and my cousin, her husband, and their other child were on the lower bunk. I slept on a canvas bed, squeezed in at the side. Outside there was a makeshift lavatory for the whole house, and if anyone wanted to take a shower, they had to wash there as well.

My top priority when I arrived in Hong Kong, was to find work and my first job was in a garment factory in Tsuen Wan. The conditions were terrible, and many workers worked in the same place all their lives. The air was thick with dust, and 'misty', because of all the particles of cotton that were flying around. Since I was testing the products while they were being manufactured, I didn't have to spend all day on the assembly line, but, whenever I went in there, I came out with my hair totally white. The masks were far too uncomfortable to wear all day: in fact it was almost harder to breathe with them on! I worked around eleven and a half hours a day, from 7 a.m. to 6.30 p.m., and was paid four Hong Kong dollars and fifty cents a day, which averaged HK$130 a month. In those days a dish of rice in some makeshift restaurant next to the factory cost about a dollar or a dollar twenty. As I couldn't afford to have breakfast or a substantial lunch, my routine was that, for two days, I'd treat myself to a dish of rice, and then on the third day I'd have bread.

There were some girls who were clearly below the legal employment age, but, since they were desperate to work, they brought their mother's or their sister's identity cards when they applied for a job. They were really exploited, and were paid a lot less than I was earning. It was quite common in those days during the 1960s for children to work seven days a week, twelve hours a day, in a factory.

I was under a great deal of pressure from my bosses to do a good job, and to do it correctly, but this pressure was entirely different from that which I had experienced in China. At least I knew that I wouldn't die because I was being politically persecuted. Whereas in China the so-called 'class struggle', meant an ideological struggle between capitalism and Communism, in Hong Kong the class struggle was materialistic, between the rich and the poor.

The first time I came into contact with the social movement in Hong Kong was early in 1969. I was working on a magazine which acted as a forum to fight for the legal status of the Chinese language. Since I don't speak English I thought that Chinese should be treated as a legal language in Hong Kong. The movement was started by a group of intellectuals and students. However, although they initiated the campaign, it was people like me, the workers, who were being exploited and who suffered because Chinese was not an official language. I realized there was a need to form a coalition between workers and students, so I started to get involved in order to represent the workers' interests. That's when I wrote my first pamphlet. A group of us put some money in, wrote it, had it printed, and we distributed it ourselves. It was not until 1974 that Chinese was recognized as an official language, jointly with English. [It was not until 1989 that the process began to issue laws in both English and Chinese.]

I was not involved with the trade union movement at that stage, although sometimes I used to get together with some of the other workers to support people who were on strike. I remember, for example, visiting the Cross-Harbour Tunnel workers who were on strike in 1970, but we didn't actually form ourselves into a strong movement.

The main labour organization then was the Christian Industrial Committee, led by Dr L. K. Ding, and I joined them in 1971. The CIC was advertising for a community organizer. The recruiting terms were very odd: no need to know any English, no need to be religious, only a basic education was needed. I thought I fitted the bill, and applied. During the interview, I was asked how I was going to be able to communicate if I spoke no English, and I was worried because that had not been one of the recruitment terms. I did however get the job, working on the CIC publication, *Workers' Weekly Bulletin*, as a reporter, interviewing workers and writing articles.

There was a great deal of work to be done to try and improve the lot of the worker. Labour laws then were very sketchy, and gave the worker little protection. All power lay in the hands of the employers.

It was not until the mid-1970s that there was any noticeable improvement in employment conditions, although the real turning point in government thinking had come during the late 1960s. After the 1967 riots there was a change of policy. The Government realized that it had to address some of the social problems which existed, and had to treat people better. It was the former Governor, now Lord MacLehose, who gave a lot of impetus to this, and I think that was why he was appointed. I think we were helped as well by the fact that there was a Labour Government in power in Britain, and under the then British Prime Minister, Harold Wilson, it was far more concerned at that time with social issues and workers' rights than the Conservative Party.

The effect that organizations like the CIC had on the movement for reform cannot be minimized. They worked hard to push for greater protection of workers, and, slowly, improvements came like rainwater in spring, moistening the land. For the first time in 1970 we saw the introduction of a mandatory day off every week, although maternity leave did not come on to the statute books until 1981.

We also realized that the people themselves had to be educated so they could understand their rights, and support our campaign for improvements. This was the hardest task. We began the process by setting up various social centres. We also made sure that the issues we were promoting were ones which could easily be understood and directly affected people's livelihood. Maternity leave was an important issue since women then were not paid for any time they had off to give birth. Slowly, through the education programmes we organized, women started to realize their rights. Many were then willing to participate in a survey conducted by the University of Hong Kong on the situation of pregnant working women at that time. The results of the survey were later submitted to the Government, and it was on that basis that changes were made.

From the late 1960s and throughout the 1970s, we concentrated on education, to get people to fight for their rights, and to press for legal changes. In the 1980s we centred our efforts on mutual cooperation between all the different trade unions and political groups.

The June 4th protests in Beijing in 1989 had a profound effect on the labour movement, and resulted in a change in our policies. Tiananmen brought home the fact that there was a need for a truly independent trade union in Hong Kong before 1997. We saw during June 4th that the so-called trade unions in China, which may have seemed independent, were in fact controlled by the government, and some were even organized by the Chinese Public Security Bureau. It was therefore impossible for the trade unions in China to function as independent bodies.

We realized that, if we wanted to maintain a strong independent voice after 1997, we needed all the trade unions to form a coalition under one umbrella organization. [In fact a decision to set up a formal affiliated body had been made at a trade union seminar held in 1988, but the events of 1989 accelerated these plans]. Until then, the independent trade unions in Hong Kong were organized under a rather loose structure. The Trade Union Education Centre, set up in 1984, was really more of a talking shop and used as a forum to discuss labour issues. We only took seriously the idea of setting up a formal body, the Confederation of Trade Unions [CTU], in 1989. The CTU was therefore inaugurated in 1990, comprising thirty-nine trade unions. In 1996, it had more than 120,000 members.

Looking at labour conditions today, of course we can say that workers now are no longer poor people, but at the same time their status in the community is not commensurate with the development of Hong Kong. Workers do not negotiate with employers on equal terms, so the boss takes a bigger cut.

I really don't think much about the future of Hong Kong, or whether it will turn out good or bad. I think everyone has to decide whether to leave or to stay. I want to stay because I do care about the future, and I want to play a part in that. I care about democracy, the democratic development of Hong Kong, and I want to remain so that I can keep fighting.

It may seem like a contradiction in terms, but my childhood experiences make me want to stay all the more. Since I have already been through a kind of hell, I think that I want to continue to help other people so that we don't have to go through the same thing again. I can assure you, though, if anyone who has lived under communism tells you that there is no fear, he is either ignorant or a liar.

Sister Mary-Edna Brophy
The Greatest Gift

At the turn of the decade, when the Government was hard-pressed to handle the thousands of incoming, destitute Chinese refugees, it had to rely on the help of many charitable and religious organizations to provide basic social and medical services. The Maryknoll sisters played their part, and it was that crisis with which Sister Mary-Edna Brophy was immediately involved when she first arrived in Hong Kong in 1959.

Mary-Edna Brophy was raised on a ranch in a small Canadian town. Her mother died when she was just three years old, and she was brought up by her aunt. She qualified as a registered nurse in Toronto, and joined the Maryknoll Order in 1955 because she liked the look of the religious habit the sisters wore! Sister Mary-Edna was assigned to Hong Kong at the age of twenty-nine, one month after taking her vows. Since coming to the Territory she has worked as a missionary sister mainly in the resettlement areas of Kowloon.

The Roman Catholic Maryknoll Order had been long established in Hong Kong, since before the Second World War, and during the Japanese occupation many of the Maryknoll sisters were interned in the Stanley camp. The Maryknoll sisters were expelled from China in the aftermath of the Communist revolution, and came to work in Hong Kong where every extra pair of hands was needed. The Order played an important role in the rehabilitation of Hong Kong after the war. The missionaries helped provide immediate relief to the general public and to the new arrivals from China. They set up small schools for the children, classes for the women, and helped those who worked in small factories.

Gradually the sisters extended their work in Hong Kong, building a large primary and secondary school in Kowloon Tong to match the pre-war school the sisters had established in Happy Valley on Hong Kong Island. As a result, more of the Maryknoll sisters became involved in teaching and pastoral care, as well as medical clinics.

Sister Mary-Edna, however, worked as a nurse in health education. When she came to Hong Kong, the Maryknoll ministry was in the process of building its own hospital in Wong Tai Sin in Kowloon. It opened in 1961, two years before the large government-run Queen Elizabeth Hospital was completed. In 1996 the Maryknoll Hospital celebrated its thirty-fifth anniversary: Sister Mary-Edna had admitted its first patient.

During her time in Hong Kong, Sister Mary-Edna witnessed the many social and medical changes which have taken place in the Territory since the 1960s, and has a deep respect for the industry, energy, and community spirit of the Hong Kong Chinese people. For Sister Mary-Edna living in a largely non-Christian society has been a rewarding experience. 'The Chinese do not give up', she says. 'Neither do I.'

THE MARYKNOLL HOSPITAL opened in 1961 at a time when refugees from China were swarming over the mountains into Kowloon. They came because they were oppressed and starving. The refugees were easily identifiable: they were terribly thin, spoke different dialects, and wore big black hats and poor clothing which was mostly in tatters and rags. They were desperate. They just parked on the ground, and put up shanty huts, which littered the urban areas.

When I first arrived in Hong Kong two years earlier, I had never seen such poverty. The people, the clothes they were wearing, they were just so poor. Later, I visited the Poor Schools, started by our sisters, and the little children all seemed dirty and bedraggled but so eager to learn. However, looking back, those who had been here a while were not nearly so poor-looking as the new arrivals.

The squatter homes, made of cardboard and pieces of wood, often went up in flames because of the little gasoline lamps they used for cooking. When there was a fire nearby, we gave temporary refuge to the homeless in our out-patients department. They came with the few belongings they possessed, kettles, pots, or whatever they had been able to snatch up before their homes were engulfed by flames. I remember, after one large squatter fire, we were accommodating many of the victims in the Maryknoll Hospital.

One of the women said to me, 'It's so convenient here, and the little basin over there has already got water in it to wash our rice bowls. It's so low down and handy, and easy for us to squat beside while we wash the dishes.'

I told her, 'That's not for washing dishes. It's a toilet!'

We found some wash-basins for them to use instead. They had never seen a flush toilet.

Ignorance was born of poverty, and they had no idea of hygiene. We were treating peo-ple in those early days who were suffering from terrible infections and boils often caused by poor hygiene. These sores had become more infected by the leaves and herbs used in tradi-tional Chinese medicine. They had all sorts of things wrong with them,

Health Education with Sister Mary-Edna

and had often been in pain for a long time. I remember many of the young boys had rashes all over their legs from working in the rice pad-dies, and many had diarrhoea and vomiting.

There was one old lady whose cheeks and lips were bruised, and the skin was ulcerated and bleeding. She had been suffering from toothache for weeks, and had been told to rub an onion really hard on her mouth, and it would help to take away the pain. She had rubbed so hard, it had irritated the skin which had bled and become infected. That pain was greater than the toothache, so naturally the toothache wasn't hurting her as much! There were all sorts of superstitions and Chinese remedies, but I think they thought we could perform magic!

The top priority for the Government was to try and prevent the outbreak of disease. We helped with the drive to immunize the refugees as the government centres were overwhelmed. We also tried to stress the importance of general hygiene. There were very few children, for instance, who wore shoes in the countryside in China, so it took some time for them to catch on that if they didn't wear shoes they'd get worms more easily.

People were so appreciative of any help you gave them, and they seldom complained. After surgery, I would ask, 'Do you have a pain?' And they would reply, 'Just a little.' Most of the Chinese had never been without some kind of pain, so perhaps they were better able than Westerners to endure suffering with patience. Often, in the out-patients department, after we had treated them and given them some simple medicines, they would bend over and whisper, 'Thank you, Sister, but could you give me some milk powder and food. I don't have enough to eat'.

There were many difficulties, and we were coping with just minor problems. The Government was trying to set up as many clinics as it could, other churches and the Jockey Club were also helping to provide essential medical services.

The Government also had to focus on getting people off the ground because it was clear from the number of squatter fires, and the conditions under which people were living, that something had to be done. The early public housing resettlement blocks left much to be desired. They had common lavatories with no door, the water taps were out on the common veranda where you did your cooking, and the disposal of rubbish was inefficient.

In the early estates like Shek Kip Mei and Lok Fu there was so little space. One day, when visiting a family near Ngau Tau Kok, I asked how five of them could live in such a small area.

'You Westerners will never understand,' the father said. 'We don't care how small it is as long as we have freedom.'

That was around 1966.

We also had to take our own precautions, particularly as hepatitis was a serious problem. We were careful where we bought our vegetables, and soaked them in potassium permanganate, which was bright red. This meant we then had to rinse them thoroughly before they were cooked. Often the eggs tasted like sawdust, because some people poured sand down the hens' throats to make them weigh more!

In 1961, we had only just opened the out-patients department of the Maryknoll Hospital. By August 1962, about half a dozen sisters were working hard to get the in-patients department up and running. The pharmacy, kitchen, and all the other departments were ready to open when, on 2nd September, our opening day, Typhoon Wanda struck

Hong Kong! The weathermen warned that the eye of the storm would make a direct hit on the Territory. It did, and the effects on Hong Kong and Kowloon were disastrous. No one was allowed out on the streets as the high winds whipped up signboards, scaffolding, and trees.

It could not have been a worse day for us to open the new section of the hospital. The strength of the wind forced the rain in through the tightly closed windows of our immaculately clean wards, all with brand new bedding. The floors were flooded, and we spent the rest of the day trying to mop up, with every available bucket and pail we could lay our hands on.

In the midst of all this, at half past four in the afternoon, our first patient arrived, a sixty-year-old lady, Shau Au Suk. She had tried to get treatment from the Kwong Wah Hospital, but they were so overwhelmed with patients seriously injured during the typhoon that she was referred to us. Our first patient was also a victim of the wrath that Wanda wreaked on Hong Kong. The roof of her wooden squatter hut had caved in on her head, and she had been badly injured from all the falling debris. Her eyes were so badly swollen that she was unable to see, and her daughter had to physically guide her to hospital. She was obviously in a great deal of pain, but she never once complained. We treated her injuries, tried to relieve some of the pain, and gave her an eye compress every three hours. She was extremely grateful for all our care.

Typhoon Wanda gradually ran out of steam once it had made landfall, but we were left with a massive mopping-up operation. We spent days cleaning up the mess. Many people were killed and injured during that typhoon, and, of course, it was the people in the squatter homes who suffered the most. It took a while for the Territory to return to normal.

Our wards were soon filled with patients mainly from the Wong Tai Sin Resettlement area. We only had one registered nurse on each of our three shifts during those early days, but we were able to cope. However, we will never forget Typhoon Wanda and the havoc she wrought!

There were only a few government hospitals in the sixties, and the conditions were quite pitiful. The Kwong Wah Hospital, which at that time was privately run by a philanthropic society, was so poor and relied on donations. In the early sixties I remember there was such a shortage of space, there were often two patients in a bed. There were few stretchers, and the patients had to be carried by the rather elderly Chinese amahs. Maternity patients, who had just given birth, were brought back from the delivery rooms in the arms of the amahs! The nappies they used for the new-born babies were so tattered, they were like the cloths that were used to clean the floor. The bed linen and the wards were badly soiled too. The problem was that the philanthropic society at the time had to rely on Chinese friends to help provide medical and welfare services. Later the Government stepped in and subsidized the hospital, upgrading it, and now it is one of the highest standard, with skilled medical staff in all departments.

Looking back, changes in medical and community care developed gradually over the years. There was better clothing, better food, better health education. I don't think the Government could have done more; it was overwhelmed with the sudden and continuous influx of people. The main thrust was to get them housed. There was also emphasis on better health education and health education programmes. The Government originally didn't have the luxury to be able to deal with eye or dental care or many of the benefits provided today: those services and other specialist clinics were developed gradually over the years. By the 1970s there were more trained nurses, better clinics, and better; housing. Finally the Government started subsidizing more hospitals and clinics.

Our daily routine was not interrupted at all by the 1967 riots, except for the fact that we had to observe the curfew when it was in force. We were still able to make our regular once or twice a month outing to the beach to swim! I suppose we were really quite a sight—a bunch of women dressed in our religious habits driving out to the ten and a half mile-stone along the Castle Peak Road towards Tuen Mun, swimming costumes in hand. On Wednesday afternoons we could borrow a beach hut where we could change. I really enjoyed those afternoons on what was then a clean, empty beach out in the countryside. Today, people wouldn't dream of swimming there, it is now one of the most polluted beaches in Hong Kong.

When I arrived in Hong Kong we were warned against preaching because we came to serve and help the people. I used to hear many of the patients whispering behind my back, calling me a 'Jesus person'! I used to explain to them that we respected their culture and religion, but if they ever asked to hear about the Gospel then we'd help. I used to tell them, 'We would welcome you, introduce you to the Gospel, and in special situations I will even coax you a little, but never force you!'

Some were really interested to learn more, while a few unfortunately, were labelled 'Rice Christians'. On the whole, people in the early sixties were desperate for a 'security blanket': they were searching for other values as well as food, and were less materialistic than they are now. When we talked to people we told them that money wasn't everything, and you certainly couldn't take it to the grave with you. You had to stop and think what the real values of life were, the everlasting values.

I remember a drug addict once asking me 'Sister, do you think God will forgive me?'

He was thirty-two years old, and had been injecting himself with drugs for ten years. His liver was completely damaged, and, by the time he was admitted to the hospital where I was working, his skin had turned bright orange. He'd had a very troubled childhood: his father had had two wives, and he had been shifted about during his life and brought up by different relatives. He had managed, though, to marry a nice girl, and they had a little boy. At some stage he had turned to drugs, and his addiction eventually had got the better of him, and his life and marriage fell apart. He later—too late—realized his mistake, and asked me to teach him more about the Bible and baptism.

He knew he would never get better, and I visited him frequently. One day he told me he had heard about the Gospel while he was at school, and he asked me whether he could be baptized. I said, 'Yes, you can, but not yet because you really don't know who Jesus is, and you'll have to learn a little about his Gospel and how He fits into your life and can enrich it.'

He asked me to go and see him every day to help him learn.

Later, when he knew he was going downhill, he asked me to give his wife a message: 'Please tell her I really do love her'.

I was so touched and just overjoyed with happiness to bring such a beautiful message to his lovely wife. I said to myself, 'Thanks Lord, for using me. I'm your instrument. It's such a privilege to help this young man.'

His wife was outside weeping in the corridor. She said to me, 'Sister, I sat in there for half an hour, but he never said a word to me. He wasn't even asleep, he was wide awake. As I sat there, he just turned his head the other way. I don't know why he wouldn't talk to me. Did he say anything to you?'

I said, 'Yes. Now listen carefully, this is very precious. He asked me to tell you that he really loves you.'

'Oh, Sister, did he really say that?' And she burst into tears. I just sat there and allowed her a little peaceful silence. It was so precious. Then she said, 'Oh Sister, don't worry about me, these tears aren't sad tears, they are tears of joy. Did he say anything else?'

And I replied that he told me to be sure to pass on his message to her.

Then she dried up her tears and said, 'Sister, would you go back and tell him that I also love him?'

I said I'd be delighted, and she ran off to pick up their little boy from school.

I was bursting with joy! I went back in and the young father had been waiting for me to return. 'Was my wife out there?' he asked anxiously.

I was just beaming and savouring the moment. 'Yes she was, she has gone out now to pick up your little boy.'

He asked, 'Did you tell her what I said?' He was just waiting to hear what had happened.

'What did she say?' He was so concerned to know whether she had accepted.

I explained that as soon as I had passed on his message she had burst into tears.

His face fell, 'Oh, she didn't accept it then?'

I said, 'Oh yes she did, and she told me her tears were joyous tears.'

His head went right back on the pillow. 'Sister, thank you so much.'

I said, 'But that is not all. She also said something else.' I was bursting with excitement! 'Listen carefully, she asked me to tell you that she really loves you too.'

Well, it was like giving him the ultimate gift of peace. He put his head back down on the pillow, and said, 'Sister, I am so grateful. Thank you very much, I'm so happy.'

They had found the greatest truth of all, that Jesus forgives us, and that in forgiving one another they loved each other.

He died three days later. I will never forget him, I was so moved by it all.

I feel that many of the Chinese become very sincere Christians once they have converted. It seems to go right to their hearts. There is now a certain amount of concern about the future of religious freedom after 1997, although I don't worry about those concerns. Many Christians in Hong Kong are forming a kind of safety net for the future, and there are some organizations which have become very active in preparing for the future. For instance they have organized a network of families who hold prayer services in their own homes for fear that something may happen to their churches in the future. They share their life experiences and how Christ's Gospel has changed their lives, and enriched their whole outlook on life.

Hong Kong is becoming more affluent, but I think there will still be a role to play for our pastoral ministry, because, amongst all the material- ism, there has to be some reminder of what the real values are. It's not just a mat- ter of preaching the Gospel, but of help- ing someone, finding time to listen to them, and bringing them kind- ness and patience. There's a great sense of accomplish- ment helping someone like a drug addict who feels he is a fail- ure, and that his life is wasted and

nobody wants him. When he learns the meaning of reconciliation, for-
giveness, and eternal life in heaven, through Christ's Gospel message,
his whole life changes, and death takes on a whole new meaning of ful-
fillment and peace!

Lee Fai Ping

Victory over Vice

Lee Fai Ping is a former drug addict and triad member, and a convicted criminal. He spent his teenage years in the 1960s in the notorious Kowloon Walled City, where he fell into the clutches of the 14K triad society, and the underground world of drugs and vice.

The Kowloon Walled City was once a bucolic village, which became a refugee squatter area after the war, and, by the 1960s, had grown into a treacherous, teeming slum. The area was excluded when the New Territories were leased to Britain in 1898, so the small enclave remained legally a part of China. When Britain tried unilaterally to take control the following year, the Walled City became the subject of dispute. In deference to Beijing's sensitivities, the Hong Kong authorities always kept their distance, and did not try to administer the area.

Outside the rule of the law, the Walled City became an infamous centre for drugs, gambling, and prostitution. The traditional Chinese-style houses were replaced in the 1950s and 1960s by a patchwork of crudely constructed multi-storey buildings. These provided homes for more than fifty thousand people, as well as shops, brothels, massage parlours, gambling dens, and workshops. Denizens flouted fire precautions and any other health and safety regulations, creating a maze of dark, unsanitary alleys and passageways. Masses of tangled wires, which illegally tapped electricity, dangled dangerously overhead. The buildings were packed so tightly together, it was virtually impossible for any daylight to come seeping through, but overhead, the noise was deafening, as aircraft taking off and landing at Kai Tak Airport, skimmed over the rooftops.

The Walled City's cheap attractions lured the curious as well as the poor. People came to be treated by the unlicensed doctors and dentists who operated within its limits; tourists and local people alike went to view its seedy curiosities and take in a strip show. Many young people like Lee Fai Ping, enticed by the powerful triad societies which in effect managed and policed the area, went for thrills, and ended up hooked on heroin.

The Walled City loomed large over Lee Fai Ping's young adult life. Now he is happy to consign it, and the lifestyle that enslaved him, to his troubled past. Following his conversion to Christianity, he became a social worker, and, in 1993, he became Deputy General Secretary of the Wu Oi Christian Centre, which helps young drug addicts kick the habit.

The old 'den of iniquity' no longer exists. Following an agreement between Britain and China in 1987, the Walled City complex was razed and the grounds have now been transformed into a city park.

I'VE BEEN sent to prison eight times—for being a triad society member, for selling dangerous drugs, for assaulting people. I've got a lousy record. In the sixties and seventies the prisons were more corrupt than the police. They used to say it was safer to smoke dangerous drugs inside than out. Nobody really cared, and there was no real attempt at rehabilitation as we would understand it today.

Once when I came out of prison I realized I didn't have any friends because they were all in prison. So it was easy to drift back into the bad ways of the Walled City. I had to live, people needed drugs, and so did I.

The last time I went to prison was in 1972 when I served four years in Stanley Prison for robbery. One day I was summoned to see the superintendent. There was a pile of files on his desk and I realized that they were all my records.

That night in my prison cell I couldn't sleep. I felt very low, depressed, and isolated. I thought it would be better to die than to live. It was two o'clock in the morning, and the image of all those files on the desk just stuck in my mind. I started to count on my fingers, not my age, but the number of times I'd been in prison. When I reached eight I thought that even when I was released, I'd still be a menace to society. There would be nothing for me to do except to go back to drugs.

That night I tried to kill myself. I tore my blanket into strips and tied them together so that I could hang myself. I tried to stand on top of the night soil bucket in my cell, but it slipped, and I fell and hurt my back. It made such a terrible racket that I lost my courage to die.

The cell door burst open, and a prison officer rushed in. When he saw what I had been trying to do he beat me up. 'Don't give me trouble by trying to kill yourself on my shift,' he shouted. He removed the bucket and the torn blanket, and slammed the heavy prison door behind him.

I lay there, aching and bruised, and I started to think about the value of my own life. Drugs had ruined my life. I had no home to go to because my relationship with my family was virtually non-existent, and no job. I wondered whether things could change and whether I could go straight. I made up my mind that this time when I finally got out I'd try to make a go of my life, although I knew that it would not be easy.

I'd never had a decent job until I came out of Stanley Prison. I borrowed some money from a friend, bought a small cart, and started work as a food hawker in the factory areas. Each morning I bought food from the wholesale market and was busy for much of the day. I was able to keep out of the way of my former friends from the Walled City, and keep off drugs.

Just as life was beginning to look up, I was arrested for illegal hawking. I was fined in court, and my cart and goods were confiscated. I was filled with anger because this was my first decent job, and I felt cheated. I screamed at everyone around me, including the magistrate, because I really believed that society neither accepted nor wanted me.

The next day, I was summoned back to court. I thought perhaps the magistrate might have changed his mind and my fine might be cancelled, but I was only asked to take away my cart, which by then was piled high with rotting fruit. I felt desperate, and there was only one answer. I went back to the Walled City and turned again to drugs: it was a well-trodden path to familiar surroundings.

I started going to the Walled City in 1960 when I was a young teenager. I wasn't a drug addict then, I was just attracted to the area. I found the place very special because it was full of contrasting and, I suppose, very exciting things for a young man. There were pornographic movies, live strip shows, and opium dens. It was an infamous den of iniquity. Many organized groups from other areas in Kowloon used to come on tours of the area, just to see the strip shows and the other things on offer.

In those days there were still a lot of wooden structures in the Walled City, and old-style Chinese houses with tiled roofs. There were no high rises, and the buildings were so tightly packed together that hardly any daylight could shine through. It was just a maze of tiny dark alleys, but, if you knew where to look, you could even find parts of the old city wall still standing. The risk of fire was a real danger in such a confined area. I remember there was a man who struck a gong every hour to let people know the time, and he was also responsible for giving the alarm when fire broke out.

The city was at a lower level than the surrounding urban area so when it rained there was always a lot of flooding. There was no sewage system, and sewage had to be taken away from the public latrines and buildings each night by bucket and truck. There were rats everywhere, and even they seemed to be addicted to the drugs, just from the fumes! That's an indication of the amount of drugs used in the city!

It wasn't until 1956 that the police actually started to patrol the Walled City, but the place was effectively run by the triads who were all powerful. Law and order didn't exist inside the city walls. It was a dangerous place to go on your own, and, if you wanted to enter the Walled City, you really had to be escorted by a triad.

I became a member of the 14K triad society when I was thirteen years old. The older members made sure you had free lunches and free dinners, and that you had money to spend. In return I had to carry out orders from my big brothers. These involved gang fights, protection rackets, and many other criminal activities. But I felt like a real macho guy. I knew a lot of the younger kids looked up to me, so I'd recruit them.

Then I started to get involved with drugs. The triad bosses used to smoke opium, and I felt my status would be elevated if I did so too. By the time I was sixteen years old I was a heroin addict. Then I started selling opium as it was very profitable. When you sold drugs at that time, it was just like selling vegetables. I had to pay off the police but, despite this, it was still a good trade. In the early 1960s I had to pay $5,000 a month to the police on each shift—so that was $10,000 a month in all. It was a great deal of money, but it was worth it for the police protection. If a rival started up, the police would quickly squash him.

My life changed drastically in 1976 when I met one of my rivals one Saturday evening. We had fought each other many times and our lives had followed similar paths. The main difference now was that I was on drugs, and he had converted to Christianity. He was so strong and fat I thought he'd just come out of prison! He was working for a Christian organization, and invited me to a service. How could this man have changed? I was very suspicious.

Curiosity got the better of me and I went to the service. When I entered I realized that I knew many of the people there as they had all been triad members and had been with me in prison at one time or another. At the end of the service they came over and shook hands with me. They had changed beyond recognition.

It was the difference in their attitude which impressed me. They urged me to stay with them, and I agreed to go back the next day. That night I started to think about my life and whether Jesus did really exist. If Jesus could change them, why not me?

I went back to join them, but trying to quit my addiction was hell. The withdrawal symptoms hit me badly during the first couple of days, and physically I felt terrible. I thought I could never go through with it, and would have to get out, but I also knew that the minute I gave in I'd be finished for ever. My friends held on to me. They encouraged me to pray. When I closed my eyes I started to cry. I'd never cried so much in my life. I prayed to God to save me, and to relieve me of the pains inside my body. I was very quiet, and my heart was tranquil. That was the day of days.

It was the start of a new life. I knew nothing about the Bible, but gradually I found that, just as Jesus loved all the different people in the Book, he loved me too.

I got a job working in a dry seafood store in Western district. That was only my second real job ever! In the evenings I'd go round talking to my ex-friends trying to persuade them to follow my example. It wasn't easy as an ex-convict, ex-addict, and ex-triad society member to influence peo-ple, but I did, and later I became a full-time social worker.

I never thought I'd get married, but now I have a very good wife who is a great support to me, and I'm reconciled with my family.

The Kowloon Walled City was a wicked place, and I was pleased when the Government announced in 1987 that it would be razed to the ground, and the area it occupied turned into a park. This does not help the fact that the drug problem remains, and is much worse now than it was when I was a kid. The drugs available today have a lot more impurities in them and are much more dangerous. The drug situation is even worse in China, so there is much work to be done, and many difficult challenges.

Young people should not be fooled into thinking that taking drugs is fashionable or exciting since it is neither. I lost many things in life because of drugs and those things can never be brought back.

Tsang Yok Sing

Coming of Age in '67

1967 was a political turning point for Hong Kong. It was also a watershed for Tsang Yok Sing, the 1990s leader of the pro-Beijing political party, the Democratic Alliance for the Betterment of Hong Kong (DAB). During the 1967 disturbances, Tsang Yok Sing came out in support of China's Red Guards, and confirmed his conversion to Marxism.

Thirty years later he still adheres to his Communist principles. He has been chairman of the DAB, established in 1992, and principal of one of Hong Kong's long-established 'leftist' schools. He was also selected to sit on the two Beijing-appointed bodies which were set up to oversee the 1997 transition to Chinese rule.

1967 heralded the advent of student politics in Hong Kong, and 'leftist' students were behind much of the discontent during the riots. It was not just Tsang Yok Sing: his younger brother, Tak Sing also first became involved in left-wing politics at the time. In 1969 Tsang Tak Sing joined one of the daily pro-Beijing newspapers in Hong Kong, while his elder brother began his thirty-year career as a school teacher.

It was a time when patriotic schools in Hong Kong flouted the colonial historical perspective, and propagated the Communist ideal. Now the original 'leftist' schools offer the same curriculum as Government schools.

Tsang Yok Sing's political interests revived with the signing of the Sino-British Joint Declaration on Hong Kong's future in 1984. He was appointed to the Basic Law Consultative Committee to canvass views on the post-1997 constitution for Hong Kong, and he spent many hours with the so-called 'Group of 38', putting forward proposals for inclusion in the Basic Law.

Tsang Tak Sing had always been seen as the 'man of action', but it was his more academic brother who emerged as the head of a political party. With his calm, intellectual approach, Tsang Yok Sing managed as chairman of the DAB to command an enormous amount of respect, even amongst his political foes. He even elicited sympathy from his opponents when he lost the directly elected seat he contested in the 1995 Legislative Council elections.

Tsang Yok Sing's political activities have put enormous strain on his family, and the events of June 1989 affected him deeply. It was then that he and his family decided to emigrate, though not, he says, through fear, but despondency. Although Tsang Yok Sing subsequently changed his mind, his wife and daughter were granted Canadian citizenship. However, he has always been a family man. He still meets his father every day for breakfast, and his parents continue to support both their sons, as they did throughout the 1960s.

WHEN THE 1967 riots broke out, I was already a committed Marxist and was in total sympathy with the workers who were only protecting themselves against the oppressive colonial government of the time. I was deeply affected by the dramatic events of '67. My brother, aged eighteen, was arrested during the riots, and locked up in Stanley Prison for two years, and my sister was imprisoned for a month, aged only fifteen. Don't talk to me about human rights!

I never thought I would be involved in politics at all, despite my political ideology. I wanted to become a scientist and had planned to serve my country, China. My role model was the famous rocket scientist Qian Xuesen, who had studied and worked in the United States [before being expelled on allegations of spying]. However, since his return to China in the early 1950s, he has been at the forefront of developing China's space and weapons programme.

It was not until I went to university that my interest in Chinese affairs developed, but the seeds were sown during my childhood. My parents came to Hong Kong in 1949, but, unlike many, not for political reasons: they had lived in Hong Kong before I was born. My father was apolitical and had quite simply returned here in 1949 because he thought it would be easier to find work. He started as a junior clerk, in what later became the Chinese General Chamber of Commerce [a pro-China business organization set up in 1949]. The Chamber used to subscribe to the pro-China daily newspaper *Wen Wei Po*, and my father always brought a copy home. I always read many newspapers including the *Wen Wei Po*.

My teachers at St Paul's, which was then a prestigious school, mostly belonged to the older generation who had graduated from university in China before the war, and had come to Hong Kong to escape Communist rule. They always spoke negatively about China and the Communist Government. This rubbed off on many of my fellow students. I felt differently. I realized that from reading the *Wen Wei Po* over the years at home, and from other publications, my knowledge and understanding of China was not the same as theirs.

When I went to university in 1965, I found a few birds of the same political feather, but our views were very different from most of our peers. I often found myself on the defensive, and even isolated. Many of my fellow students would be very critical of China, and this used to sadden me a great deal. Human rights didn't feature in those days, but it was the poverty, the low standard of living, hunger, and so on, which they criticized. I tended to see the brighter side of things in China—the scientific and technological achievements, the projects, the dams, the rivers, the bridges, the railways, and so on—because that was what I had read about.

The turning point in my life came in 1967, during my second year at university, when I decided to visit China. I had read a great deal about the motherland, and had heard so much conflicting information, that I wanted to find out for myself what was actually going on there. I planned to go to Guangzhou with my mother, but in those days it was dangerous to go to the Mainland, not because of things that could possibly happen to you there, but because of what would happen to you after you returned to Hong Kong. Many friends of mine advised me against the trip because there were reports of students who, having gone to China from Hong Kong, were branded as 'leftists' by the British administration once they returned. This could make life difficult later on. There was one story of a student who had been granted a student visa by the United States, but, when it was discovered that he had been to see a Mainland Chinese film, his visa was subsequently cancelled.

I went to China, but made a detour via Macau, so there would be no record with the Hong Kong Immigration Department of my visit. The journey took eight hours by bus. It was very impressive. It was shortly before the Cultural Revolution, and I think it was perhaps the best time in China. The people I met, both those I knew and those who were complete strangers, gave me the unmistakable impression they had a lot of faith in the Government. They knew their country was poor and backward, but they had the confidence that under the leadership of the Communist Party, China was going to be strong. I talked to some of the young people. All of them told me of their plans to go to far-flung places in China, where the country needed them most, after they had finished their education. People there, including my family, who knew about my educational background, tried to encourage me to go abroad after I had graduated, and do research in my field of interest, with the aim of returning eventually to the motherland to serve the country. I was so impressed that everybody I met seemed to be working with a purpose, that the idea was quite attractive to me. It was quite unlike the attitude of people in Hong Kong. When I returned from my trip, I found the whole atmosphere, and what was happening around me, quite distasteful. Most people spent all their time talking about how to make money and how to raise a family. That was when I planned to go abroad and equip myself with the aim of then returning to help contribute towards China's development.

I don't know whether it was fortunate or not, but when I returned to Hong Kong to resume my studies, the 1967 riots broke out. The demonstrations of that year marked the first time I had ever taken part in any political activity.

At university, there were three or four of us with the same political inclinations, and we became very close. We met often, we bought Mao's books, and would read together writings by Marx and Engels. We watched political developments in Hong Kong very closely, and clubbed together to send money to the *Wen Wei Po* in support of the [left-wing] trade unions. We even took part in some of the street demonstrations, led by the local Communist organizations.

I remember my father being absolutely horrified to see my photograph on the front page of the newspapers in the front ranks of the demonstrators. It was the first time I had taken part in a demonstration, and my father was very nervous.

The Government handled the riots in a very high-handed, colonial manner. I felt that it was protecting the interests of the capitalists, and, in doing so, suppressing the workers. I personally knew many of the people, the workers and trade unionists, involved in the violence, and they were very good people. When we were together, none of those people was prone to violence. They were simple workers who had been exploited all their lives. Yes, they harboured a lot of resentment towards their employers and capitalists, but, no, they were not bandits; they were not taking to violence for violence's sake. They were oppressed so they had to protect themselves.

The prevailing view now is that the police acted with a great deal of restraint at the time, and that people in the leftist camp were just a violent mob, throwing bombs and escalating the violence. This is not true, and the Government's firm action was neither necessary nor justified. We saw how the workers started with a peaceful sit-in. They just sat there with the 'little red book' [of Mao's quotations] in their hands, chanting and singing. I saw the riot police come and beat up the workers. When some police officers were killed by terrorist bombs, many of us thought they deserved it because they were working for an oppressive government. I understand now that public sympathy generally did not lie with leftists, but, because I took sides with the rioters then, we had just the opposite view. Whenever one of the workers or trade unionists got killed, we all mourned him, and many people wanted to seek revenge.

The greatest shock during that time was the imprisonment of my siblings. My brother was arrested for distributing anti-government leaflets. He was a Form 6 student at St Paul's, and was a timid boy. He was seldom involved in political arguments. Everyone linked his actions to me because I was obviously leftist by then and I didn't hide my political views. In fact I had no idea what my brother was doing. His actions surprised everyone. He printed some leaflets at home calling for the reform of the school curriculum, denouncing the British for the Opium War, and so on. He got a pile of those leaflets and handed them out during lunchtime at school. Of course, everybody saw him doing this, and, when classes resumed, the riot police were there. The other students had told the school principal that one of the school prefects had distributed leaflets, and the principal had called the police. The prefects were all summoned and told to line up in the staff room. A couple of the younger boys were then asked to identify the culprit. My brother was arrested straight away, tried, and sentenced to two years.

He was sent to Stanley Prison which was then full of trade unionists and non-violent workers. They protected my brother because he was just a child.

A couple of months later, my fifteen-year-old sister was also arrested. She was a form 3 student at Belilios Public School. She was in the playground with thirteen other girls, and when the school bell rang they refused to go back to the classroom. I cannot quite remember what they were asking for, but anyway the headmistress decided they were making trouble. She called the police, and all fourteen were tried, found guilty of breaching the emergency legislation in force during 1967, and sent to the women's prison in Lai Chi Kok for one month.

My parents were very supportive. When my brother was arrested, they still knew nothing really about politics. They were typical working-class parents, but, because of my university education, they respected me and the views I held. I told them my brother had done the right thing. I think the judge, when my brother's case was heard, had expected my father to plead for mercy, but he stood up and said, 'My son did the right thing and we are all proud of him.'

However, after my sister's arrest, my mother began to break down. Any sympathy which family and neighbours might have felt had turned by then to suspicion. Long-standing friends rejected her. When she went to the marketplace, she was ostracized. She was in tears all day, and my father decided that it was going to be too difficult to continue living in Western district where I'd lived all my life, so we moved to North Point [also on Hong Kong Island], to a new neighbourhood.

It was also a very difficult period for me. After my brother's arrest, I was shunned at university, and spent most of my time at the hostel where I was living. When I entered the common room I would find groups of people talking, but, as soon as they saw me, they dispersed. On the other hand, I found lots of warm friendship, comradeship, and sympathy amongst the leftist circle. I remember joining the [Chinese] National Day celebrations in 1967. Seeing the national flag being hoisted was a very moving moment for me.

My experiences drove me more to the other side. I worshipped Mao Zedong and he became my idol. This was not in the same manner as many of my leftist friends who thought of him as God and refused to criticize him in any way. They would walk around with badges of Chairman Mao pinned to their chests. I greatly admired the man, and I believed in Marxism, but I could not accept the idea that he was infallible.

After I left university, I gave up my plans to study in the United States. It was at the height of the Cultural Revolution and it went against Mao's beliefs. So I had to look for something to do after I got my degree, but, because my brother was in prison, my options were restricted. It was impossible for me to join the civil service, or even to become a teacher in a government-aided school. I am not sure that I would even have applied for a job in one anyhow: we used to call the teaching in the mainstream schools 'enslaving education'.

It was therefore quite natural that I took a job in a leftist institution. I started to work at Pui Kiu School [in North Point] in 1969 where I found the teachers warm: they made me feel at home. However, many of my leftist friends disapproved. They thought the teaching job in Pui Kiu could be filled by many other people in the leftist camp and that with my educational background I should be doing something else. I never intended to stay there very long anyway: I thought that the school, with its very strong links with the Mainland, would be a convenient springboard for me to start working in China.

The late 1960s and early 1970s, were really the heydays for the leftist schools, although Pui Kiu had been founded in 1946. During the fifties and sixties, and especially at the height of the Cultural Revolution, everybody in the patriotic community in Hong Kong felt it was their duty to send their children to patriotic schools. They realized that the younger generation had very little opportunity to get to know China, and we filled this need. We expanded rapidly, but with the death of Mao and the fall of The Gang of Four, many of our parents became disillusioned with China and the Cultural Revolution.

I and my colleagues at the school felt very cheated after the fall of the Gang of Four. It was a very difficult time, and we just concentrated on our teaching work. It was not just the swing against China, but the need for our school also lessened with the introduction of free primary education in 1971, and then junior secondary education in 1978. My colleagues and I were fighting hard to survive: from the late 1970s onwards, one by one the leftist schools were forced to close, and Pui Kiu was just one of a handful to keep going.

I think one can describe Hong Kong in general, at least in the latter half of the seventies, as quiet—quieter than in the sixties—for a number of reasons. The end of the Cultural Revolution marked the beginning of a period of pragmatism both in China and in Hong Kong. The Mao craze died down, and university students seldom talked of ideals and revolutions. The Hong Kong Government under the then Governor, Sir Murray MacLehose, put a lot more effort into improving social conditions. Until then, the Government had invested very little in education, but, in the 1970s, not only did we see the introduction of free education, there was a very large-scale school-building programme, the start of free medical care, and many other social improvements.

Gradually feelings changed towards China, and there was a surge of patriotic feeling and sympathy in the late 1970s. This was helped by the movement to defend the Diaoyu Islands from Japan [disputed islands claimed by both Japan and China]. Then of course there was President Nixon's visit to China, followed by China's re-entry to the United Nations. However, despite the renewed feelings of patriotism towards China, there was still little need for our schools. As China began to open up, many people in Hong Kong were able to visit any time, and information about China was much more readily available. Even senior cadres in China were sending their children abroad to be educated.

The signing of the Joint Declaration heralded a new era. My colleagues in the school found a new sense of purpose. We had asked ourselves during those difficult years, 'Why keep the school running? What's the purpose, what's the point of maintaining a school?' By 1985 there was a need for a new generation of Hong Kong people who could understand China, who could communicate efficiently with the Chinese Government, and who could put into practice the 'one country, two systems' principle. The years following the signing of the Joint Declaration, and before 1989, were the best years, not only in our schools, but in Hong Kong as well.

After the 1989 suppression of the student movement in Beijing, we had a renewed sense of mission. It was then that we first started thinking of forming a party. We felt that, despite all that had happened, we had to start thinking in a more positive light. We needed to do all we could to make sure that the 'one country, two systems' concept would be realized but asked ourselves, 'How can it ever succeed with all the hostility that exists?' A million Hong Kong people had gathered on the streets, shouting slogans against the Chinese Government, while Beijing was calling Hong Kong a base for subversive forces. I was one of those who took to the streets, demonstrating against the Chinese Government, but I still believed we could maintain a dialogue with the Mainland authorities.

On reflection, I was more disillusioned with China after the death of Mao than in 1989. The fall of the Gang of Four and the excesses of the Cultural Revolution made me question my ideological beliefs. Tiananmen provoked a more emotional response. By 1989 China had been open for more than ten years, and we knew enough about what was happening there to have no more illusions. We knew that the country was fraught with problems, we knew that corruption was very bad, we knew the people had a lot of resentment towards the bureaucracy. Although it came as a shock, the impact of Tiananmen was rather different from the death of Mao.

Many ask me why I set up a political party, and why I believe so strongly in Hong Kong's future. There is a Marxist belief that where there is conflict, or competition between two systems, the better system always prevails. China is now moving forward, opening up, moving towards a market economy. You can already see how much Hong Kong has influenced China's development. In many of the major cities in China you can see Hong Kong culture spreading very extensively. I have friends in Hong Kong who have come here from China over the past ten years or so. Now they tell me they find it very frustrating to do business with their counterparts from across the border. They can see the deficiencies in the systems which operate in China; they have become Hong Kong people.

There's another Marxist principle that holds that your existence determines your thinking. Members of the Chinese Communist Party are looking at the world and re-evaluating China's role and position in the international community. The trend, I believe, is irreversible. So I cannot see any reason to be pessimistic about Hong Kong's future. We can't convert the pessimists, but we can let history prove itself.

Sir Jack Cater
The 1967 Riots

For nearly forty years Jack Cater has been involved with almost every aspect of Hong Kong government. He arrived in the Territory during the months following the Liberation to join the interim military administration, which governed the Colony until the colonial Government was restored in 1946. He was the first Commissioner of the Independent Commission Against Corruption, established in 1973, and he became Chief Secretary in the late 1970s. He retired in 1984 after serving as Hong Kong's Commissioner in London.

Sir Jack, as he was eventually to become, played a prominent role in the Government's efforts to contain and handle the 1967 riots. The events, which, for the first time since the war, threatened the authority of the British administration, underlined once again just how vulnerable Hong Kong was to China's internal affairs.

It seemed almost inevitable that by 1967 the effects of the Cultural Revolution, in particular the patriotism and devotion to Mao, would spill over into Hong Kong, and influence a proportion of the population who held patriotic feelings towards the motherland. Extremists in Hong Kong saw 1967 as an opportunity to take advantage of the social and economic conditions to enlist support for the overthrow of British colonial administration. They resorted to violent measures, terrifying the majority of the population for four, hot, summer months, to achieve their ideals.

The Government maintained that it combined determination with restraint, using as little force as possible, to respond to the threats and to preserve law and order. It was helped along the way by the Beijing leadership's resistance to exporting the Cultural Revolution. Radio messages to Communists in Hong Kong, thought to come from Premier Zhou Enlai himself, seemed to hold an underlying message to help the British administration contain the situation. Indeed, the local Communist party was also split as to how far the Revolution in China should be brought to Hong Kong.

Ultimately, it was left to a small circle of Hong Kong officials to deal with the serious disorder and riots. Many in the Government, worried by what was becoming an increasingly dangerous situation, took advantage of their summer leave to go back to Britain. Amongst those who left was the Commissioner of Police and the Governor himself, Sir David Trench. However, although he was deemed to be unwell, his departure at a time of crisis subsequently came in for much criticism.

Sir Jack Cater (left) with Governor David Trench

It was Jack Cater—who by then had assumed the role of Personal Assistant to the Governor with direct responsibility for the disturbances—who took charge of the situation.

IN MANY WAYS the 1967 disturbances were the most far-reaching occurrences to affect Hong Kong post war. I say this for two reasons. First, there was a very real danger that Hong Kong could have been lost to the Chinese Communists in the Red Guard period, just as Macau had been lost in 1966. Macau has never been 'Portuguese' in the same way that Hong Kong has been 'British', and since 1966 there has really only been a facade of Portuguese authority there. This is why there is no 'problem' over the enclave's future: the die was cast many years earlier.

Second, Hong Kong's 1967 riots proved to be a watershed in its social development. They made the Government here responsive and aware of the needs of the people as never before, and were the catalyst for the enormous changes which took place in the 1970s.

The so-called Star Ferry riots of 1966 were the first indication of the pressures which were building up, but I think that the Hong Kong Government may well have gone to sleep again thereafter had it not been for the events of the following year. To understand the situation pertaining then, one has to consider the economic problems and social pressures Hong Kong had faced since the end of the Pacific War.

When I arrived in the Colony in 1945 the situation was, as you can imagine, not good, following four years of Japanese occupation, all the privations of wartime, and wholesale looting in the hiatus between the Japanese going and the British military administration, of which I was a member, taking control. We had to get going quickly to start 'governing' Hong Kong. The population then was estimated at about 460,000; by 1946 we were up to about 1.7 million. Most of the increase was accounted for by people coming back from China where they had spent the war years, but who had previously been living and working here. It therefore became a sort of status quo ante, and, in those terms, a size of community that we could eventually expect to cope with given time and much hard work.

From 1948 onwards, however, with the civil war raging in China, Hong Kong began to be inundated with refugees. Social welfare assistance both from government and from non-governmental agencies was only minimal, although we and they all tried our best.

It has to be remembered how very little money we had in Hong Kong in the late 1940s and early 1950s. Britain itself was on its economic knees after the Second World War, and was in no position to be generous financially to its colonies. The aid which the Americans gave to France, to Germany, to Japan, and to other parts of the world did not extend to Britain. In Hong Kong we did receive one welcome piece of assistance in the shape of a loan from the Colonial Development and Welfare Fund, which had partly to be repaid. Better than nothing, though, and we did what we could afford to do, but there was so much need in every sphere that we had to be deliberately cautious in giving and not wasting our small resources. It bears recalling, too, that it was not only the refugees from China who were in a pitifully poor way: we were none of us affluent. There were few cars, minimal public transport, especially in the New Territories, a scarcity of medical facilities, and a severe shortage of accommodation of all kinds; and jobs were hard to come by.

And here I must give credit to the arrival of the Shanghainese. Possibly many Cantonese may even now disagree with me, but it was those people from Shanghai, mostly textile manufacturers, who brought the industrial revolution to Hong Kong, and made it possible for us to see ourselves through those tremendously difficult times of the 1950s.

As the 1960s began, Hong Kong was showing signs of becoming a flourishing entity, and we all spoke a lot about our hard-working population, our determination to overcome the privations of the past, and pull together, come hell or high water, to succeed in the world, not just in our own region. By the way, hell and high water we also had in good measure by virtue of the terrible and destructive typhoons with which this part of the world was visited with dreadful regularity at that time.

In 1966, the year of the Star Ferry riots, I found myself far away from Hong Kong attending the Imperial Defence College in London [now the Royal College for Defence Studies]. It turned out that I was in a most fortunate position in more ways than I could have known. I saw the start of the Cultural Revolution from a different standpoint, and had the opportunity to observe and to think about urban disturbances in general, and especially when news of riots in Macau were reported.

The incident which gave rise to the outbreak of the upheavals in Macau had to do with a school which the Communist trade unions had built on one of Macau's islands—country areas then, not linked to the Mainland by bridges as they are today. The school was small, and, according to the Portuguese authorities, the premises had been built on a plot of land which exceeded the boundaries allocated for the school. It seemed that the school was therefore encroaching on an adjacent village path, probably, from what I could tell, by a very small margin. Nevertheless it had been built over the permitted limit, and the Portuguese authorities ordered that the whole building be torn down. That did not make much sense, especially when the Cultural Revolution was booming away almost literally across the road in China. A thoughtless decision and the start, possibly the excuse for the start, of Macau's ensuing uproar. Next day there were demonstrations throughout the main urban areas. People thronged the streets shouting 'Down with the Government', and considerable chaos reigned. In a further unwise move, the army were given instructions to quell the riots: permission to shoot. Some nine people were killed, and many more were injured.

Having studied similar situations I had learnt a few lessons, one of which is that one never allows the bodies of the dead to get into the hands of those who are rioting. Regrettably this happened, and the bodies were paraded around Macau. The Governor of Macau was made to look ridiculous in every imaginable way, including effigies and street 'plays'. He had no real adequate military or police force to protect him, and he retreated to the comparative safety of Government House.

Early in January 1967 I returned from the UK to take up my duties in the Hong Kong Government as Defence Secretary. One of my priorities was to continue to examine the possibility of evacuating the Portuguese from Macau. Fortunately this never had to be done, but nevertheless I went there with my wife so that we could see the situation for ourselves. The rumour was that the Portuguese had tried to hand Macau back to China but it had not been established if that was so. We soon found out that it was true when arrangements were made for us to meet secretly with the Portuguese emissary who had been sent to Beijing. His story was one of discourteous and embarrassing treatment. Together with the Portuguese Ambassador, he had gone to the Ministry of Foreign Affairs. They were asked by two, very young officials what they were doing there, and they started to present their credentials, making it clear that they wanted to see a senior official to talk about Macau. An hour and a half later a junior officer came and said simply, 'We don't want Macau back. You are to leave and go back to Macau at once!'

Back in Hong Kong at my office, I found that instead of being 'Defence Secretary' I was to be retitled 'Personal Assistant to the Governor' with direct responsibility for 'confrontational matters', and then in June, on the departure of the Governor to the UK, my title was changed again, this time to Deputy Colonial Secretary (Special Duties). Whatever my designation, it was pretty clear what my job up ahead was likely to involve: there was no doubt that the troubles Macau had suffered were on their way to us.

During the months of January through April the local Communist organizations, such as trade unions, teachers from Communist schools, film stars from the Communist studios, and so on, had been very difficult whenever they could, causing problems and orchestrating sporadic industrial disputes, any and all of which were potentially dangerous. They continued and escalated their activities, although they did not receive the support of all the Communist organizations in Hong Kong. [Chinese business interests, for instance, wanted to keep the Cultural Revolution out of Hong Kong.]

Throughout April and May there were many demonstrations going on, by and large very orderly if loud, but gradually they got increasingly more raggedy. The population of Hong Kong in general was becoming less and less enamoured of all this disruptive behaviour, and, much to our surprise and delight we received on May 21st a most heartening message of support from the University of Hong Kong Students' Union. It was the first, and therefore for me the most memorable, of all those that followed. They began to pour in from all kinds of groups, 640 of them in all, representing a cross-section of our people, and proving to us, if proof were needed, that they were behind us all the way. It gave us a wonderful boost during those dark, exhausting times.

Support came too from many members of the Legislative Council who spoke out publicly and bravely on behalf of the efforts being made to contain the Communist confrontation. Their names were later [in August] to be seen on the list published in a left-wing newspaper of prominent people said to be marked for assassination.

Then we had a problem with a Mr Ng ensconced on the fifth floor of the Bank of China, who used a loud speaker in order to address the vicinity and make threatening verbal assaults on, amongst others, our Political Advisor, Tony Elliott, and myself. Whenever we walked through Statue Square, there he would be bellowing down at us. In order to drown him out, we started playing loud Chinese music from the rooftop of the Supreme Court [now the home of Legislative Council]. The noise was horrendous! After we had been 'broadcasting' our music for four or five days we noticed that the people in Central district had become rather more cheerful: some smiles were detected. Thus encouraged, when the Communists, being good trade unionists, closed down their daily broadcasting at 5.30 each evening, we used to finish up our programme by playing Colonel Bogey which we were assured was greatly appreciated, at least by some!

Well on into the disturbances in May, the call came from China's hierarchy, 'Let the masses decide'. This was the word not only to their own revolutionaries but was also taken to apply to their supporters in Hong

Kong, and was the signal that things were hotting up considerably. The Communist trade unions were still bent on making revolution here although Zhou Enlai had said publicly that the Cultural Revolution was 'not for export'. •

Then something happened that made us sit up. Word came that Hong Kong would receive radio messages from Beijing at specified times which would be delivered at dictation speed. It was somewhat fascinating, if ludicrous, that, amongst others, special messages were sent to members of the local Communist hierarchy instructing them to demonstrate, and this they obediently did outside Government House. They dutifully took along their 'little red books', and women were observed arriving in such plebeian transport as their personal Mercedes Benz limousines to do their stuff at the gates of Government House. Hoi poloi, of course, simply walked up the short hill to Upper Albert Road.

More and more demonstrations were held there and they became more and more disorderly. Throughout the whole of this period the Hong Kong Police acted most bravely, I would say magnificently. By now we had a line of them stationed along the route to Government House trying to keep the crowds in reasonable order. The police held their tempers and behaved with great restraint, even when the occasional teenage brat went up to them and poked fingers at their eyes, and otherwise taunted them. Adopting the agreed policy, we remained quietly sensible and issued perspex goggles to the police on duty there to protect their eyes. When the crowds became riotous and started breaking through police ranks, we issued the order to dump hobnailed boots and don rubber-soled non-slip footwear. We were trying in every possible way not to give any excuse for escalation, and make sure not to create any incidents.

At the end of the month [May], it was clear that there was going to be a very big demonstration over the weekend. Crowds built up in the vicinity of Statue Square. Surprisingly, a large number of youngsters, school students, had been called out, and these groups had caught the attention of the American television station NBC, which had a camera at the ready outside the Hilton Hotel at the foot of Garden Road. They were waiting their turn to march up the road when the police formed up to control the crowds. Suddenly, when the police were fairly near to them, these kids dropped to the ground, brought out bandages doused in mercurochrome and 'bloodied' themselves, especially their heads, while some clearly expectant local media members stood by to record this documentary for world distribution and history. Fortunately, NBC got the 'before' as well as the 'during and after' on tape. It was worth an enormous amount to our credibility, and knocked theirs for six. Great good fortune!

By now they were prepared to use a great deal of violence. By mid-July when the bombing started, there were some terrible tragedies. One, in fact, brought a big backlash against the Communists. A man took his children with him while planting bombs in the North Point area of Hong Kong Island. The bombs exploded prematurely, killing his children.

As the bombs increased, so did the work of our bomb disposal experts, unbelievably brave men doing appallingly hazardous jobs. Not all the bombs were the real thing, but all had to be treated as if they were, and there were many dreadful casualties. The total of real bombs and explosions amounted to 1,167 and 253 respectively, plus 8,074 suspected bombs, which all had to be dealt with. The death toll was 51 with 832 injured. We held grimly on to the policy of not over-reacting, but there was understandably a certain amount of agitation for positive action from our side.

It was not only in Central district, of course, that major troubles were happening. On July 8th there was an incursion across the border by the Man Po [Chinese Militia Guard]. A message came to us that a senior officer of the People's Liberation Army had been seen earlier in the morning on the Chinese side of Sha Tau Kok [a border village] talking to members of the Man Po, and, at about one o'clock, the Militia Guards, together with a large mob, began forming up on the border itself. There was going to be more trouble. A typical local approach to organizing such a confrontation consists of rounding up a lot of women, preferably obviously pregnant women, and pushing them to the front. As this was happening, the Man Po suddenly opened fire at the Sha Tau Kok police post at the border, and attacked the police officers manning the post, killing five of them and injuring eleven.

Having overrun the police post, the Man Po spread out, and it was necessary to contain them. We sent the Gurkhas into action, and within an hour and a half it was all over. A short-lived but very worrying incident. We then put the army on the border, and there they remained until the early 1990s. Predictably there were some stupid reactions. The British Sunday Express of 9th July reported that several thousand PLA troops had come across the border.

There was, I suppose, a general feeling that the situation was worsening here. Meantime in Western district we had raided a bomb-making factory, and tracked down a number of Communist schools in which the students and their teachers were also busy making bombs.

Even now, we believed that we had to hang on, that sooner or later quiet would return to China, and that, in turn, quiet would therefore return to us. But the messages coming from Beijing during August were ominous: 'We are unable to be helpful'. We knew then we had to prepare ourselves for worse troubles up ahead, and to be ever more vigilant in holding the line, and doing whatever we could to ensure that very serious upheavals did not occur. Always, too, there was the threat that a change of generals in one of the southern Chinese provinces would see the arrival of a militant revolutionary who could order a flood of his troops across our border. There was no way we could have resisted that for long: it would have been heroic but bloody.

August also saw one of the leading communist newspapers, together with a number of smaller ones, printing articles calling upon the people

of Hong Kong to 'rise up against the British Administration'. This could not be tolerated, and we decided to take action against three very virulent if small left-wing newspapers. The editors of these papers were arrested, charged, put through the courts and imprisoned. Beijing didn't like this, and on 22nd August they virtually destroyed the British Embassy [in Beijing]. Some years later I was introduced by the then British Ambassador, Richard Evans, as 'the man who got us the new Embassy building'! Of course I had no idea that the reaction to our dealing with three seditious newspaper people in Hong Kong would be to burn down the British Embassy in Beijing.

It is an ill wind which blows nobody any good, and, in the case of the 1967 disturbances, the opportunity was offered and seized with alacrity to take forward a number of reforms. These included the provision of compulsory, free primary education, and the setting up of the City District Officer system—in addition to the existing District Officer network outside the urban areas—as well as several other innovations which might otherwise have taken light-years to achieve, not least of which was a mandatory day off each week! It was very clear that the New Territories people and the fishermen came out of 1967 in much better shape than the townspeople did. We put this down largely to the fact that they had always been treated as people 'in the round', as it were, rather than as health problems, fire risk problems, and so on. There is no doubt that the City District Officer scheme has served us extremely well over these past twenty-eight years.

Some of us hoped that increased governmental contact with all the people of Hong Kong would inevitably mean better and continuing interaction, leading to a more democratic situation. When I was appointed the first Registrar of Cooperatives in 1950, my involvement initially was with the fishermen's and farmers' cooperative societies, but later on societies were formed among government servants, and in many other sectors of the community. Credit unions followed thereafter and quickly proved a great success. That early experience confirmed me in the belief that Hong Kong people could and would act in a democratic way, given the opportunity. I still hold to that view.

Roots of Stability, Seeds of Change

the 1970s

Hong Kong's social and economic features were dramatically transformed during the 1970s. A combination of domestic factors— political stability and measured reform—and China's new 'open door' policy fostered a new dynamism in Hong Kong. The decade saw the emergence of an increasingly affluent middle class, the beginnings of institutionalized social welfare, and the start of Hong Kong's transformation into an international financial centre as manufacturers began to move their factories into southern China at the end of the decade. Most significant was the shift in attitudes towards China. The people of Hong Kong began to recognize that China had become an important factor in the Territory's economic development, and Deng Xiaoping's 'open door' policy and the normalization of Sino-British diplomatic relations encouraged this change. But, as the 1970s drew to a close, concern over Hong Kong's future increased as the expiry in 1997 of the lease governing the New Territories drew nearer.

The man who dominated the Territory's developments in the 1970s was Sir Murray (now Lord) MacLehose. He governed Hong Kong from November 1971 to April 1982, becoming the Colony's longest-serving governor, exceeding Sir Alexander Grantham's tenure by just a month.

Sir Murray's appointment to succeed Sir David Trench in November 1971 marked an end to the long line of British colonial officials who had traditionally occupied Government House. The Foreign and Colonial Offices had merged in 1968, and, although Sir Murray had begun his career in the Colonial Service, by the time he became Governor, he was a trained Foreign Service diplomat. His appointment heralded the involvement of a close circle of Foreign Office sinologists who were to dominate Britain's policy on Hong Kong for two decades. Sir Murray had served in China during the war, and was familiar with Hong Kong. He had been seconded to the Hong Kong Government by the Foreign Office in the 1960s to serve as Political Adviser on the Territory's external relations, mainly with China.

Sir Murray brought with him a fresh approach, which discarded the Governor's colonial image. Terminology, too, had changed. Hong Kong was no longer described as a 'Colony', rather, the more diplomatically sensitive 'Territory' was adopted. In 1973, the title of 'Colonial Secretary' was finally abolished and the post was renamed 'Chief Secretary'. It was not until 1974 that, for the first time, Chinese was recognized as an official language, together with English.

Rapid progress in housing, education, and social welfare reforms marked Sir Murray's long tenure, but he opposed far-reaching political reform. The long held *laissez faire* beliefs of Sir John Cowperthwaite, who had dominated fiscal policy in the 1960s, were quietly modified by his successor, Sir (as he was to become) Philip Haddon-Cave, who was in charge of the public purse throughout the 1970s. The realization that the Government had to provide for the community had come in the aftermath of the 1967 disturbances. A number of reforms had already been set in motion (as outlined by Sir Jack Cater earlier in this book), and public spending had increased. Under Sir Murray, added impetus was given to the reform programme while government spending, helped by the growth in the economy, continued to rise. The overall results created enormous improvements in the life of the average citizen.

The appalling living conditions of much of the population shocked the new governor, and after a year in office, and with a great deal more money in the public coffers than his predecessors, he set about an ambitious ten-year housing programme. More than a quarter of a million people were still living in squatter huts, and just as many, if not more, were housed in hastily built, overcrowded tenement blocks. Many people had been rehoused in the 1960s, but only in the most basic way, with roughly 120 square feet [11.3 square metres] of space for a family of five, and communal washing and cooking facilities.

During his first policy address to the Legislative Council in October 1972 Sir Murray outlined his plans to house 1.8 million people over ten years: 'The inadequacy and scarcity of housing and all that this implies, and the harsh situations that result from it, is one of the major and most constant sources of friction and unhappiness between the Government and the population.'

The bulk of the new housing was constructed in the 'New Towns' in the New Territories, initially in Sha Tin, Tsuen Wan, and Tuen Mun. At first organizational constraints together with the economic downturn in late 1973, triggered by the oil crisis, frustrated the achievement of targets envisaged. However, by the end of the decade, and the start of the 'second generation' New Towns, which included the development of Tai Po, Fanling, and Yuen Long, nearly a hundred new flats were being completed each day. Many people benefited from a significant improvement in living conditions as a result of the programme which continued well into the 1980s.

Improvements to education and health-care facilities were also targeted by Sir Murray. Compulsory free education at a primary level was introduced in 1971, and he ensured that plans were kept on track to extend this by 1978 to junior secondary education for all children up to the age of fifteen. This in turn necessitated expansion at the tertiary level. At the beginning of Sir Murray's tenure, demand far outstripped the existing facilities, but by 1978 the number of tertiary education places had tripled.

In addition, cultural venues grew in number and major improvements were made to the Territory's transport system. Sir Murray officiated at the opening of the Cross-Harbour Tunnel shortly after his arrival in 1972, and, in a timely move to avoid worsening traffic congestion in Hong Kong and Kowloon, the underground Mass Transit Railway started operation in 1980. This provided a clean and efficient means of transport, revolutionizing the lives of the travelling public.

The Governor's programme of reform included an overhaul of the civil service, many of whose procedures he described as a 'legacy of history'. He brought in outside consultants to suggest improvements and to expand the scope and scale of the Administration. However, some senior officials who served under Sir Murray later complained that many of the consultants' recommendations were not implemented, while changes which were introduced did not go far enough, touching only the higher echelons of the service.

Sir Murray's tenure was not without its crisis. His attempt to clean up deep-seated corruption, especially within the civil service, was one of the more dramatic, though successful aspects of his governorship. Some, however, have stated that Sir Murray refused to recognize just how serious a problem corruption had become, particularly in the police force, until there was a crisis. The dramatic flight from Hong Kong of Police Superintendent Peter Godber, who was being investigated for unaccountable sums of money he had amassed, forced Sir Murray to act. In 1973, internal police investigations revealed that the high-ranking officer had accumulated more than HK$5 million in bribes. Godber fled the Territory to avoid arrest, but was later brought back to Hong Kong to stand trial.

Sir Murray's response was to set up the Independent Commission Against Corruption (ICAC) in October 1973, and he brought back Jack Cater, who had resigned from the civil service, to head the new organization. Sir Jack, as he was to become, had long campaigned for a tough clampdown on what he saw as an evil that was eating its way through society.

The ICAC's success in uncovering large-scale syndicated corruption proved just how well-placed Sir Jack's concern had been. In 1977 he revealed that at the height of corruption activities in Hong Kong, syndicates of corrupt civil servants had amassed what amounted to 'many hundreds of millions of dollars each year'. The Public Works Department, among others, was notoriously corrupt: it was in the police force, however, that corruption proved most prevalent. Of the twenty-three cases of syndicated corruption investigated in 1976, eighteen had involved the police. In some cases, middle-ranking officers were paying HK$250,000 for what Sir Jack described as a 'lucrative posting to a district which had a reputation for vice', where they were able to recoup the money from bribes within a couple of months. And there was certainly money to be had; some officers who escaped abroad to avoid prosecution were believed to have made up to HK$80 million. One station-sergeant boasted that he had accumulated some HK$500 million, 'enough to ensure that my family won't have to work for five generations!'

But, despite the promises made in early 1977 that the campaign to root out the corrupt would be merciless, many did escape justice. In the face of a threatened police mutiny later that year, Sir Murray announced full amnesty from prosecution for any policeman who had committed corruption offences before 1 January 1977.

Sir Murray has been commended for addressing areas of social concern, but he has also been criticized for not introducing simultaneously more far-reaching political reforms. The constitutional structure remained almost intact, as it had done for the preceding decades. The Governor's top advisory body, the Executive Council, was made up of senior government officials, and appointees, representing mainly business interests. Almost half of the members of the Legislative Council were government officials, while the unofficial members represented, by and large, a very narrow band of the community. Those people maintained that, rather than be constrained by party politics, which the advent of democracy would inevitably bring, they were free to vote according to their consciences on what they believed was right for the people of Hong Kong.

The new generation of Hong Kong people, many of whom were articulate, educated, and keen to become involved in the governing of Hong Kong, were not convinced by this argument. The lack of political reform meant that they were effectively denied a means of directly influencing the formulation of government policy. Despite the support of a small but senior group of officials led by Sir Jack Cater (who by then had become Chief Secretary), Sir Murray refused to countenance proposed changes to the Legislative Council, and thus the opportunity was deemed to have been missed.

The modest reforms introduced in the early 1980s allowed for a small amount of participation in government at the lower, grass-roots level. Partially elected District Boards were established, which strengthened local administration, and limited elections were extended to the Urban Council.

The boost to Hong Kong's economy at the end of the decade was a result of the changes in China. The death of Mao in 1976 resulted in the subsequent emergence, in 1978, of Deng Xiaoping, whose pragmatic new 'open door' policy invited foreign investment in China. Hong Kong was ready to take advantage of the increased trading opportunities, and moved towards becoming a leading financial and service centre. In 1979, banking restrictions were removed, and within two years there were more than a hundred licensed banks in Hong Kong, the vast majority based overseas.

When Sir Murray arrived as Governor, Britain and China had already begun moves towards normalizing relations. This could only be to Hong Kong's benefit: for the first time, a post-war governor was not faced with tension across the border. Following the formal establishment of full Sino-British diplomatic relations, the leader of the opposition, Edward Heath, visited Beijing in 1974. (It had been envisaged when the invitation was made, that he would be making the trip in his capacity as

Prime Minister.) Ties were strengthened as China embarked on its 'open door' policy. As the decade drew to a close, Sir Murray made his historic trip to Beijing, the first by a Hong Kong governor.

Sir Murray visited Beijing in March 1979, returning to reassure investors that paramount leader Deng had urged them to 'set their hearts at ease'. Although notice had been given that the 1997 issue would have to be addressed, the *status quo* would remain for the time being. However, there was still an undercurrent of concern that the question of Hong Kong's future could not be postponed for long.

Lord MacLehose
Social and Economic Challenges

When Sir Murray (now Lord) MacLehose arrived as governor in November 1971, Hong Kong was already set on a course for wide-ranging social improvements as a result of the extended civil disorder in 1967. However, while 1967 may have been the catalyst for the changes, it was Sir Murray who gave the added impetus to carry forward many of the programmes on a large scale. When he departed in April 1982, he left behind him a more affluent Territory, on its way to becoming one of the world's leading economies, and well placed to benefit from the modernization of southern China.

Sir Murray had a reputation for being an extremely forceful governor. He was resented for the way in which he coaxed, and sometimes rammed, his ideas through a less than vital colonial bureaucracy. Many admired him, some were afraid of him, while others simply found his methods hard to accept. The system of government, which remained almost intact throughout his tenure, left little opportunity for dissent, and, together with his personal style of government, meant that his views nearly always prevailed.

Sir Murray has been credited with the ability to cut through any impediments to implementing his policies. As a result, he carried forward—at a much greater pace than would otherwise have been possible—the development of the New Towns and better transport infrastructure, and he enhanced recreational and cultural facilities.

Bound by the Official Secrets Act, Lord MacLehose has been less forthcoming about his visit to Beijing in 1979. His now famous speech on his return in which he quoted Deng Xiaoping's exhortation to 'set your hearts at ease' has, with the benefit of hindsight, been seen as a misleading message of confidence to investors. What was not known at the time, but is now common knowledge, was that during a courtesy visit to Deng Xiaoping, Sir Murray had raised the question of the New Territories land leases, due to expire in 1997, at the same time as Britain's main lease over the New Territories. Britain argued that the matter was affecting business confidence, although others have questioned whether the time was right to

raise the issue in 1979. If it had been generally known then that the Chinese had rebuffed Sir Murray's request for a so-called 'blurring' of the 1997 deadline, confidence would have nose-dived, not soared, as it did.

WHEN I ARRIVED in Hong Kong as Political Adviser in 1963, the Territory had already recovered from the scars of war, and had well started along the lines that made its future so remarkable. By then the United Nations embargo had already abolished Hong Kong's original entrepôt position to the China trade, but the Territory was well established as a worldwide export centre for raw materials, and the basic services for supporting trade and investment were also already in place. This growing prosperity was producing a satisfactory revenue for the Government, but, despite this, the problems facing the administration were quite daunting. The massive increase in population caused by the flood of refugees from China meant that something had to be done to provide some sort of services for the large number of squatter settlements which had sprouted on the hillsides. The Government then was doing what it could to tackle the problems, though there was a long way to go.

When I came back in 1971 as Governor the situation had greatly changed. Trade and manufacturing and financial success and, indeed, services, had resulted in a large increase in Hong Kong's international status and self-confidence.

I did not come then with any set of instructions from London, or a list of things to be done. When I arrived at the airport I was asked what my priorities were, and my reply was that my first priority was to learn the job, and to see and familiarize myself with the people and the place. At the press conference someone had read *Who's Who* and knew I was a fisherman. They asked, 'Will you go fishing in Hong Kong?' To which I replied, 'I certainly will go fishing, but it will be simply for information!' A plan of action emerged in the course of much discussion, briefing, and visiting during my first year, and the results were set out in my first speech to the Legislative Council in October 1972.

I pushed very hard to achieve quick expansion of social services and housing. All this seemed to me right and essential on its merits. It was what a British colonial power should do for the population. However it

was very much in the
back of my mind
that a fairly dra-
matic social pro-
gramme would
help in fending
off attempts to
restrict our
exports on the
grounds that they
were the outcome of
unacceptable social condi-

tions. This would have been extremely dangerous and injurious to people in Hong Kong.

In terms of expanding the public housing programme, my problem
was not so much the money, but in ending the fragmented aspect of its
administration. It was not easy to persuade the different departments
and personalities that a concentrated effort by a single department
would be in the public interest, since it removed power from some
people. However, in the end, everyone was very reasonable and helpful.

The housing programme certainly had serious teething problems,
and was held back by financial constraints that were unavoidable in
1973 and 1974 when the drastic increase in the price of oil caused a
worldwide slump. It was thus not really until the end of the 1970s that
the programme got fully into its stride, but it then did admirably, and I
think has continued to do so ever since.

There was simply no room in the older urban areas of Hong Kong and
Kowloon, and so we had to plan for the development of new areas in the
New Territories. We were determined to build not just dormitories but
communities, with all that was necessary for a community. Each 'New
Town' would include space for industry, and also the schools, recreation
areas, and public services which support a community. We developed
the concept of building the New Towns on a 'modular' principle, such
that the production of schools, police stations, fire stations, and public
amenities generally kept pace with the development of housing. This
was a new concept in Hong Kong, and I think it was extremely
successful.

I should mention that it became clear that it was not enough to move people from squatter huts to modern housing in new cities whether on Hong Kong Island or in the New Towns. Steps had to be taken to make people feel at home and secure in spite of new surroundings and new neighbours. I remember a group in a squatter area of Hong Kong Island asking me to promise that they would not be moved unless the whole of the squatter settlement was moved together. I pointed out that their present conditions were dangerous and unsanitary, but they replied they felt safe with their present neighbours and feared what the situation might be like in a new housing estate with neighbours they did not know. One could not wait for good neighbourly relations to develop in the new estates in the course of time: the Government had to help. Thus the architects were encouraged to build new housing according to designs that favoured neighbourly contact rather than privacy. Similarly District Officers were tasked to promote neighbourly contact, and to encourage the development of cohesive communities.

Promotion of sport and recreation was something that helped this process, and so did promotion of the arts. In both cases it brought people together who otherwise might have had little in common. There was great support for this type of approach from the private sector. The Jockey Club gave great encouragement to sport through the donation of the Sha Tin Sports Centre, and they gave similar encouragement to the arts by funding the Academy for the Performing Arts. In parallel with these developments a group of enthusiasts promoted the idea of an international arts festival in Hong Kong. Under the expert management of Sir Run Run Shaw and the administration of the Urban Council, this developed into a very large and popular event at which Hong Kong people could see international artists of the highest calibre. This helped to boost interest in teaching the arts in schools, and created a public demand for high-grade performances in the town halls of the New Towns. The creation of the country parks was also intended to encourage people to widen their enjoyment of Hong Kong, as well as to have healthy fresh air and exercise in Hong Kong's lesser known and very beautiful wild places.

I admit to being an enthusiastic supporter of these fields of activity not normal in most governments because of the new opportunities for health and pleasure, and also the pride in their city that they brought to Hong Kong people. Hong Kong also earned a reputation in the world as a place where there was more to life than manufacture and money. I think this made a considerable contribution to the international credibility of Hong Kong.

The development of major new roads in the New Territories, and the upgrading of the surface railway to the border were essential to the success of the New Towns. In the urban area the development of the MTR was likewise essential as there was just not enough room on the surface—even with the very considerable road-building programme that was undertaken.

Sir Murray taking part in the 1973 Keep Hong Kong Clean Campaign.

Oddly enough, there was not much about corruption in the briefing I received before I went to Hong Kong. The new law on corruption—placing the onus for proof of innocence on persons discovered to have greater wealth than their legal income could explain—was already in place, and, though there was much talk about corruption on my arrival in Hong Kong, very few specific instances were brought to my attention. I was concerned about the rising crime rates, and about the people's fear of crime, and it was my first objective to deal with that situation.

The extent of corruption only became evident after the establishment of the Independent Commission Against Corruption [ICAC], which launched a large-scale, and technically very efficient, investigation. I think many people in high positions were appalled when it was revealed just how deep-rooted corruption had become, affecting every stratum of society.

Prior to that the task of detecting corruption had been the responsibility of the anti-corruption department of the police, but the force was discredited by the Peter Godber case. When Godber escaped while being questioned by the police—though he had not, at that stage, been charged—the public believed, quite wrongly, that the police had engineered his escape. Consequently no major effort to combat corruption led by the police would have commanded the confidence of the public, and that was what led to the establishment of the ICAC.

The ICAC, as set up under Jack Cater and John Prendergast [the former Director of the Police Special Branch], was a formidably effective organization. Its successful investigation of the corrupt, and subsequently its drive to instill management procedures that made corruption more difficult, did achieve a turnaround in corruption in Hong Kong. This, like the improvements in social services, certainly helped Hong Kong's image in the rest of the world.

Without going into a lot of detail, the partial amnesty for the police in 1977 worked. It would have been feasible to go on prosecuting people for offences committed long ago, but the risk of such prosecutions had resulted in an alliance between the formerly corrupt and the presently corrupt which was at the heart of the near mutiny of the police. The amnesty split off these two rather different elements and simplified the ICAC's ability to press on with the prosecution of current corruption.

The influx of Vietnamese boat people did present an almost insoluble problem. They could not be deterred from coming, and there was clearly a limit to the extent to which they could be accommodated in Hong Kong, especially considering the restrictions that were rightly imposed on immigrants from China. The solution reached in the Geneva Conference was that if Hong Kong gave the boat people temporary asylum, other countries outside the region would eventually provide for permanent asylum. Many thousands of boat people were settled elsewhere under the Geneva agreement, but efforts to stop them coming from Vietnam, or to repatriate them to Vietnam, were ineffective.

The impact of Deng's 'open door' policy on Hong Kong was very great. Not only did it result in mainland companies investing in Hong Kong, but, perhaps more important, it resulted in Hong Kong companies investing in China, and doing so on such a scale as to transform the southern cities of China.

My visit to Beijing in 1979 was at the invitation of the Chinese Government. Its objective appeared to be to show that the hostility towards Hong Kong manifested, for instance, in the Cultural Revolution, was a thing of the past, and to accept that Hong Kong had a lot to offer China in helping Deng's modernization programme. While the visit demonstrated China's wish for better relations with the United Kingdom over Hong Kong, it did not start negotiations about the future. These were only begun in the visits of Humphrey Atkins [a junior Foreign Office minister, who visited Beijing in January 1982], and, eventually, of the then Prime Minister, Margaret Thatcher [whose visit took place in September 1982].

Looking back, my time as Governor contrasted with that of my predecessors in several ways.

Economically and politically the 1970s was a different scene. Commercial success had produced larger revenues which made possible expanding government expenditure. The relationship vis-à-vis China and the United Kingdom itself, and so of Hong Kong, had been greatly improved by Edward Heath's success in changing British policy so that full Sino-British diplomatic relations were established. This relieved the bilateral tensions of ten years before, just as the tensions in the whole Western Pacific area had been reduced by the policies of Nixon and Kissinger which had greatly improved Sino-US relations.

My impression is that the style of governors was very much a matter of personality and background. Certainly Black differed from Grantham, and Trench differed from Black, and, no doubt, I, in turn, differed from Trench. While my predecessors had experience of other colonies, I had experience of working in a comparatively large number of countries, including China itself. Unlike them I also had considerable experience of working in Whitehall and, as Principal Private Secretary to the Foreign Secretary, of the way the British Government worked.

My predecessors tended to be heirs to the Colonial Service attitude of muted hostility towards London and the Westminster of the Colonial

Office. My own familiarity with the personalities in Westminster and in the Foreign Office was undoubtedly helpful in that respect.

Many observers have commented that Hong Kong was seen to transform during my time as Governor from 'a colony to an independent city state'. I would not agree with this. The Colonial Office had ceased to exist in the 1960s, and as Hong Kong had not been dependent on any financial assistance from the UK, it did not call for any specific supervision from London—and little was given. Whilst this did not amount to independence, it did amount to a 'high degree of autonomy', which was subsequently written into the Joint Declaration.

Looking to the future, Hong Kong has the physical, social, and academic infrastructure to maintain and improve on its present prosperity. It also has an enviable geographic situation on the edge of both China and the emerging economies of the Pacific Rim. Its present problem is the uncertainty accompanying the forthcoming political change, albeit change within the limits defined in the Joint Declaration.

For my part, I believe that Hong Kong people will dispose of this uncertainty as they have disposed of so many difficulties in the past, and that Hong Kong's future under Chinese sovereignty will be as prosperous as under British.

Yuen Kong Ming

My Home in Lok Fu

Yuen Kong Ming grew up during the 1970s on one of the first public housing estates. These 'Resettlement Units' were built hastily in the 1950s in response to the urgent need to clear wooden squatter huts from the hillsides following the Shek Kip Mei fire in 1953. They housed thousands of people for more than thirty years.

When Sir Murray MacLehose arrived as Governor at the end of 1971, there were as many as half a million people housed in the so-called 'H-blocks'. The flats were basic, small, and unhealthy, and the need for change was underscored by the general feeling then that life in a squatter hut was preferable to conditions in some of the early government public housing estates.

Despite these conditions, Yuen Kong Ming and his family thrived for more than two decades in their public housing flat. Born in 1966, Yuen Kong Ming had never known any other life. It was not until 1989 that the building in which he grew up was demolished, and his family moved on. Yuen Kong Ming now owns his own flat, and works as a hairstylist in Central District.

MY PARENTS WERE delighted when they moved into the newly constructed Lok Fu housing estate in 1963. They thought the flat was very luxurious because they had a whole room all to themselves. My mother lived there for the next twenty-six years. I have six brothers and sisters, and each of us, except the eldest, was born and brought up there.

A family photograph with Yuen Kong Ming on the far right.

My mother had had a rough time before she was able to move into the flat. She had come back to Hong Kong in 1958. She had actually been born here during the war, but Hong Kong was in chaos at that time, so my grandfather had returned with his children to his old village in southern China where at least they could find something to eat. By the time my mother returned to Hong Kong she was already married with a daughter. My father was unable to leave China at that time, so she left him, and came with my eldest sister.

My mother moved around a lot, to wherever she could find a job, while my grandfather looked after her child. She lived in a tiny bed-space apartment, and subsequently moved into a wooden squatter hut in northern Kowloon. She had a job then as a construction worker on the Lion Rock Tunnel [which links urban Kowloon to Sha Tin in the New Territories]. It was while she was working on the tunnel that she was able to apply for public housing, by which time my father had left China and joined my mother in Hong Kong.

My first twenty-three years were spent in that Lok Fu flat. It was really just one room of around 120 square feet [11 square metres]. That didn't leave much space, and we had to sleep on the floor since there were at least four of us in our flat at any one time. There was only one tiny window in the room, and in the summer it was oppressively hot and airless. The men, including myself and my brothers, used to sleep out in the corridor on fold up camp-beds, where it was cooler. There were no kitchens, and people used to cook in the corridors. All the residents on each floor shared a communal toilet.

As our family grew, my parents were able to rent the room next door, so eventually there were nine of us living between the two rooms. At that time they paid HK$18 rent for each room, which still amounted to quite a lot in those days.

The blocks were very simply constructed. Each floor of our building had two long parallel corridors and each corridor was partitioned off into ten cubicles housing ten families, so there were a lot of people living on each floor. There was a staircase at each end, and, linking the two corridors across the middle, were two rows of toilets. We lived at the top, on the eighth floor, so we had to walk up eight flights of stairs. People left the doors of the flats open, to let in more light and air; even when they went out, they left the main front door open and just closed the iron security gate. This meant inter-personal relationships were either very bad or very good, because people lived in such close proximity.

H-block public housing

Generally speaking, neighbours mixed a lot better than they do now because they didn't lock themselves inside their flats. Everybody knew everybody else, and there was a feeling of being part of one large family because we all lived so closely together. Whenever the ladies next door were cooking something delicious, they would give some to me; or sometimes the 'uncles' next door, my parents' friends, would take me to *yam cha* in the tea restaurants because they knew we had a big family and a lot of mouths to feed. When we went outside, we always saw lots of friends on the street, and we knew the people in the market.

There was a downside, too, since the living environment was not very good. The buildings were quite open with no security, so anyone could walk in and out. I would often find drug addicts smoking heroin on the staircases, and they sometimes fought each other. I was quite young at the time, but I was still aware of what they were up to. I don't remember there ever being much other crime though. There were squabbles amongst the residents, despite the family atmosphere of the place, but I suppose that was inevitable. The Resettlement Department [which subsequently became part of the Housing Authority] didn't really care about our living conditions—whether we had water or not, or the fact that the corridors were very dirty—I suppose they were just interested in trying to house people.

We never thought much about whether we would stay in Lok Fu for a short time or forever. We just got on with our lives and I was very happy. All I cared about was playing with the other kids as I had so many friends around me. We lived in Block 24, and my school was at the bottom of Block 5, and nearly all the children living on the estate went to that school. One of our favourite pastimes was going to the top of the nearby Radar Hill and watching the aeroplanes coming over. We lived almost under the approach path for Kai Tak airport so it was exciting to see the aircraft descend directly towards you, and then bank sharply for the final approach over Kowloon City to Kai Tak. I remember that we even found wild guava to pick up there.

Since our flat was on the top floor of our building I could look over to the beautiful homes along Broadcast Drive. I then wondered why I couldn't live in one of these houses and why I had to stay in such a small flat. I had an uncle from China who was a merchant seaman and whenever he visited Hong Kong, he would come and stay. The only place we had for him to sleep was on an old cot which we put out in the corridor. In winter, it was too cold for him to sleep out there, so we would have to find room to squeeze the folding bed inside our flat. Still, I understood from him that living conditions in China were even worse.

My dad leased a shop on the ground floor of the building in which we lived. He was a wholesaler of plastic flowers, which was a common occupation then. He would get a big box of plastic flowers and send them to individuals to assemble. My mother helped him, and so did we children. We only studied for half a day at school, and, as soon as that finished, we would always go down to the shop to help them. We all had to work hard to make ends meet. In addition to our daily  living expenses, we had to pay HK$50 a month protection money to the local triads who 'looked after' my father's premises. That was normal, and we didn't think anything of it, but it was a lot when you think we were only paying HK$18 in rent!

No attempt was ever made to recruit me into any of the triad societies during my time at school. I don't think any of my school friends were members in the 1970s: we were too poor to afford to join!

When I was young, people didn't travel around very much because it was difficult and expensive. My parents wouldn't let me go far away anyway as I had to help with the family or in the shop. It wasn't until I was eleven years old, in 1977, that I went by bus to Hong Kong Island for the first time. My sister and I went with our uncle who was then cleaning the windows on the Connaught Centre—what is now known as Jardine House—in Central. He took us up to the roof to see the view of Victoria Harbour and the Island, and my sister and I were really scared! In 1980, after the opening of the MTR, I started to travel around quite a bit more. [Work had begun on the Mass Transit Railway in 1975, and Lok Fu was on the first line to be constructed.]

By then I was fifteen and had left school, after completing Form 3. I'd always wanted to be a hairstylist, and I went to a salon to try to get a job, but I was too young. So I went to the Productivity Council School [responsible for promoting increased productivity by Hong Kong's industries], and later took on several factory jobs. Finally, when I had saved enough money, I started as a junior in a local hair salon. I needed my savings to supplement my small wage. I also started to learn English at an evening class with the British Council.

I trained for over a year, and was lucky enough to get a job at a well-known salon in Central. Work there was quite an eye-opener, and it was all a sharp contrast to life in Lok Fu. I'd always thought that the really wealthy people in Hong Kong were the gweilos [expatriates], but I soon found out there were lots of wealthy Chinese as well who were equally, if not more, demanding!

We left Lok Fu in 1989 when the Government finally decided to demolish our housing estate and replace it with improved public housing. We moved away from the area and took the opportunity to purchase a flat through the Home Ownership Scheme [which enables low-income families to buy homes at prices below their market value] on one of the new estates which were being built on the reclaimed land in Junk Bay on the far eastern side of Kowloon.

Living conditions there are a great deal better. There is more space and each flat has its own kitchen and bathroom, but the atmosphere is not the same. Everybody lives behind closed doors, and the same friendships do not exist. We don't even know the names of our neighbours. My mother isn't happy. She was sad to leave Lok Fu, having lived there for so many years. She had lots of friends with whom she could play mahjong, and now she is very lonely; my father has died and we are all out working during the day. She has nowhere to go in Junk Bay, and she can't get around very well because the area is not well served by public transport [it is not linked to the MTR line for example]. She just stays at home by herself.

I still live at home with my mother, but I've been able to buy a flat in City One Sha Tin [a vast apartment complex]. I'm renting it out at the moment so that I can repay the loan from my mother. It's a lovely flat of 395 square feet [36 square metres], with two bedrooms, a toilet, a kitchen, and a living room. It's three times the size of our old home in Lok Fu!

Jean Wong
Western Culture, Chinese Values

Hong Kong's economic success has repeatedly been attributed, at least in part, to the many Shanghainese refugees who brought their business acumen to Hong Kong following the 1949 Communist Revolution in China. But Hong Kong's cultural life was also enhanced by the influx of these educated, sophisticated, urban families. Jean May Wong was one of them. Having escaped from Shanghai with her family while she was still a young girl, she was brought up with a refugee mentality, perceiving Hong Kong as just a temporary stop on the way to somewhere else. But Hong Kong became her home, and, nearly fifty years later, she is one of the doyennes of Hong Kong's cultural community, and founder of the Territory's leading school of ballet.

Jean Wong and her generation are typical products of Hong Kong's bi-cultural background. Like her peers, she was raised in a traditional Chinese family, yet was Western-educated in one of the prestigious English schools in the Territory. She feels that this upbringing enabled her to appreciate and take advantage of Hong Kong's cultural melting pot, where East meets West.

At the end of the 1950s, Jean Wong completed her training at the Royal Academy of Dance in London, and, ten years after she had first set foot in Hong Kong, she returned to the Territory as the first Chinese person to graduate with a teaching certificate from the Academy. While in Britain, she established lasting friendships with some of the mentors of the dance world, including the late Dame Margot Fonteyn, and Arnold Haskell, the renowned balletomane and historian.

When Jean Wong began her profession, she was the only Chinese person teaching classical ballet in Hong Kong. At that time very few local students were interested in taking lessons in what was perceived as a purely Western art form. In 1960 she established her own school, which then expanded and flourished throughout the 1970s. By the mid-1990s, Jean Wong's schools stretched across the Territory giving many young people the chance to learn classical ballet taught by teachers who spoke their own language and understood their cultural background. Jean Wong was also one of the founding members of the Hong Kong Ballet Group and adviser to three professional dance companies which were established in the late 1970s. She can be credited for training a new generation of dancers in Hong Kong, and for encouraging a greater appreciation of ballet as an art form.

IT WAS SIR MURRAY MACLEHOSE, now Lord MacLehose, who was really responsible for raising cultural awareness in Hong Kong, and it was his governorship that marked the turning point in the Territory's cultural development.

I am not a political person, so it is difficult for me to give an overall assessment of his achievements, but, culturally speaking, I think Hong Kong is indebted to him. He was a great supporter of the arts, and more involved with events, such as the annual Arts Festival, which began in the early 1970s, than his successors, Sir Edward Youde, Lord Wilson, or Chris Patten. The Hong Kong Academy for the Performing Arts was established in 1984, and the construction of many of our other venues for the performing arts was set in motion at that time as well.

Hong Kong is often viewed as not a particularly cultured place, where people are more interested in making money than in the arts. I would agree with that, but does it matter? It is important to make money first: you can't say, 'I'm going to look at a da Vinci or Rembrandt', or whatever, when you don't even have a bowl of rice. After you have the bowl of rice, and become a bit more affluent, then you can afford and desire other less materialistic things. Fortunately, during the 1970s while Lord MacLehose was Governor, the economy grew, and society gradually became more culturally aware. Nowadays, there is a great deal more interest in the arts. 70 per cent or more of the people attending cultural events, such as those performed during the Arts Festival, are Chinese, whereas previously these performances were dominated by expatriates.

I was very fortunate in that from a very young age I had a wide exposure to the arts. My mother, in particular, loved going to the opera and the theatre, and I would tag along too. I adored those occasions, but, believe it nor not, I didn't see my first live ballet performance until I went to London to study in my late teens. There just wasn't the opportunity.

I spent my early years living in Shanghai. My father's position with the Bank of China meant that my family entertained a great deal and we gave many parties. These were really dancing parties, and, although I was quite young, when given the chance I would love to dance too!

I had a happy, but rather traumatic childhood because of all the moving around, initially as a result of the Japanese war, and then because of the Civil War. I was about five years old when my family moved from Shanghai to Kunming [in Yunnan province, south-west China], out of harm's way from the Sino-Japanese conflict. When we returned to Shanghai in 1945, we were there for barely a couple of years before we had to move again, south to Guangzhou, because of the Communist uprising. Two years later we were fleeing the Communists once more, and we arrived in Hong Kong in 1949 as refugees.

The upheavals in China brought a great deal of uncertainty to our family, especially for my father. I was aware of a lot of political undercurrents, even as a child, partly because my father's job with the Bank of China involved him in some political activities. I knew when we went back to Shanghai in 1945 that we would not be there for long because of the start of the Communist Revolution. So when we arrived in Hong Kong, that, too, was just a temporary home for us. My parents had no intention of staying, and my father refused to invest any money in fixed assets, such as property. His next step was to move the family on to South America! We didn't go, as it turned out, but neither did my father stay in Hong Kong all his years. After retiring from a large American stock brokerage firm in the mid-1970s, he moved to the United States. He kept saying, 'The Communists will be coming!'

We started off in Hong Kong living in the seclusion of the Bank of China quarters, out on Mount Davis on the western side of Hong Kong Island. Then it was a very rural and idyllic area. There were beautiful sea views, fresh air, and no buses, so we often walked home from the Mid-Levels area above Central. We didn't see any squalor or anything like that.

Many Shanghainese came to Hong Kong in 1949 and 1950 for the same reasons as us. We all felt very superior, very suave, and we tended to look down on the 'barbarian Cantonese' because they were not very sophisticated. The Shanghainese tended to stick together. We thought that if you didn't speak our dialect you were really quite a different creature! The first generation Shanghainese hardly spoke any Cantonese, so they rarely integrated with the rest of society in Hong Kong. It was easier for us, though: we could speak a little of the Cantonese dialect since we had been living in Guangzhou before we moved to Hong Kong. Neither my sister nor I knew much English when we came here, and that was more difficult for us since all the best schools expected a fluency in the language. I have to say, though, that I found my school years here relatively easy because the foundation I received during my formative days in Shanghai was so good: it has served me well all my life.

It was not until two years after we arrived in Hong Kong when I was eleven, that I came across ballet for the first time. It was my younger sister who first started dancing, and one day I went to watch her. It was love at first sight, but kind of late! I wanted to start learning ballet immediately, but I was already taking piano and painting lessons. It wasn't long after that I started dancing, and, without letting my father know, I used my pocket money to pay for the lessons.

Later, when I left school, I was offered a place at the Royal Academy of Dancing in London to join the teacher's training course. My father, who was really a very liberal man and always very supportive, thought that it wasn't too 'lofty an idea'. He had already been trying to discourage me from going to Rome to learn to be a sculptress. He thought I wouldn't be able to make a living out of being an artist, but in the end he was persuaded that being a ballet teacher wasn't such a bad idea in comparison!

London was quite a culture shock. I was only eighteen years old and had never lived in a boarding-school before. What surprised me most was the way the English and some of the other girls had no qualms about walking around naked! I would be taking a bath and they would just roam into the bathroom. I was so embarrassed and thought 'Ooh! That's kind of, you know, risqué!' To make matters worse, I didn't know that I'd have to wash my own clothes. There was no washing machine, and I didn't know how to wash clothes because we had always had a

Jean Wong (left) with Dame Margot Fonteyn in Hong Kong.

maid. They used to call me 'Jeanie Wongie Tongie from China, floating down the Yangtze River on a lotus bed!'

I also remember going with friends into St Martin's Lane to buy some point shoes. All I had to wear was my cheongsam, which we all thought was very elegant. However, everyone on the street just stared at me as if I was somehow indecent wearing a dress slit up to the thigh!

There were two great influences on my life when I was a student in London. One was Arnold Haskell, the Vice President of the Royal Academy of Dancing. I was a kind of novelty item, this 'thing' from the East, and we developed quite a rapport. The other was Dame Margot Fonteyn who was the President of the Royal Academy. It was one of the biggest thrills of my life when she first spoke to me as a student at the Academy. Over the years, Dame Margot and I developed a very close relationship. I think our Shanghai connections bonded us initially, as she had spent part of her childhood there with her parents.

Dame Margot first danced in Hong Kong in 1960, in one of the performances to celebrate the opening of the newly constructed City Hall. She returned in 1973 for the first Hong Kong Arts Festival. I asked her in her dressing room at the Lee Theatre whether she would agree to be the patron of the Hong Kong Ballet Group. She was not in the habit of accepting such positions, but she thought about it and agreed. The Ballet was fortunate as she was patron in more than just name. When she accepted she said, 'You should not just confine ballet to within four walls of a classroom, you should perform more. I will try to help you.' She felt that ballet should be 'taken out to the people', and, in her bid to help us, she asked her partner, David Blair, to come and help us mount a full-length ballet.

In 1974, when he came to Hong Kong, David had just finished his career at the Royal Ballet, and he treated us as if we were the Royal Ballet, which of course we weren't! Far from it in fact! We didn't even have a stage manager or ballet master or anything! However, it was a momentous occasion when we performed our first, *Giselle*. It was the first full-length ballet to be performed by any local ballet group. We did it on a very limited budget, with hardly any props or scenery, but everybody was doing it with just a pure love for dance. It was the most touching performance of *Giselle* that I have ever seen. I was so moved, because we had all been so involved, that I cried in the wings watching the performance.

This really marked the beginnings of professional dance in Hong Kong and it was from this first production that the Hong Kong Ballet Company developed. However, the Hong Kong Ballet Group got into an awful financial mess putting on that production, despite the fact that we had tried to do it on a shoestring budget. Margot learnt about this and said 'I'll come and dance for you'. She came the next year, in 1975, and danced free for us in a series of fund-raising gala performances.

When I first returned to Hong Kong from London in 1959, I was invited to join a local ballet school run by my former teacher, an expatriate. However, there was a great deal of racial discrimination. I felt that, because I was Chinese, I was never going to be given the same kind of standing as other teachers in her school, and I'd always just be second fiddle. I also felt there was great potential to introduce ballet to more local Chinese people because nearly all the people I was teaching were expatriates.

So I decided to strike out on my own. In those days, it wasn't that difficult. I remember I found a small apartment, put in a mirror and a barre, and started business with maybe eight or nine students.

I never thought it was a business, I enjoyed it so much. I loved my students and I adored the teaching. I had never had a strong yearning to perform, but I had always wanted to teach. I was so dedicated that, for a long time, I hogged all the students myself, refusing to allow anyone else near them! I was finally persuaded by a friend to allow other people to teach, and I realized that many others were just as good, if not better than me!

During the early days of my school, I think I influenced a lot of young students because of my passion for dance and for ballet. The first generation of the Hong Kong Dance Company, the Hong Kong Ballet, and the City Contemporary Dance Company, which were all established in the late 1970s, were mostly my ex-students. I feel that it was my love of ballet that empowered them and helped build up this passion they are now carrying on. Now I have been teaching for a long time, and already the children of my early pupils attend my schools.

Since the beginning, many of the children of leading Hong Kong personalities have been my students. Initially, when the school started, they were not learning ballet with the aim of becoming professional dancers, but they all went through my training. Even nowadays the parents whose children have enrolled have never seen a real ballet. It's very much a status thing. I used to be upset by this, but not now. I just think that if we educate them today, maybe tomorrow the next generation will appreciate ballet and want to go to watch performances for themselves.

The children who come to my school start at five or six, and usually stay for a good ten years. Given their background, they don't want to become professional dancers, and their parents have no such aim. That doesn't matter. I view ballet as part of a child's general education: through dance and their training, they learn to become more disciplined, well co-ordinated and, I hope, young people with a sense of integrity. I don't think I need to turn them all into ballet dancers because there will be no jobs for them. Even when students stop dancing, if they apply to other things in life the same kind of drive and will-power which goes into ballet, they will succeed. I just hope that I am able to give all my students more understanding of the art, and for them to have some love in their lives. If so, then I think I have done what I need to do.

Ballet is a Western art form. It's too alien for many Chinese. It is not in our blood, nor in our culture, but I don't think we should be aping the West. It took me a long while to realize I was pursuing an art form that was really not in my heritage. Perhaps I should have taken up Peking Opera, or something, which was part of my cultural background?

I am quite an optimistic person. China is changing and I don't feel quite so concerned about the future of artistic freedom as I did a few years ago, following Tiananmen and the crackdown on the student movement in 1989. I was very agitated then: I joined the demonstrations here in support of the students in China, and I still have a few concerns. Recently I attended a performance by the Shanghai Ballet. I told the company they had put on a wonderful show which was well suited to the Shanghai Ballet since it was in a style so typically Chinese and reflected a certain period in China's history. The dancers told me that we would be performing that type of ballet after 1997. Now that is not the official view, but if the people in China think like that, then I don't know.

I just hope that after 1997 nobody is going to bother with the artists for a while. As Deng Xiaoping said, 'Keep dancing for the next fifty years!'

Liu Ching Leung

New Towns in the New Territories

The traditional Chinese walled village used to be a familiar sight in the New Territories. Sheung Shui Wai was one of them: it was the ancestral home of the Liu clan, one of the five largest clans in the New Territories. It was also, however, one of the many villages which found itself part of a growing New Town of nearly a quarter of a million people. Liu Ching Leung, a village leader, was closely associated with the development of Sheung Shui from a remote farming community to a thriving New Town. He emerged as one of the leading spokesmen on rural affairs, and, after the conclusion of the Sino-British Joint Declaration, he, along with many of the New Territories politicians, developed a trusting relationship with China.

In the early 1970s the Government embarked on an ambitious programme to build 'New Towns' in the rural areas of the New Territories. Housing was urgently needed for Hong Kong's growing population, and Sheung Shui, together with the adjacent village of Fanling, became one of the 'second generation' of New Towns built. The concept was that each New Town should be self-sufficient, providing not just homes, but a commercial base and employment, as well as social welfare and recreational needs for those who lived there.

Although the New Towns encouraged some commercial and industrial development within their boundaries, and the Government invested in roads and community facilities, self-sufficiency was not achieved, and most remained vast commuter towns. The speed and scope of development in the 1970s also led to tensions with indigenous New Territories residents who fought to preserve their political privileges, the environment, and their rural lifestyle.

Liu Ching Leung was among those who tried to protect the New Territories' interests. His own village was hundreds of years old and based on the traditional Chinese clan system, whereby groups of families with the same name and common ancestry lived together, generation after generation. The tightly packed rows of houses were surrounded by a wall

and moat. These inward-looking communities reflected age-old beliefs and
Confucian ethics, which included filial
piety and ancestor worship. There was
typically an ancestral hall and a village
temple in the midst of the houses inside
the walled village.

In 1976 Liu Ching Leung became
the Sheung Shui representative on the
Heung Yee Kuk—a council which
advises the Government on rural
affairs—and was elected Vice
Chairman of the Kuk in 1982, a position he held until 1995. He has also
served as an ex-officio member of the
North District Board, and he became a Regional Councillor in 1986, when
the Council was formally established to provide environmental, hygiene,
and recreational services to the New Territories. In 1995 Liu Ching Leung
was appointed by Beijing to sit on the Preparatory Committee, the body set
up by China to oversee the transition to Chinese rule. Sheung Shui Wai in
1997 is a very different place from the one Liu Ching Leung remembers in
the 1970s.

I WAS BORN and brought up in Sheung Shui Wai in the 1940s when it was
still a very remote farming village in the north-eastern New Territories.
Over ten generations of my family were born there, and I am the
twentieth generation of my clan to live in the New Territories. I can
trace my roots in China back to around AD900.

Sheung Shui Wai was a typical old Chinese walled village, where over
four hundred people lived. The protective wall was some five metres
high with two strong iron gates, and surrounded by a wide moat.
Although roving bands of robbers had long since disappeared when I
was a child, we still kept some muskets ready in the event of an
emergency. Inside the village there were a number of wells which
meant that the villagers could hold fort for several months. We lived in

a typical single-storey rural house which was just beside the storm-water nullah which ran through the village.

My most vivid childhood memory is being washed away into the nullah. I was out walking one windy morning wearing a brand new hat, and it blew into the nullah. I went to retrieve it, but was swept up by the water, and washed away to where the water went underground. I would have disappeared for ever, had it not been for my large hat which stuck in the drain. A passer-by saw my hat, and we were both rescued!

The New Territories then was very quiet and remote; people living there were largely unaffected by the rapid urbanization in Hong Kong and Kowloon, and the major changes in China. Refugees from across the border swept through the New Territories on their way to the urban area where they hoped to find work.

Nothing changed very much during my childhood. My family was very poor. My father was an ambulance driver, and, after normal working hours, he was employed in a flower shop to try and earn some extra money. Life was quite peaceful then, although we had a simple existence. Every day I walked to Sheung Shui Railway Station and took the train to Tai Po where I attended the government primary school. After school I came home and tended the cattle. The countryside was very fresh and green. There were even fish in the rivers which are now mostly polluted. When the fruits on the twenty-foot tall lychee trees which surrounded the village were in season, the children ganged up to steal them.

The most important custom in the New Territories was family pride and unity with the clan living together and helping each other. This helped with the maintenance of law and order. Every child born in the village was known to everybody else and there was never any need for documents such as birth certificates. If there was a 'bad apple', he would never dare make trouble at home because he could be identified easily and bring shame on his family. At the major Spring and Autumn festivals [Ching Ming and Chung Yeung] all the adults in the village came together for a major feast, and made offerings to the ancestors.

In the 1960s rural people were very poor. It was difficult to make a living from farming, and many went to Europe to work as chefs or to start Chinese restaurants. While most stayed on in Britain to have their children educated there, some did return to their old villages. When those who had been born abroad came back, they tended to look in amazement, and often disdain, at the simple cramped village houses where their parents had been brought up.

When I finished school, I became a primary school teacher, and then a merchant, but I gave up my career in 1973 to become Sheung Shui Wai's Village Representative on the Sheung Shui District Rural Committee, a locally based management committee. I've often asked myself why I took up this post, but I had a lot of encouragement from the villagers, and the support of my uncle, Liu Yun Sum, who had been the Village Representative for many years.

As Village Representative I had to run the communal property which totalled over a million square feet [some 93,000 square metres]. This included the Liu clan's ancestral hall, which provided a focus for clan activities. I took charge of village meetings, and at the Spring and Autumn festivals offered gifts to the ancestors. I also helped mediate in disputes between villagers and with the Government, and I acted as a contact point for members of the Liu clan living overseas.

It was partly because of the poverty and lack of opportunities for younger people that, in the late 1950s, community leaders, and the rural council, the Heung Yee Kuk, pressed the Government to develop the New Territories by building New Towns. Many people think that the first New Towns in Hong Kong were developed in the New Territories, but this is of course untrue. The Government built a New Town in Kwun Tong in the early 1950s. But many of the lessons learnt in Kwun Tong had to be relearnt in the New Territories when Tsuen Wan, Sha Tin, Tai Po, and Fanling were developed in the sixties, seventies, and eighties. In particular, planners realized that it was no good just building homes— other facilities and community needs had to be integrated into the development plans. If this was not done, the New Towns would only pose a great deal of inconvenience to the people living there, and would not encourage those in the urban areas to move out.

The Government worked hard to consult the New Territories villagers about the design and layout of the New Towns, and many people benefited financially when land was taken over by the Government for development. But the development was not without its problems for the people in the rural areas, particularly in the early stages when land was being formed. Villagers were often affected by dust and noise, and Government officials were blamed for not adequately supervising the construction work.

In general, expatriate Government officials had a very good general knowledge and understanding of the people of the New Territories. Villagers treated the expatriate District Officers as very senior officials, even though they held only middle-ranking positions in the government structure. The District Officers held a great deal of power in the 1970s, and, although the needs of the people were minimal, most officers helped when difficulties arose. Of course there were some District Officers who thought themselves very superior and they were not so easy to deal with. However, overall I believe the old colonial District Office system was a lot more efficient and effective than the present local government system.

The New Towns have brought prosperity and lots of newcomers to the New Territories, and both indigenous villagers and people moving to live in the area have benefited. There are probably few other places in the world where this type of development could have taken place so quickly, and on such a scale, as in the New Territories in recent years—and the process is still continuing.

The traditional New Territories' Rural Committees and the Heung Yee Kuk have helped that process, looking after the interests of the original inhabitants. However many newcomers did not feel accepted by the Heung Yee Kuk because of its mainly rural focus, so other advisory and consultative bodies have been established for them. I believe the elected District Boards in the New Territories, which were inaugurated in 1982, and more recently the Regional Council, have played a useful role in meeting local political aspirations, and have provided a sounding-board for all shades of opinion in the New Territories. There was a general feeling, especially among members of the Kuk, that the Government tried deliberately to undermine the Heung Yee Kuk by introducing and funding these new political entities. If this is true, the attempt was unsuccessful. The New Towns occupy about 90 square kilometres in total which is only about 10 per cent of the land area of the New Territories. The Heung Yee Kuk has always maintained the unswerving support of the indigenous people in the area, and that is extremely hard to break.

The indigenous population of the New Territories is generally more optimistic about the future than the urban people. A large proportion of the urban population were refugees from China, who fled from the Communists. New Territories people have never had this experience: they have never seen the cruel side of Communism. In fact almost the opposite has happened. Since the 1980s, they have come into closer contact with the Chinese Government's 'open door' policies, and as a result have become more confident that the New Territories will survive as an entity within the Hong Kong Special Administrative Region.

I will continue to play my part in the community, and have no higher political ambitions. I've been fortunate in being part of the New Territories' achievements, and gaining positive, concrete results which have benefited the lives of ordinary people. My life has been bound up with New Territories affairs for so long that I doubt I would want to do anything else.

Jimmy McGregor

Fighting 'the Vermin of Society'

Jimmy McGregor first came to Hong Kong with the Royal Air Force in 1951. Three years later he joined the Hong Kong Government as a junior officer in the Commerce and Industry Department. He has been involved in the Territory's development for more than forty years. During the 1970s his first-hand experience of the effects and extent of corruption drove him to become one of the most outspoken and tenacious fighters against its perpetrators.

Jimmy McGregor's fight against corruption began during the 1960s. He recognized that the whole fabric of government was being undermined by corrupt practices, but fighting such established and accepted crime was difficult. He received menacing threats, including legal action. During the 1967 riots, he played an important role on the Government's 'counter-propaganda committee'. He received death threats, and was vilified by left-wing activists who described him as 'the Governor's Jackal', 'a wolf whining in the night', and a 'vagabond and criminal'. But it was the accusation that he himself was corrupt that caused him to retaliate. He successfully took a left-wing newspaper and its publisher to court.

The investigations of the Independent Commission Against Corruption (ICAC) focused particularly on the police force. As a result, in October 1977, following an unruly attack on the ICAC Headquarters at Hutchison House in Central, the force threatened strike action. According to Jimmy McGregor and others, Sir Murray buckled. His response was to grant a partial amnesty to all the police, expunging any corrupt activities by officers which had taken place before 1 January 1977. This effectively meant that many officers suspected of being involved in corrupt practices prior to that date could reach the highest echelons of the force through into the 1980s.

Jimmy McGregor left the Government in the mid-1970s to become the Director of the Hong Kong Chamber of Commerce. He entered the political arena when, in 1988, he won the Legislative Council seat representing the Chamber. Against fierce competition from conservative businessmen, he won again in 1991. He bowed out of the 1995 elections, and the same year he was appointed by the Governor Chris Patten to the Executive Council. Jimmy McGregor has always been a firm advocate of democracy, and has been critical of the business sector throughout the 1990s for protecting its own interests, and for its reluctance to stand up and speak for the people of Hong Kong.

Looking back over his years in Hong Kong, he still maintains a high regard for the determination and effective leadership of Sir Murray MacLehose during his lengthy term as governor, and believes that Sir Murray's only major mistake was the granting of the partial amnesty to the police during the corruption crisis.

SIR MURRAY MACLEHOSE was the first Governor to take a direct and very personal, controlling grip on the way the Government developed. He led from the top, with a sense of conviction. When he indicated, in the clearest way on government files and minutes, what in his view was necessary, that was the view which then prevailed. When the Governor put his marker on something, people paid considerable attention.

Sir Murray was the right man for the times. When he became Governor the administration was expanding so rapidly, in concert with the economy and society, that the need for sound and high-quality direction from the top became paramount. The checks and balances within the government system were under strain, and incompetent officers were beginning to appear. By the mid to late 1960s, there was a considerable amount of corruption within the civil service, especially in the uniformed services, and, by the turn of the decade, there was gathering pressure on the Government to do something about it.

When I first came to Hong Kong in the early 1950s, corruption was

Jimmy McGregor (left) with Governor Murray MacLehose

already quite endemic. There were a million and a half people in the streets, on rooftops and on the hillsides: refugees who would do anything to have a job and some means of earning a living. Many of them became small manufacturers, or small businessmen. Their little businesses, which they had perhaps worked on for several years, were going along quite well, and they were able to provide for their families and educate their children. However, with growth came bureaucracy, and these people then suddenly found they needed a piece of paper, or a licence, which they had to get from some obscure official. One day that official would appear and say, 'You need such and such a permit. By the way I'm going to have to put a report in about you: you're occupying these premises illegally'—whether they were or not. That officer was in a very powerful position.

So corruption started at the lowest level. There was no such thing as human rights, there was only the right to live, and you had to create it for yourself. Survival was the watchword through the 1950s and into the early 1960s.

However, corruption had reached such a stage by the early 1970s that, if it had been left unchecked, it would have posed a very real danger to the growth of Hong Kong's export trade. For instance, certification of exports was a key documentary requirement for Hong Kong. When foreign countries received the goods, they got a Certificate of Origin, or a Certificate of Processing, issued by the Hong Kong Government. Those countries expected the documents to be accurate. They would not expect the goods to be Chinese products which had been brought into Hong Kong and remarked, or reworked, and then despatched to the importing countries, such as the United States, as Hong Kong products. We had 'Most Favoured Nation' trading status with many countries, which meant we were given a privileged rate of duty, whereas China had to pay a much higher rate. So the certification system was of great importance to the viability of our exports and the acceptability of these products overseas.

It was vital that we were able to trust our own inspection system to ensure the integrity of all the supporting documents and certificates of authenticity. If we couldn't, all would be lost. The problem was that we couldn't trust our own system. The certification of these exports involved hundreds of millions of dollars of exports, and corruption was rampant.

Our officers would go to the factories, which would be warned in advance that they were coming. The inspectors would go over the books and records, and would look at the products. They might find major irregularities—that they were Chinese products, for instance, remarked, or wrongly packaged, and exported as Hong Kong products. The officers would turn a blind eye, if they were paid a certain sum, which they passed on to the syndicate.

The Americans were on our backs because that was our principal market, and they had their surveillance people here. Hong Kong was so dependent on its exports that, as access to foreign markets became more competitive and official requirements more stringent, corruption became worse and worse, leading to large-scale syndicates. There were sometimes dozens of officers in a syndicate, so just imagine how profitable, but how damaging it all was.

I was absolutely determined to tackle corruption head on. There were other people around me who were also totally opposed to corruption: some were effective, some were not. Looking back, some ideas were laughable. We would, for example, introduce extra rules and regulations with the aim of eliminating corruption, but there was no means of enforcing the new rules, or administering them effectively. All we did at times, was to give the corrupt new barriers which could be seized upon and exploited.

We obtained much of our information from informers, people who gave information usually because they were angry or jealous. They were pretty awful most of them. When information was given to me I had to be careful as it was difficult to know which of my own officers I could trust to help me investigate what was going on. I had to work with people I knew well and could rely on.

Information was once given to me that a syndicated racket existed in jade and ivory products. I found there was something very wrong, so I brought all the principal jade manufacturers in to a closed-door meeting. I told them I knew what was going on. They confirmed that each exporter was paying 2 per cent of the value of the exports to the officer who came to inspect the products. I calculated that the exporters were paying in total several million dollars a year to the syndicate, which at that time was a great deal of money.

Some jade exporters laughed at me when I confronted them with the facts. While they admitted that they were paying my officers 2 per cent on the documentary value of the goods, they were deliberately under-calculating the official value of the goods, so they didn't have to pay my officers as much as they should. It was a situation of 'crooks on crooks'! Not only that, but, because the exported products were undervalued, it also meant that the duty the manufacturers had to pay at the other end was also considerably less.

The Anti-Corruption Branch of the police worked closely with me, and we had some success in stamping out this syndicate. But unfortunately the police themselves had an enormous problem, because they were often men who had been transferred into the Anti-Corruption Branch from other places, and were themselves suspect.

As a result of the action I took with the jade exporters, a deputation of my officers involved in the syndicate came to see me. They threatened me with legal action and all sorts of other things. I said, 'Go ahead. But think very carefully about it.' They didn't do anything!

The other problem I had in my battle against corruption was persuading others of the extent of the problem. The Director of my own department gave me a great deal of authority to beat the racket, but even he needed some convincing. At one stage, he told me a report I had given him was, 'unbelievable and extremely damaging'. He told me he couldn't accept the extent to which corruption had corroded the department.

I asked him whether he would like to listen to somebody who knew the system better than I did. He hesitated and agreed. So I bugged my own home, and asked my Head to come over one evening, having told him that my place was bugged. He sat hidden in the bedroom while I entertained an officer from my own department, who knew a great deal about corrupt practices. This officer knew I had a great deal of information, some of which might have been damaging to him, and he was very frank with me. I think he thought I was going to help him. We held an hour-long conversation, while the Director listened to every word.

I said to the officer, 'How many in a particular unit may be corrupt?'

He laughed and said, 'How many are not? You should be asking that question!'

I said, 'All right, how many are not?'

He said, 'None.'

There were dozens of officers in that unit, mostly inspectorate staff, and he was at quite a senior level. I obtained a great deal more information about the extent and nature of the activities which were going on.

Afterwards, my Director was absolutely shocked. He was an honest person, who had lived in Hong Kong for a number of years and he was stunned by the revelations. Subsequently, he helped by adopting new methods to try and beat the problem within our own department.

Corruption pervaded many other sectors of society. The import and distribution of drugs in Hong Kong, and the use of drugs, had an inevitable connection with corruption. If hundreds of millions of dollars were being spent by importers and financiers on bringing drugs into Hong Kong, then Hong Kong was going to be the drug centre of Asia. People with that kind of money would do everything in their power to clear the way for their trade, and to prevent their products from being seized. The drug syndicates were among the worst of all the dangers in terms of corrupt practice.

Second to that came prostitution, blue films, and other vice-related activities. In the case of prostitution, it was obvious that brothels had to advertise themselves, or at least ensure they were known, if the businesses were to be lucrative. The brothels tended to be in one particular area, such as Wan Chai or Mong Kok. The last thing they wanted was harassment. The pressure was on the brothel organizers to pay off and seek protection, or have the District police cooperate with them. The worst situation was when the District Commander of that particular area was on the take, as frequently happened. That posed a huge threat to the integrity of the police. The police were in the front line of the battle against drugs, prostitution, and other malpractices, but in many districts corruption was the norm, and very substantial sums of money were paid in protection money.

Those who declined to participate in, or tried to expose corrupt practices, were often hurt or penalized.

I remember two young policemen who decided, before they left the Police Training School that, if there was any corrupt activity, they would record it and do something about it. They had been fired up to believe that they could honestly stand against corruption.

Each was posted to a different Division, but they kept in touch. Within the first month they received payments of $500. 'That's for you, from the boys, from the lads,' they were told.

They said, 'What is it for?'

'It's not for anything,' was the reply. 'These are just payments which you can expect each month. You are important people, senior officials, you know.'

They decided to open a joint bank account, and pay in all the monies they received. Separately they kept a note of when and from whom they had received each payment. After six months, they wrote to the Queen saying they were disgusted with the whole procedure, enclosed the evidence, and asked that the matter be investigated. Buckingham Palace referred the matter to the Foreign and Commonwealth Office which referred the matter to the Governor, who in turn passed it on to the Commissioner of Police.

They were summoned for interview.

'What on earth is this all about? We hold you responsible, among other things, for these sums of money which have no connection with any corrupt practice, or anything you were asked to do. Were you asked to do anything?'

The boys replied, 'No, we were not asked to do anything, Sir, but clearly they are not regular payments.'

'You should have reported that immediately to your superior officer.'

'But, Sir, we didn't know whether the superior officer was perhaps involved in some illegal practice.'

They were told quite simply, 'That's not for you to decide; that's for me to decide.'

Their lives were made miserable. One resigned whilst the other was rotated round a series of posts—'a thoroughly unreliable person, keep him moving'. I eventually came across the chap, and the upshot was that he too resigned from the police, and I helped him get a job in Canada. He had tried to ring the bell and the bell fell on top of him.

In case anybody needed to be reminded, the message was clear: if you are not on the bus, run beside it, but don't stand in front of it.

There were determined people within the Government who were keen to fight corruption. Jack Cater was one of the most senior, determined, in his words, to stamp out 'the vermin of society'. I greatly admired him. Sir Murray was given continuing evidence of corrupt practice from the time he arrived. The problem for people like Jack Cater and me was that there were not enough people in Government, from the top down, who had a clear impression of the way corruption was developing and how serious it had become. Sir Murray was a good administrator, and I am sure that, had others also told him he had a really corrupt Government, he would have acted before there was a crisis and the situation blew up. There were obviously others who were giving him advice to a different effect.

I know that from my own experience. A Financial Secretary had written to me saying he totally disagreed with statements I had been making, and that the extent of corruption was nothing like as serious as I had been suggesting. That officer had come into Government at a senior level, as part of the British Colonial Service, and had served previously elsewhere. He had no grass-roots experience in Hong Kong, as some of us had, of having to deal day by day with petty and dreadful corrupt practice, and seeing it develop the way it had. He, and others, did not understand how it was affecting the way Government worked.

It was only after the exposure of Peter Godber that Sir Murray announced the establishment of the Independent Commission Against Corruption (ICAC) in October 1973. Jack Cater, its head, took to the task with great energy, and the new organization really gave things a jolt.

I respected Sir Murray for his determination and leadership during this difficult time in Hong Kong. My criticism of him was the partial amnesty he granted to the police, following the revolt against the ICAC's work in 1977. I think the Governor was ill advised. I know that some of the people who gave him advice felt that a way had to be found not to alienate the police altogether, and they wanted to avoid chaos and the breakdown of law and order. 1967 was still in people's minds.

That argument did not wear with me. Many of us felt that Sir Murray should have taken a hard line. Let them stand down, let them go on strike, and let the Governor give warning that any police officer who didn't report for duty on the Monday morning would find himself without a job! We were convinced that after a period of chaos, the police who were not afraid, because they weren't involved, would come back to work. I knew some policemen who were drawn into corruption through no basic fault of their own, and would have been happy to see an end to it all. Many of us felt an opportunity to tackle police corruption head on had been missed.

The work of the ICAC, and changing public attitudes, have led to a reduction in the level of corruption in Hong Kong, but I have very serious concerns about what will happen in the future.

The Chinese Government has a different concept. The Chinese authorities are much less sophisticated than ours. We have met the challenge, and done much about dealing with what is a very specialized form of crime. It becomes highly sophisticated and permeates the whole of society. Over the years, quality of life is seriously affected if corruption is left unchecked. Hong Kong has slowly built up the apparatus to bring corruption under control—to such an extent, that the public has felt free to report corruption, without fear of reprisal. The ICAC has had thousands of reports coming in every year, which have illustrated the public wish for a clean society.

In the past, Chinese officials had power, but nobody ever had enough money for corruption to develop. The 'Chinese way' has always existed: favours are asked of relations, to look after this, give training to my girl, or put my boy on the board of a family business. It's simply straightforward corruption: you pay this, you get that. That has all changed. Now in China there is the opportunity and power. There has been a devolution of authority, and many officials now find themselves in a position of influence. It is the inevitability of corruption in China which is so frightening. Corruption has gone out of control because of the changes which have taken place. There is the huge desire by millions of people to make more money, even at the risk of a bullet in the back of the head.

At the moment we have a border, and in Hong Kong there is the ICAC to control corruption. I question whether in the future China will be willing to see the huge difference which continues to exist between the Chinese way of dealing with corruption and the Hong Kong way of dealing with corruption. Can the Hong Kong system prevail with the huge opportunities that will exist for people in Hong Kong and for those in China?

That is one of the biggest problems Hong Kong faces. There are going to be huge additional pressures on Hong Kong from corrupt elements within China. A lot will rest on whether the high degree of autonomy, promised in the Joint Declaration, will be permitted, and whether the Chinese authorities will allow Hong Kong to direct this particular boat; or to what extent Hong Kong will be seen as a ripe plum to be plucked, by officials from all over China.

There is a real danger that if corruption advances steadily, then the kind of social order we have constructed over the last forty years, and which stands as a monument to British administration and Chinese ingenuity, will come under pressure. It's under pressure now.

Anna Wu

Government by Whom?

Hong Kong was built by dint of the energy and entrepreneurship of the diverse immigrant class who, having adopted the city, quickly set to the task of creating better lives for their children. Anna Wu comes from one of these families. She represents the new, vocal generation of the politically aware, which came of age in the 1970s. A few of them went on to become legislators in the 1990s.

Many of this generation, like Anna Wu, see themselves as neither British nor Chinese. They are first and foremost Hong Kong citizens and products of its bi-cultural society. They received a typical Western education at Hong Kong's church schools where the language of instruction was English, but were raised in the Chinese family tradition. Many went abroad to study at universities in the United States and Britain, but returned to the Territory, and now make up Hong Kong's professional class. Anna Wu went on to study at the University of Hong Kong, and is a qualified lawyer.

There may not have been much general public desire for political reform in the mid-1970s, but many of the professional, middle class began to question their lack of participation in the policies which governed their lives. In 1975, Anna Wu was one of the founding members of the Hong Kong Observers, a group of young professionals who promoted informed discussion on issues of the day. It was the first pressure group of its kind, and it faded away a decade later with the emergence of political parties in Hong Kong. Several of its former members, including Anna Wu and the former Chairman of the pressure group, Christine Loh, were appointed to the Legislative Council in 1992 by Governor Chris Patten. In the 1995 Legislative Council elections, Anna Wu stepped down to pursue her legal career, but Christine Loh went on to win one of the directly elected seats which she contested as an independent candidate but on a democratic platform.

In many ways the middle-class professionals of the 1970s have been thwarted in their political ambitions by history. The colonial Government of the day was not used to being questioned about its policies. One of the criticisms of the Governor, Sir Murray MacLehose, was that he did not respond early enough and fully enough to the demands of this new force. By the 1990s, growing concern over 1997 and China's mistrust of any democratic form of government dashed any further hopes for political reform.

IN 1973, MY FAMILY left Hong Kong and emigrated to the United States where they have settled. I was in my last year at school and was under a great deal of pressure from my parents, relatives, and friends to go with them. I refused. I made up my mind to remain in Hong Kong on my own.

I had lived the first two decades of my life in Hong Kong and yet I didn't think that I knew Hong Kong very well. It was like a blank sheet of paper to me. I knew my own sheltered life, my small environment in high school, my small circle of friends, and my home. But I didn't know Hong Kong. I thought if I stayed I would be able to fill out those twenty-odd years of my life a little better and learn more about the Territory. I wanted to continue studying and to complete my university education here, then I could decide what I wanted to do and where I wanted to live.

Anna Wu (left) with pro-democracy campaigner Emily Lau at school in 1971

My parents viewed Hong Kong from a different perspective. They had come here as refugees from Shanghai in 1949, and they had had to start from scratch. Hong Kong was home to them in practical terms for a long time, but, they always viewed it as a transient place. They have no plans to return to Hong Kong at all, but they still have a house in their old village in China. They've never relinquished that, although they have never returned to the village. At the back of their minds, they still see China, that particular village, as their ultimate home.

I am from the second generation of Hong Kong people who were born and brought up here. We consider Hong Kong our home. Our lives have been much easier than our parents'. They had to suffer the hardships of the 1940s and 1950s, but, as Hong Kong became more affluent, so did they. It has been my generation which has been able to benefit from those who came and worked so hard. We benefited from whatever tax was paid, and the growth of the economy. It provided us with an education, and during my time everybody paid for schooling.

The introduction of mandatory schooling and free education in the early 1970s happened just as I had started university, and it was a watershed in my own thought process. It was not until then that I realized that I had been in a privileged position. It made me aware of all we had not had before. I had been through a decent education all the way from Grade One through to university, and it seemed to me almost improper that those opportunities were not open to everyone.

In the 1970s there were what I classify as ordinary student movements, much more like universities outside Hong Kong. In the 1960s we had the off-shoots of the Cultural Revolution, and student demonstrations reflected the struggle between the Left and the Right. Social activists were more concerned with livelihood issues. The emphasis was on people who needed help—the squatters, factory workers—and concern over industrial safety and transportation issues. In the 1970s there was a search for some kind of stability and identity, and the development of a community spirit. That came through to me in the early 1970s, and I was glad I stayed in Hong Kong to go through university at that time.

There were many factors pushing people onwards, to look for some kind of identity for themselves in Hong Kong. People like me had been pulled in different directions throughout our lives. There had been the colonial British influence, the impact of the Cultural Revolution, and the repercussions of that; and then there were our parents, who kept on telling us what they did in China, why they had run away, and then their plans to leave once again.

In short, the demographics had changed, and people like myself no longer associated ourselves with China in the same way that our parents had. I've never thought of myself as someone who was a Chinese national. I thought of myself as a Hong Kong person, and there were many who thought like me.

Together with the sense of belonging and identity came the wish to participate in the running of government. We were the second generation. We had grown up in Hong Kong. We were more affluent, better educated, more inquisitive, and it was quite natural to want to have a role in the running of Hong Kong, whether through community affairs, social affairs, or politics. It was one of the major issues that I, and others, became concerned with while I was at university in the early 1970s.

Many have argued that Hong Kong people were not interested in elections or in politics. I would dispute that comment. Ever since I remember, from the 1970s on, quite a lot of people were talking about politics. We began to wonder why 98 per cent of the population could not participate fully in community affairs or government administration.

One of the main problems was the language barrier. The language of Government, the courts, and commerce, was solely and exclusively English. It was one of the main factors controlling social mobility. It still is in Hong Kong, but then it was far more significant. It was impossible to get into Government at that point unless you spoke English. Now there is a greater emphasis on the use of Chinese, and we are trying to preserve English as an alternative language.

It was in 1974, that Chinese was recognized as an official language. Since then, although we started the policy in the early 1970s, we never fully implemented bilingualism in Hong Kong until recently. Now we're trying very hard to catch up, particularly in the translation of laws.

It was in these circumstances that a group of us came together and started to get very agitated. We weren't happy that we were barred from expressing a view. We were particularly unhappy that there were no alternative policies to those proposed by the Government. Whatever the Government said was implemented. There was no political participation, and few avenues for the public to express their views.

The only elections we had then were those to the Urban Council, and they didn't mean that much to us. The Council dealt with libraries, streets, urban services, and cultural services. They are all important, but the Council didn't help to determine Territory-wide policies. It didn't help to formulate the philosophy behind the laws.

In 1975, we formed the Hong Kong Observers, and we started behaving like lobbyists. It was the first pressure group of its kind in Hong Kong. It looked at political issues and political participation; it questioned the Government, asked for accountability, and asked for dialogue. In particular we started making proposals on alternative policies, and questioning government policies.

We generally tried to make it very difficult for the Government to hide behind its own bureaucracy. We went straight to senior officials and asked to meet them to discuss policies, and we spoke out quite publicly. We wrote a lot of letters to newspapers in English and Chinese asking them to respond. We didn't just take on specific issues such as housing, education, or transport, we also looked at the general philosophical aspects of accountability, dialogue, participation, and the supply of information.

It was an uphill battle. Trying to discuss an issue sensibly with a Government official was extremely difficult. We would ask for information and the response would be, 'What right do you have to know?' We had to justify why we were asking the question! That summed up Government mentality at that point.

Frankly, the Government didn't know how to handle us. They thought of us as a group of rebels who were creating a lot of problems for them. They also feared that our group might undermine the *status quo*.

The activities of the Observers and other groups led the Government to form a Standing Committee on Pressure Groups in the late 1970s. It was a secret, high-level committee, comprising very senior Hong Kong Government officials, including the police, Special Branch, and the British Military Representative in Hong Kong. It was formed to monitor the activities of the pressure groups, and we were number two on the list of groups to be investigated. The first was the Society of Community Organizations (SOCO). Even the Heritage Society was on the list.

I don't know what the nature of their surveillance operations was, but the Committee's report was leaked some years later. The reports relating to the Observers implied that the administration viewed us as a potentially subversive organization. The report stated that 'one of the objectives of the Observers was to oust all expatriate officers in Hong

Kong, and independence for Hong Kong.' This was completely inaccurate. They were also checking Communist infiltration into some of these groups including the Teacher's Union. I was named individually in that report together with my husband, Frank Ching, who was also a member of the Observers.

To me the report revealed very clearly the attitude of the administration at that time. The Government would not tolerate a different point of view, which might endanger its power and authority. The report highlighted the level of political surveillance and the monitoring of political activities. I viewed the matter very seriously. We didn't have a privacy law or a personal data protection law at that point. I was concerned that the Government's collection of sensitive information relating to your family life, your political views, your financial information, your health problems, or whatever, could be gathered up and used against you in a way that you might never know about.

Subsequently, I took up the issue in the Legislative Council. I asked the Government whether it did keep personal data on individuals, and whether it had undertaken political surveillance on individuals. The replies were 'No', and I was told that the files compiled by the Standing Committee on Pressure Groups had been destroyed. There are copies of those reports still around, but there was little I could do to press the Government to open up these files because they claimed they had been destroyed.

For me, that was one of the significant events of the late 1970s and 1980s. It illustrated how difficult it was to deal with Government. You really didn't count at all.

The policies which were formed in the 1970s to combat the threat we posed were more an exercise in damage limitation than any commitment to introduce fundamental political reform. There were improvements, for example, to nominations and the appointment to Advisory Boards, which led to a little more willingness to disseminate information about Government policies.

I was aware that different types of reforms were being proposed during the late 1970s, and this eventually led to the extensions of the franchise to the Urban Council in 1981, and the establishment of the

District Boards in 1982. This didn't go anywhere near to meeting our aspirations. District Boards dealt with district-level issues, not Territory-wide policy issues. There was also the problem that even if individuals were willing to start off with District Boards as a move to acquire political expertise, there was nowhere else for them to move on to. There were no elections to the Legislative Council at that stage.

The Government had three main arguments for resisting electoral reforms. First, it maintained people were just not interested in politics and that we were just a vocal minority. That's a chicken-and-egg argument! The more opportunities we provided for people to participate in Government affairs, the more people's interest would grow. Interest comes with the ability to participate as well. You learn more and you become more mature. That was one factor which the Government did not accept, but I think that was quite wrong.

Second, the Government never accepted, until recently, that we had a right to participate in the running of Government. It was considered a privilege; it was considered a gift, if it came to that. It was never considered a right.

The other argument was the political situation. The British Government had always been concerned about possible conflicts between the Nationalist and Communist China in Hong Kong.

Therefore political activity among Hong Kong people and the grooming of Hong Kong leaders to take over the administration was never a priority for the British Government in Hong Kong.

I and members of the Observers were extremely critical of the lack of channels for political participation, and of the lack of Government accountability. The 1970s could have been used as an opportunity to establish a wider base for consultation, but all that came through was the negativism. The Government under Sir Murray MacLehose looked at the issue of reform as a very destructive exercise for themselves.

The effect has been disastrous for Hong Kong. If the Government had started opening up elections to the Legislative Council gradually in the 1970s, we would have had a fully directly elected Legislative Council well in advance of 1997. We wouldn't have had the problems which have dogged the 1980s and 1990s over political reforms and which have resulted in the breakdown in relations between China and Britain during the last stages of the transition to Chinese sovereignty.

It would have given us a more stable and a more mature alternative Government to British Colonial rule, and we would have been far better prepared for the future SAR Government. We would have had leaders who were more politically mature, and politics would have been part of our lives and culture, not a new concept. There would also have been more opportunity to establish a balanced relationship between the Executive Branch and the Legislative Council.

Perhaps the most serious consequence of the lack of political reform in the past is that it has given more credence to China's stand against a faster pace of political change now. Britain had always ruled Hong Kong that way, so why should changes be made just a few years before 1997? Why shouldn't China just substitute itself for Britain and rule Hong Kong as it has always been governed? The political changes of the last fifteen years have led to a deep feeling of mistrust, with Beijing suspicious of British motives behind the move for change. China has seen everything that happens in Hong Kong as a political struggle, rather than from the perspective of what is best for the community.

It has been very frustrating and disappointing for people like me, who wanted to give something back to the community, wanted to participate. We had so much positive energy. But you come to a point where you can't do any more: you suddenly reach a dead end, and that's how I've felt for a long time. I think that will always weigh on my mind. Why should it have been that way? Why shouldn't people like me, who wanted to contribute one way or another, have had the opportunity to go all the way to the top of the political hierarchy? We have been robbed of the opportunity. A political career has simply not been an option in Hong Kong. It has never been for anybody.

I'm not sure how much of an option it is going to be in the future either, particularly for the democratic forces. China still draws a very clear line between those who would uphold a particular ideology and those who think differently. The view is you cannot work within the system unless you uphold the same ideology and the same objective. The tolerance for pluralism is simply not there. Unless attitudes change, this could be very dangerous for Hong Kong because we have thrived on pluralism, not on a single ideology.

I think the future is going to be increasingly more restrictive at a political level, particularly as we get closer to 1997, and beyond. Tactics will be applied to those with dissenting views to push them out of the mainstream—push them out of Hong Kong if it comes to that. And I think those pressures will become stronger than they are now.

Those are uncertainties we have to live with. We just have to hope that China will continue to open up, and that in doing so it will accept more international standards.

I still believe that whatever we do, we shouldn't stop fighting for what we believe in. The more pressure we put on those in control today, the more difficult it will be for them to ignore these views and possibly it would make the ultimate result just a fraction of an inch better. That's how I look at it despite the personal sacrifices which might come along the way. And I'm sure there will be individuals who will be sacrificed in this process of democratization in Hong Kong.

Chinese Shadows, Foreign Ghosts

the 1980s

The year 1997 and the future of Hong Kong dominated the 1980s. The 1984 Sino-British Joint Declaration, returning the Territory to Chinese sovereignty, forced Hong Kong to come to terms with its history. Thus began the political awakening of the people of Hong Kong.

The optimism following Sir Murray MacLehose's visit to Beijing in 1979 was short-lived, as Hong Kong became gripped by uncertainty over its future. The announcement in January 1982 that British Prime Minister Margaret Thatcher would visit Beijing in September, and that Hong Kong would definitely be on her agenda, was the first public signal that Britain no longer intended to ignore the fifteen-year deadline on the expiry of the New Territories lease. It was also announced that a high-ranking Foreign Office sinologist, Sir Edward Youde, would succeed Sir Murray as Governor in May of that year. Sir Edward was seen in London as a safe pair of hands able to deliver, which he did, a workable agreement with the Chinese on the future of the Territory.

The fact that Britain had already been considering Hong Kong's future was not public knowledge. Even the Governor's top policy-making body, the Executive Council, had been kept in the dark. Later, in 1982, when the councillors were given a background briefing paper, it is said that they were shocked to learn the extent to which, without their knowing, the future of the New Territories lease had already been raised with the Chinese.

Sir Edward's first task was to pave the way for Margaret Thatcher's historic trip to Beijing, the first by a serving British Prime Minister. Her visit achieved as much or as little as Britain had intended. It was a blunt rehearsal of each side's position. Sir Edward had made it quite clear to Mrs Thatcher, prior to the Beijing visit, that it was impossible to draw a line between Hong Kong Island and the Kowloon Peninsula, which had been ceded to Britain, and the New Territories, which was on lease until 1997. But relinquishing sovereignty over the whole of Hong Kong was not something Mrs Thatcher was prepared to accept during her 1982 trip to China and Hong Kong.

What the visit did achieve was the formal opening of talks between Britain and China over Hong Kong. Two years of tense and difficult negotiations followed, during which the people of Hong Kong were neither consulted nor involved in the diplomatic negotiations that governed their future.

While some have argued that Sir Edward, as a Foreign Office man, was prepared to protect Britain's interests over those of Hong Kong during the negotiations, many who worked closely with him believed that he fought earnestly and tirelessly for the Territory, reflecting the advice of his cabinet, the Executive Council. He had insisted at the beginning of the negotiations that the Executive Council should be consulted on the negotiations, a move which those involved have said was opposed by some of the other Foreign Office mandarins. Sir Edward's sudden death from a heart attack during an official visit to Beijing in December 1986 shocked the community; the spontaneous outpouring of grief was a manifestation of the high regard and respect in which he was held.

By the time the substantive talks on Hong Kong's future opened in July 1983, it was apparent that Britain was prepared to relinquish sovereignty over Hong Kong, but was pushing instead, and at the insistence of the Executive Council, for continued British administration of the Territory. To China this was not negotiable. Deng Xiaoping had made it clear that the principle of 'one country, two systems' would be applied for the resumption of sovereignty over Hong Kong. In short, Hong Kong's capitalist society would continue and co-exist with Communist China. The Territory would be a Special Administrative Region (SAR) of China, with 'Hong Kong people ruling Hong Kong'.

The Sino-British Joint Declaration signed by Margaret Thatcher and her Chinese counterpart Zhao Ziyang on 19 December 1984, enshrined that concept. The agreement was hailed as a guarantee that Hong Kong's social, economic, and judicial systems would remain intact and continue for fifty years after 1997. Opinion polls had shown that, given a choice, most people would have preferred Hong Kong to remain British, but, by the end of 1984, the public had accepted political reality. In the absence of any alternative, the Sino-British agreement was well received, and many took comfort from the number of specific guarantees it contained.

It was not until the following year when China began the five-year process of drafting the Basic Law, the post-1997 constitution for Hong Kong, that some inherent weaknesses in the Joint Declaration became apparent. There were areas in which it had been difficult to reach agreement in the negotiations and those had been deliberately left vague. The ambiguities allowed Britain and China to interpret the terms of the Joint Declaration in different ways.

The crux of the problem which dogged the thirteen-year transition was a difference of opinion between Britain and China on the appropriate extent and pace of institutional change in Hong Kong prior to the handover. China insisted that it should inherit the Territory and the systems exactly as they were when the agreement was signed in 1984. The British and Hong Kong Governments argued that Hong Kong was a dynamic place which could not be put in cold storage for thirteen years; Hong Kong had to move with the times, and that meant some progressive social and institutional reforms.

China's stance was rooted in a deep-seated mistrust of Britain. The Chinese leadership believed Britain was constantly conniving to ensure a continued presence after 1997, and any move to change existing legislation, introduce new laws, alter the political system, develop the infrastructure, or improve welfare benefits, was viewed with grave suspicion in Beijing.

One of the first and most contentious issues which arose from the differing interpretations of the Joint Declaration was the question of electoral reform. Britain, having denied the vast majority of the Territory's population a say in government for almost 150 years, moved swiftly in 1984, before the completion of the Sino-British negotiations, to propose a more representative system of government. It was a belated move designed to pave the way for 'Hong Kong people ruling Hong Kong'. This included modest reforms which introduced limited democracy through indirect elections to the Legislative Council in 1985. While the Government did not extend the reforms to include the election of representatives by universal suffrage in 1985, it clearly envisaged that the political process would move forward much faster than actually happened with the next elections in 1988.

Britain and China had agreed that by 1997 the Legislative Council would be 'constituted by elections', but it became apparent that this phrase was interpreted differently in London and Beijing. Any talk of holding all elections by universal suffrage brought an angry reaction from China.

In early 1986, the British Foreign Office Minister responsible for Hong Kong, Timothy Renton, publicly announced a policy of 'convergence' with the Basic Law, whereby Britain would consult China on matters relating to the transition, with the aim of ensuring a smooth handover in 1997. By accepting the idea of convergence, Britain was seen to have allowed China an opportunity to redefine the grey areas of the Joint Declaration and a veto over major pre-1997 policy decisions. Britain had no say in the drafting of Hong Kong's future constitution, yet for any new initiatives introduced during the transition to survive after 1997, they had to comply with the Basic Law. The 'through train' concept, to prevent as little disruption as possible after the handover, had been established.

The man who many believe was responsible for negotiating the policy of convergence was David Wilson, the leader of the British side in the Sino-British Joint Liaison Group, the body set up under the terms of the Joint Declaration to oversee all matters relating to the transition. It was Sir David, as he was to become, who succeeded Sir Edward Youde as Governor in April 1987.

Sir David arrived amidst the 1987 debate on the pace of political reform. In 1984, the Government had clearly envisaged the introduction of direct elections to the Legislative Council, starting in 1988. By the time Sir David had become Governor, the policy of convergence made it almost impossible to introduce major political reforms until after the publication of the Basic Law in 1990. Indeed, it is widely known that Britain had entered into a secret understanding with China in late 1985 to delay major constitutional changes until then. Britain has since argued that the delay in 1988, whatever its background, resulted in China's eventual agreement to the acceleration of democratic reforms in 1991—at a much faster pace than Beijing would otherwise have allowed.

Publicly though, Sir David was seen to have taken 'the politically correct course', by the decision to defer direct elections until 1991. The result had a damaging impact on the Government's image.

By 1987 people had accepted the reality of the future and had begun voting with their feet. Those who could emigrated. The majority were middle-class professionals, many British passport holders, who were denied the right to live in Britain by a succession of British Immigration and Nationality Acts which had gradually eroded their residency status. Some intended to return to Hong Kong once they had secured an 'insurance policy' in the form of another passport, usually from Canada, the United States, or Australia. 45,000 people emigrated in 1988, and, by the end of the decade, this had leapt to 65,000 a year.

The irony was that, while Hong Kong people were anxious to obtain some form of security should they become political refugees after 1997, there was a popular campaign in the late 1980s to refuse asylum to Vietnamese boat people, and forcibly repatriate to Vietnam the thousands already in Hong Kong. Those arriving in record numbers in the early 1980s were deemed mainly to be economic migrants, rather than genuine refugees, and, as the numbers in Vietnamese detention centres swelled, the boat people were seen as a drain on the Territory's financial resources. An international agreement—the Comprehensive Plan of Action—brokered by the United Nations, and aimed at resolving the region-wide problem in the longer term, was eventually reached in 1989. This provided for the resettlement of all genuine refugees languishing in camps throughout South-East Asia, and the repatriation to Vietnam of those deemed to be economic migrants.

Whilst there were a few years of budgetary constraint in the 1980s, on the whole Hong Kong was hardly short of funds. By the end of the decade, plans had been put in place for the establishment of a Hospital Authority, to improve efficiency and reduce chronic overcrowding in public hospitals, and the provision of tertiary education places for 25 per cent of all secondary school leavers, while a strategy was formed to improve the environment, including a HK$8 billion fund to overhaul the Territory's ancient and unsanitary sewage system. Throughout the decade, Hong Kong continued to become an increasingly affluent society; more than 40 per cent of the population owned their homes by the early 1990s.

Hong Kong's infrastructure and skyline were changing dramatically too. The second cross-harbour tunnel, the Eastern Harbour Crossing, opened in 1991, providing an important road and rail link to eastern Kowloon, and a second road tunnel, Tate's Cairn, linking urban Kowloon and the New Territories was completed in 1991. The prestigious new Bank of China Building was topped out on the most auspicious of days—the eighth day, of the eighth month, of 1988.

The Hong Kong Convention and Exhibition Centre, the largest in Asia, was opened by the Prince of Wales in 1990, whilst the establishment of the Academy for the Performing Arts in 1984 provided a venue for aspiring performing artists. The opening of the Arts Centre in 1978 and the Hong Kong Museum of Art in 1985 provided venues for Hong Kong Chinese visual artists to exhibit their work. During the 1980s, greater financial resources were devoted to promoting all forms of art. Money was provided by the newly established Hong Kong Arts Development Council and the American-based Asian Cultural Council, which not only provided cash grants but also exchange programmes for local artists.

Hong Kong had survived the dramatic swings in the stock and property markets, which had slumped during the early 1980s amidst the concern over the Territory's future. The uncertainty was symbolized in 1984 by the decision by the oldest British *hong*, Jardine Matheson, to move its holding company to Bermuda. Following the signing of the Joint Declaration, however, the economy boomed until the worldwide stock market crash in 1987. Even then, Hong Kong bounced back as the economy reverted ever more closely to its traditional role as the gateway to southern China, and assumed its new position as a leading financial centre. By the middle of the decade China was Hong Kong's largest trading partner, and, by the end of the decade, the Territory was the main channel for all of China's imports and exports.

Hong Kong's economic integration with southern China was further strengthened by investment in Guangdong by the Territory's businessmen. Labour shortages and rising costs led local manufacturers and service companies to look over the border. By the end of the decade more than three million mainland Chinese people were employed across the border by Hong Kong companies.

Despite the increasing economic integration, however, the political honeymoon in Sino-British relations came to an abrupt halt in June 1989.

Hong Kong's worst fears were seen unfurling in Beijing with the military suppression of the student movement. Thousands took to Hong Kong's streets in mid-May, in support of the students, who were calling for greater democracy in China. On 4 June, after the tanks had rolled into Tiananmen Square, around a million Hong Kong people came out to mourn the tragedy. The record turnout for the demonstrations displayed a strength of public feeling never before witnessed in the Territory, and underlined just how badly confidence had been shaken.

With this came an almost universal call to accelerate the development of democracy in Hong Kong.

Tiananmen united the people of Hong Kong, but marked a turning point in China's policies towards the Territory. The events of 1989 showed just how far Hong Kong had been brought into China's political orbit, and how the internal politics of China impacted on Hong Kong. For Beijing, there was no choice other than to harden its line on Hong Kong. As the final years of the transition approached, Britain was left with fewer cards to play, while China's shadow power increased.

Lord Wilson

Learning to Live with China

Sir David Wilson's five-year tenure as Governor of Hong Kong saw enormous changes in the Territory's development. When he arrived in 1987, there were no formal political parties or well-established political leaders; these did not emerge until 1991, when direct elections (for eighteen of the sixty seats) to the Legislative Council were introduced. That year, for the first time, the majority of the Council was elected by one form or another.

Sir David arrived as Governor with a reputation as an eminent sinologist and experienced diplomat. He had accompanied Sir Murray MacLehose on his historic visit to Beijing in 1979, and, in 1984, was appointed leader of the British team in the Sino-British Joint Liaison Group, established to manage transitional issues prior to the handover.

During his first year in office, Sir David's governorship was clouded by the decision to defer from 1988 to 1991 the start of direct elections to the Legislative Council. Democracy advocates were enraged by the move, and many felt the Government had used the results of an official public opinion survey supporting a delay to mask its own self-interest in postponing democratic reform. Britain, by deferring major political changes until China eventually decided the way forward in the Basic Law, was seen to be bowing to Beijing's demands.

Ironically, it was not the contentious electoral reform issue, but Sir David's actions after the Tiananmen Square protests—when he appeared to be assuming a stronger role in defence of Hong Kong—that saw his downfall. To assuage local anxieties about political uncertainties after 1997, Sir David pushed a reluctant Britain into offering the protection of nationality to fifty thousand key Hong Kong people and their families. In October 1989, his Government also set in motion a Bill of Rights to shore up civil rights guarantees. That same month, Sir David announced plans for a new port and airport, a move he denies was contrived as a confidence-boosting measure.

Chinese distrust of Britain's intentions intensified after 1989, and Beijing reacted angrily to the British initiatives. The result was a long-running argument with China over the financing of the new airport.

The obsession in the 1980s over the Territory's future tended to overshadow the achievements of Sir David's tenure. He would rather be remembered for the solid improvements in education, social welfare, and the environment, than for his response to the troubled politics of the era.

I HAD NEVER THOUGHT, when I first came to Hong Kong as a language student in the 1960s, that I would return one day as Governor. I arrived on that first trip, as a carefree student, in the traditional, old-fashioned way by sea from Saigon. When I returned in 1987, after an intervening posting as Political Adviser in the late 1970s, it was in very different circumstances, following the unexpected and tragic death of Sir Edward Youde. I approached the onerous task of succeeding him with a good deal of trepidation.

To be Governor of Hong Kong is a colossal job. It is quite unlike anything else because of the degree of personal responsibility, and to some extent the loneliness. In most other jobs, even if you are at the top of a pyramid, you can get away from it, and there are always people you can go and chat to informally. As the Governor of Hong Kong, that is not so easy: you are always at the top of that pyramid.

There's no real training for being Governor. The traditional Colonial Service training was no longer possible nor relevant; so there was a very steep learning curve at the beginning. My earlier experience in Hong Kong as Political Adviser helped since I knew a good deal about how the system operated.

If you were to ask me whether I was at a disadvantage because I had dealt with Chinese officials previously, because they knew me and my negotiating style very well, I would totally disagree. It was an advantage to have known personally most of the senior Chinese officials dealing with Hong Kong as a result of my involvement in the final stages of the Sino-British talks on Hong Kong's future and my leadership of the British side in the Joint Liaison Group. That helped because working away at the same problems over a longish period of time gave you a degree of trust and confidence in each other.

The negotiations in 1984 had been a fascinating and exciting experience. I came into them in the later stages, when the broad framework for the Joint Declaration and the basic principles had been agreed. What hadn't been established was how on earth it was going to be dealt with in practice. My job was to work out with my Chinese counterpart how we could write down, in as much detail as possible, precisely how the 'one country, two systems' principle would operate.

We were working under a great deal of pressure. There was a time limit set by the Chinese, who had said the negotiations must be completed before 1 October 1984, otherwise they would make a unilateral declaration. This had originally been stated by Deng Xiaoping at the end of 1982. He had given a two-year deadline for the talks, and that was carved in stone. In the end, it turned out to be a great help to us because the Chinese side was under pressure to complete the negotiations within their own time frame.

There were some obvious lessons to be learnt from the experience of those negotiations. The key was that each side had to understand the problems faced by the other if a solution was to be found. There were times when we put forward a proposal which the Chinese objected to, but we didn't understand why. Eventually we would discover that the way we had put something across had aroused suspicion in the minds of the Chinese, or had a possible consequence which they had seen, which we hadn't intended. 90 per cent of the time the problems were solved once we found out what was at the root of their concerns.

There was one incident which illustrates this point. We were meeting, during this intense period of negotiations, in what was then the old International Club in Peking, very close to the British Embassy. In this sense it was extremely convenient, although in other ways it was not. There was no air conditioning, the journalists gathered immediately outside the door of the meeting room, and there was no security of any sort. The chief Chinese representative on the drafting group, Ke Zaishuo, came to me one day in the middle of our talks and said, 'We have made special arrangements which are much more convenient. We are to start meeting in the State guesthouse, the Diao Yu Tai, out in the western suburbs of Peking.' He said it would be quieter, there was air conditioning, better security, and food could be provided if the negotiations went on. I pointed out that this might pose a communication problem since we needed to be near the British Embassy. We were keeping in constant touch with the Foreign Office in London and the Hong Kong Government on the details of the talks. I told him that driving to the west of Peking would not be very convenient. This discussion went on for several days, and at the end of it Ke Zaishuo said, 'Well the real problem is we only hired this room at the International Club for a limited period of time and we can't renew it.' We moved off to the Diao Yu Tai, but it was an interesting example of how you need to get to the real problem!

We established a set routine during the talks. We'd meet in the morning with the Chinese, and go into very detailed negotiations. We would then go back to the Embassy in the afternoon, do a report, and give our recommendations to Hong Kong and the Foreign Office about what should happen next. We agreed with the Chinese that we would 'leapfrog' the subjects that we were discussing. So on Day One negotiations would be on subject X and we would come back to it on Day Three; on Day Two we would do subject Y, and come back to it on Day Four. This gave time for Hong Kong and London to react. We would then go very early each morning to the British Embassy, pick up all the telegrams which had come in overnight, sit down, and work out how we were going to deal with the issues that day. This went on day after day after day. It was very intense and absolutely exhausting. The British Embassy in Peking was sending about as many telegrams during this period as the Embassy in Washington, which is a colossal organization.

Matters were complicated by the fact that the Chinese text of the agreement was as important as the English, and would be read by more people in Hong Kong. We didn't want a separate negotiation on a Chinese version of the text after an English one, however, so the two were negotiated together. We were aided by the use of modern technology with a computer in the Embassy which could transmit in cipher the Chinese text of what was being agreed. The Chinese side either had to use a typewriter or revert to pens. I believe the use of this sort of information technology for diplomatic negotiations was probably unique at that time.

On the day that the Joint Declaration was signed, I had two feelings. The first was a tinge of sadness. I was nostalgically sad to think that this signalled the end of the period of British administration of Hong Kong. On the other hand, I felt immensely pleased that we'd managed to get an agreement with so much detail written in, and so many of the key points. It had looked at various stages in the negotiations as though we might have failed and that there might have been no agreement. That would have been bad for Hong Kong.

I flew down from Peking to Hong Kong with Sir Edward Youde to be there when he announced what had been agreed. Most people who had been involved in parts of the negotiations were surprised and pleased to find how much detail there was in all the other parts. Some people had been involved in negotiating on the judiciary, or on the civil service, or the monetary system, but hardly anybody had the overall picture. It must be remembered also that there were two very different starting positions at the outset of the talks. We had wanted to write a book— which would have looked rather like the *Encyclopedia Britannica*—while the Chinese wanted about two or three sides of A4 paper. We had to bring these two points of view together. As we discovered during the negotiating process, it was almost as though the Chinese side had an editor sitting back there who said, 'You can have so many words in this article, but no more.' When we were able to boil down the real essence of what was important to us to a few words, then we could get it agreed. If we had an endlessly long piece of prose like one of Cicero's speeches, it was always rejected. I think actually, at the end of it, there was, for an international agreement of that sort, a quite astonishing amount of detail.

When I returned as Governor in April 1987 one of the first issues I had to tackle [which has been perhaps one of the more contentious areas of the Joint Declaration] was the future political structure. The Hong Kong Government was already committed to conducting a public consultation exercise to review what the next step should be in Hong Kong's evolution towards more representative government. That review was about to happen when I arrived with the release of a Green Paper putting forward various options to find out what people wanted. The key question was whether to introduce direct elections to the Legislative Council the following year in 1988, or to wait until 1991.

Without re-running all the political and the emotional battles, one or two points need to be clear. The Chinese were against a review because to them it pre-empted the Basic Law, the future constitution for Hong Kong. Equally, it was clear enough to me that we were committed to the review and that we should go ahead with it. The results showed Hong Kong opinion was very divided over how quickly we should move towards a more representative government. That didn't surprise me at all, but the result was that we had to take decisions which were not going to make everybody happy. Those who wanted us to go faster, criticized it; those who would have liked it to go more slowly, were also critical, but much more quietly because they were those sort of people. Lastly, we had a real issue in terms of China's concerns. We wanted, if possible, to produce a situation which could continue beyond 1997. So we had to keep an eye on the China dimension, and I think we came out of it with something which did achieve that.

Some, I think unfairly, have said we simply came up with the result Beijing wanted. I don't think that's the right way to look at it. China quite clearly didn't want the review at all, and didn't want any commitment to direct elections in advance of the Basic Law. What was achieved, and people can criticize it as they like, was something which met the growing aspirations in Hong Kong, but managed to fit them in with what was tolerable to China.

Such decisions need to be a balancing act between trying to meet the needs of Hong Kong, while at the same time protecting its survival. You're trying to achieve the best you possibly can for Hong Kong, otherwise you would simply be setting something up that would just be pulled down in 1997.

To call this a policy of 'appeasement' is to my mind just talking in crude headlines. People often see these issues as a black and white contrast between, 'Are you confronting China or are you trying to agree with China?', as though confronting was somehow better and braver than agreeing. What is necessary is to put forward what *you* think is right for Hong Kong, but in such a way that it does not get a total veto from China—so that it does survive, and is therefore beneficial to Hong Kong.

Unfortunately the political climate dramatically changed in 1989. This was a particularly difficult and tense period in Hong Kong's history. It was no surprise to me that the Chinese authorities took action against the demonstrators in Tiananmen Square, but I was appalled at the way in which it was done and at the deaths of so many people as a result. It's a tragedy, too, that those who were demonstrating didn't have the foresight to see that they could have made their point and then withdrawn from occupation of the centre of the city. I realized as soon as I heard the news early that morning of 4 June that, not only had a great tragedy occurred, but that it would have a very dramatic effect on people's views in Hong Kong, as indeed it did.

One of the immediate concerns was the safety of Hong Kong people still in Beijing, and of the need to ensure they came out as quickly as possible and didn't get caught up in the aftermath of what had happened in Tiananmen. That meant contact with Chinese officials in Hong Kong and help from the British Embassy in Beijing. I won't go into precise details, but it was interesting that, despite all the difficulties on the Chinese side, as well as ours, we were still able to communicate and make arrangements to airlift out Hong Kong residents stuck in Beijing The logistics of organizing an aircraft to fly up there was the easier bit. It was sometimes harder trying to explain to people in Hong Kong that everything possible was being done to help people who were stuck and needed assistance.

People in Hong Kong managed to react to all these events without getting out of hand. I think that is to their immense credit. However, the impact of Tiananmen should not be underestimated. Among people outside China, including many in Hong Kong too, there was a naïve expectation that China had suddenly fundamentally changed, and that the demonstrations in Beijing would produce a different, more liberal political atmosphere. Sadly, it was also naïve to believe that any Government would tolerate the occupation of the centre of its capital by a group of protesters over a long period of time. In the end the demonstrations were dealt with in a way which combined extreme clumsiness, brutality, and inefficiency. Of course China didn't suddenly change like that, and expectations were then suddenly dashed. Morale sunk to a very low point and this made life quite difficult in Hong Kong for several months. It was striking, though, how relatively quickly Hong Kong got back on to an even keel by early 1990. It's not that people had forgotten it, but it was put into perspective.

One of the lessons we all had to re-learn was a difficult one: Hong Kong has always had to understand the rules of its own existence. This may sound harsh, but if you are a tiny little Territory on the coast of China, there are certain rules of behaviour if you are going to survive. One of them is, you don't interfere in the affairs of China, and you do the best you possibly can to make sure that China doesn't interfere in your affairs. It's a two-way business. For many years Hong Kong has achieved that. I think there was a period, as expectations about change in China grew, when people thought those rules no longer applied and that people in Hong Kong could involve themselves in the politics of China, without cost, without penalty, either to themselves or to Hong Kong. That simply isn't true. It's a very difficult lesson for people to learn. We learnt it in the early days after 1949, when we had to make sure that Hong Kong was not used by the Taiwan-based Kuomintang as a base for sabotage operations against China. They did sometimes succeed in making use of the Territory, but they never achieved so much that it became a major provocation to China.

Ultimately, you have to realize that although events like Tiananmen are drastic and horrifying they are not the end of the world. The whole relationship has not fundamentally and totally changed. We went through a very difficult period, and we had to work to get out of it. Hong Kong cannot separate itself from China: it must deal with China, however difficult that is.

There were things which could be done, though, following 1989, in particular to boost morale. I felt it was very important that the British Government should not simply criticize what had happened in China, but should show that it was prepared to help Hong Kong in a practical way. That was why it was right to push for measures which would provide a right of abode in the UK for British passport holders in Hong Kong, and to go ahead with a Bill of Rights. Some of those things were done, although not as much perhaps as many of us would have liked. Still, in terms of British politics a huge amount was achieved.

The other key issue was the new airport. We were nearing a decision on the airport. I had said the previous year that I wanted to be able to make an announcement in my annual Legislative Council address in 1989. All the material came through, and it showed conclusively that Hong Kong desperately needed a new airport, that it should be at Chek

Lap Kok, and that we could afford it. Then, after the crisis and the drop in confidence, we suddenly had to decide whether to shelve it or to go ahead. We took the important decision and went ahead with the airport, despite all the political difficulties.

I am sure that despite all the difficulties, it was the right decision, and in the long-term interest of Hong Kong. We may have made mistakes in the way we explained it, or perhaps we failed to explain it enough to China: the main problem was that we didn't realize how deep the suspicions were in China about Hong Kong. It's all back to this question of Hong Kong getting involved in the affairs of China. The Chinese had programmed their minds to think that almost anything we did was somehow directed against them or was just a straightforward reaction against Tiananmen. What we were actually saying was, 'Tiananmen or no Tiananmen, we have confidence in Hong Kong's long-term future, and we are going to put all our effort and a huge amount of resources into building for that future.'

Some people have claimed that the airport issue, and the difficulties over it with China, affected my own term as Governor of Hong Kong. This is not so. My own five-year period came to an end in 1992, and it was a question of whether I should be extended to do a further period, or whether a new Governor should come in for the final period of British sovereignty. I think there had been a feeling for some time in Britain, way before the airport issue, that the last Governor of Hong Kong should be a politician, as had been the case with last Governors of other major British territories. In no way do I believe that the decision was connected simply with the airport.

During the period I was in office there were some very important broader issues which we in the Hong Kong Government had to tackle. First of all we had to learn how to live with China, making sure that Hong Kong's interests would be looked after, understood by China, and carried out in a way that would last. This was not easy because for Hong Kong the whole process of living with China was really a very new concept.

We also had to consider how we were going to give Hong Kong a solid foundation for the future, not just in constitutional terms, but also in terms of other fundamental problems, such as education. This was vital if Hong Kong was to survive and flourish in the future. Another important issue was dealing with the massive environmental damage result- ing from Hong Kong's rapid devel- opment. We also had to consider infrastructure devel- opments that would take Hong Kong into the twenty- first century so it would continue to be the main centre of communica- tions in southern China. The natural harbour was no longer enough: what was needed was a modern airport which would play the role that Hong Kong's harbour had played in the middle of the nineteenth cen- tury.

All these, together with sound administration, without which nothing else works, were the essential day-to-day work of government. The dramas get the headlines, but the solid everyday work is what really builds the future and makes people's lives worth living.

What of the future? Prediction is always dangerous. It can never be accurate. Of course there will be change—there always is in Hong Kong, even without the major break of a change of sovereignty. Many of us associated with the old Hong Kong will probably regret some of the changes. There has been so much good about Hong Kong, the way it has been run, and the way its people have prospered. And, of course, as China prospers, Hong Kong will prosper too. What's more, the people of Hong Kong will make a major contribution to the way China itself will change over the years ahead. All of us involved with Hong Kong in its British phase will wish Hong Kong and its people well—and China too.

Sir Q. W. Lee

Banks and Bankers

Hong Kong, over the course of three decades, has been transformed from a centre of manufacturing and export, known chiefly for its output of inexpensive factory goods, to one of the world's great centres of banking and finance. One person who has watched it all progress is Sir Quo Wei Lee, whose banking career in Hong Kong spans fifty years. He played an important role in the development and reform of the growing financial sector in the 1980s.

Sir Q. W. Lee rose from comparatively humble beginnings (his family had fallen upon hard times during the war) to become Chairman of Hong Kong's largest local bank, Hang Seng Bank. He joined the bank just after the Second World War, and worked his own way up the ladder. He played a key role in negotiating the survival of the bank following a run on its reserves in 1965, when he persuaded the long-established Hongkong and Shanghai Banking Corporation to buy a controlling stake in Hang Seng Bank.

The bank developed its own measure of Hong Kong's financial health—the Hang Seng Index—which has become the standard gauge of stock movements on the Hong Kong Stock Exchange. During the 1980s, it also became an important barometer of local feeling, plunging every time there was a crisis of confidence, particularly during low moments in the Sino-British negotiations over Hong Kong's future.

In 1988, Sir Q. W. Lee was elected Chairman of the Hong Kong Stock Exchange. He had to revive international confidence after the 1987 stock market crash, and was responsible for implementing many reforms.

Sir Q. W. Lee was also involved in Hong Kong politics as a senior member of the Governor's top advisory body, the Executive Council. As an Executive Councillor during the early 1980s, he was one of the élite, inner circle kept informed of progress during the negotiations on Hong Kong's future. He took part in lobbying missions to London, and was part of the infamous trip to Beijing in 1984 where the Executive Councillors were seen to be snubbed by Deng Xiaoping himself.

Despite the troubled politics of the 1980s, Sir Q. W. Lee has always been optimistic about Hong Kong's economic future which he believes will be progressively integrated with that of China. He has maintained a cautious approach to Hang Seng Bank's own commercial developments, however— a conservatism which he believes has partly accounted for the bank's endurance, stability, and success.

I WENT TO SCHOOL at St Joseph's College in Hong Kong, but I had to leave when I was eighteen before I was able to complete my education. My immediate family, which was based in Guangzhou and Macau as well as Hong Kong, was not well off, and we were badly affected by the Japanese invasion of China in 1937. I urgently needed work at that time, so I applied and was accepted as a trainee with the then Hong Kong branch of the China State Bank which had its headquarters in Shanghai.

Shortly after I started work, I was promoted to cable clerk. This was a very important position because there was, naturally, no telex or fax in those days. I was responsible for helping to decode a cipher, which was used to protect the secrecy of the bank's business transactions. I was very junior, but my work, particularly in relation to foreign exchange, brought me into contact with important people and, fortunately for me, with other banks and customers.

During the Japanese occupation of Hong Kong no commercial banks, other than the Japanese Yokohama Specie Bank, were allowed to operate. I spent the war years in Macau where I worked for some of Hang Seng Bank's shareholders in their personal businesses. The day after Rear Admiral Sir Cecil Harcourt steamed into Victoria Harbour on 30 August 1945, I returned to Hong Kong. The place was almost deserted with only a few hundred thousand people remaining. I joined Hang Seng Bank in 1946, and have now been with them for over fifty years.

Hang Seng Bank was set up in Hong Kong in March 1933. It was not really a bank in the strict legal sense of the word as it didn't take deposits, and it dealt mainly in foreign exchange, gold bullion, and remittances. When I joined the bank after the war there were just fifty staff, and I was in a fortunate position being one of the few people who could speak or understand English.

The local banking industry, in line with the growth of Hong Kong's economy, expanded rapidly in the 1950s and 1960s, and a number of foreign banks opened up in the Territory. Regulation of the banks then was fairly loose. The 1948 Banking Ordinance set out in a couple of pages how licences were to be granted and what the charges were, but did not spell out how banks should operate. At that time the annual licence fee for a bank was only HK$5,000. There was also a Banking Advisory Committee, and that was about it! There was little, if any, banking expertise in the Government at that time, and hardly any professional supervision.

At the same time the stock markets were booming, and bank loans related to real estate and stock dealings rose at a tremendous rate. In the six-year period from 1955 to 1961 the liquidity ratio of banks in Hong Kong fell from 53 per cent to just over 34 per cent.

This situation was exacerbated by intense competition between banks which were fighting for a bigger share of the loan market, and some tended to overlend. In the late 1950s, land prices rose dramatically, as developers sought to increase the supply of residential flats for the growing population. The Landlord and Tenant (Consolidation) Ordinance was amended to allow for the redevelopment of pre-war protected buildings to the maximum allowable gross floor area. The redeveloped property could then be sold in individual units, with buyers taking out a mortgage from a bank for a loan repayable by instalments.

By 1960 it was clear that reform and better regulation of the banking industry in Hong Kong was essential if the economy was to continue to expand. Following a detailed report by Tomkins of the Bank of England, new legislation was enacted in 1964, which, among other things, tightened control over unincorporated banks which were often just family-based partnerships, and set up a Banking Commission headed by a Commissioner with regulatory powers. Mr Tomkins also thought that there were far too many banks in Hong Kong, and the Government therefore ceased to issue licenses to new banks from 1965 to 1978. But before the new arrangements could take effect, Hong Kong was hit by its worst banking crisis ever, which had really been precipitated by the crash in the property market.

The closure of the Ming Tak Bank and the Canton Trust and Commercial Bank in early 1965 [because they were insolvent] led to widespread rumours about the liquidity of six local banks, including Hang Seng Bank. People rushed to withdraw large sums of money. The queue of people withdrawing funds from our head office led to a major traffic jam in Central!

The Hongkong and Shanghai Banking Corporation pledged publicly its full support for the Hang Seng Bank, and the crisis eased. But there was a new run in April. We lost nearly 80 per cent of our deposits in two days. We had few choices because it was clear that when we opened the next day our cash would be exhausted.

Following an emergency board meeting and consultation with the Financial Secretary, we decided the best way forward was for us to dispose of some of our shares to the Hongkong Bank, and become its subsidiary. With a mandate from the board, I was up at Queen's Road Central [the Headquarters of the Hongkong Bank] for a good part of the day on 9 April 1965. They wanted to buy 76 per cent of Hang Seng Bank's shares; we offered 51 per cent. They valued Hang Seng at sixty-seven million dollars; we valued it at one hundred million dollars. I stuck to my guns, and the deal went through on our terms—but not until midnight!

If the Hongkong Bank had turned down our offer, it would have been a disaster for Hong Kong. Hang Seng Bank would have closed, and this would probably have had a domino effect, and a number of other banks would have collapsed as well. In these circumstances, Hong Kong's banking system would have probably fallen apart causing tremendous damage to the community and economy overall. Our relationship with the Hongkong Bank has been a very happy one. Apart from residual representation on our board, they have left us alone, and we have concentrated on developing our own niche in the market. We have maintained a cautious approach to our future development, and this helped us to weather the property and stock market crashes in the early 1970s and during the 1980s.

One of the areas in which Hang Seng Bank has been able to make a positive contribution to Hong Kong has been through the stock-market index which bears our name. Initially, we constructed the index in 1964 for our own use, but decided in November 1969 that it might have a wider application. The Index was quickly recognized in Hong Kong and internationally where it has the same status as the Financial Times Index, the Tokyo Nikkei Index, and the New York Dow Jones Industrial Average.

Over the years, I have known all Hong Kong's Financial Secretaries. I worked closely with John Cowperthwaite, Philip Haddon-Cave, John Bremridge, and Piers Jacobs. Each of them was very good, and each had to face difficult problems. Probably John Cowperthwaite had the easiest time. Given the growing tensions in the market over the apparent lack of progress with the Sino-British negotiations in September 1983, the Government did an admirable job in arranging, at very short notice, for the linked-rate system in October 1983, when a market was established for Hong Kong dollars at the linked rate of HK$7.80 to the US$1.00 However, for some time the Hong Kong dollar has been traded around 7.73 and 7.74 which is almost 1 per cent stronger than the linked rate.

The linked-rate system has worked extremely well, and has ensured that the Hong Kong dollar remains strong. Suggestions that the Hong Kong dollar should be linked to a trade-weighted basket of currencies is not practical because it would involve very detailed calculations without much apparent benefit. Again, the argument that the linked-rate system leads to imported inflation is not really sound as the extent of imported inflation is low. Unless the system now in place has a negative impact on Hong Kong's economy it should continue to serve us well long after 1997.

Following the 1987 stock market crash, I was elected Chairman of the Stock Exchange of Hong Kong for a three-year term. It's no good arguing with hindsight whether it was the right decision or not to close the stock market for as long as four days, but, once I became Chairman, we concentrated on implementing the recommendations in Ian Hay Davison's report [he was consultant to the Hong Kong Government on securities regulation reform, and former Chief Executive of the London Stock Exchange], and in cooperating with the then newly established Securities and Futures Commission. The outcome has been a very well-regulated exchange which commands international confidence, and has enormous potential given the 'open door' policy in China.

The early 1980s were an extremely demanding time, not just in banking and economic terms, but in a political sense as well with Britain and China negotiating the Joint Declaration.

I was a member of the Executive Council at that time, and we were involved closely with the progress of the negotiations. We sometimes used to meet seven or eight times a week, and some of the meetings went on at Government House until eight or nine o'clock at night. The Executive Council was sounded out by the British Government every step along the way, during the negotiations. We were very fortunate in having as Governor Sir Edward Youde who was a first-class diplomat and China scholar. He was extremely dedicated, very impartial, and he tried to defend Hong Kong's interests to the hilt.

On several occasions in the 1980s, the Executive Councillors went to London to put their views directly to the then Prime Minister, Margaret Thatcher. Sir Geoffrey Howe [then British Foreign Secretary] and officials from the Foreign Office never said very much at these meetings. Mrs Thatcher did all the talking; she was very dictatorial and had her own views. Certainly, she was a very strong woman.

I also accompanied Sir S. Y. Chung and Lydia Dunn on the historic visit we made to Beijing. It was the first time that unofficial members of the Executive or Legislative Councils had held a formal meeting with Deng Xiaoping. We went at the invitation of the Chinese Government, in June 1984, so that we could explain some of the concerns in Hong Kong [in particular the fear that China might not stand by its promise of 'one country, two systems' in the future]. To the public it may have looked as if we were snubbed by Deng Xiaoping, but we didn't see it that way. We never expected to be received as members of the Executive Council, although we made it clear that we were going to China in that capacity. I think both sides were just taking a political stand, but it gave us a chance to say what we wanted to say. I think the Executive Council did a marvellous job at the time, and that China did its best to accommodate Hong Kong's views as far as possible.

Looking to the future, I am confident. Hang Seng Bank has been a little slow in expanding into China. We only recently set up representative offices there, and our first branch was opened in Guangzhou only in 1995. But we do a lot of China business in Hong Kong, financing clients who wish to invest there. In that way we have exposure to China, but with little risk because we have Hong Kong jurisdiction on most of our borrowers.

China is a huge market; Hong Kong is a small place. Eventually our traditional market will be saturated. But development in China has only really started in the past ten years, so we have to look to the future since the market potential in China is enormous. As a service economy Hong Kong is well placed to take advantage of the developments that will undoubtedly happen in the China market in the future, but competition is likely to be intense.

I have seen the ups and downs of the Hong Kong economy, and I believe Hong Kong has approached international standards. Hong Kong continues to provide its established markets with exported products, and has been able to take advantage of cheap labour and land in southern China. Moreover, the Territory has provided South-East Asia with financial services for the past century, and will continue to do so in the future. But as a Special Administrative Region of China, the long-term strategy for the development of Hong Kong's economy should focus northwards towards China.

As I have predicted before, China will become a giant economic dragon of the world economy. Hong Kong and Shanghai, as the core cities of the Chinese economy, will be the eyes of the dragon, and the stars of the twenty-first century.

Anna Sohmen
My Father, Sir Y. K. Pao

By the 1980s commerce and trade in Hong Kong had been dominated for more than 140 years by long-established expatriate companies (or hongs), such as Jardine Matheson, Swires, Hutchison Whampoa, and Wheelock Marden. In the early 1980s, however, after the previous decade of rapid economic growth, the hongs became takeover targets for a new generation of wealthy Hong Kong Chinese businessmen who were unwilling to accept the dominance of British companies. The shipping magnate, Sir Yue Kong Pao was one of the local tycoons who challenged that dominance.

Sir Y. K. Pao had come to Hong Kong as a refugee from Shanghai in 1948. By the early 1980s he had a shipping fleet second only to the Russian navy, and was poised to diversify his business activities. The recollections of Anna Sohmen, his eldest daughter, travelling companion, and business confidante, reveal the sheer entrepreneurial drive typical of so many of the émigrés, particularly the Shanghainese, who had sought refuge in Hong Kong.

In 1979, in a surprise move, Sir Y. K. Pao took over the Hong Kong and Kowloon Wharf and Godown Company, an off-shoot of Jardines. The takeover shook the British *hong*, especially since it had been backed by the British-owned and operated Hongkong and Shanghai Bank. This was swiftly followed by the takeover of Hutchison Whampoa by property tycoon Li Ka Shing. In 1985, another of the British hongs fell into Sir Y. K.'s hands when he gained control of Wheelock Marden.

Sir Y. K. Pao's experience as a refugee permanently affected him and perhaps led to his great business success. He displayed a continuing insecurity about placing his funds in fixed assets—which are vulnerable in wartime—and instead he settled upon shipping as a safe alternative. It was not until the 1980s that he felt confident enough to invest in Hong Kong property.

During that decade, Sir Y. K.'s international social and business dealings brought him into close contact with world leaders—including President Ronald Reagan, Prime Minister Margaret Thatcher, and Chinese leader Deng Xiaoping—and he became something of an ambassador-at-large. He closely consulted with both the Chinese and British, playing the sensitive role of intermediary, during the difficult talks on Hong Kong's future. In 1985, he was invited by China to sit on the Basic Law Drafting Committee, and was an Executive Committee member of the Basic Law Consultative Committee, set up to canvas Hong Kong people's opinions.

Anna Sohmen maintained a close and warm relationship with her father until his death in 1991. Sir Y. K.'s business empire lives on, and his family has maintained close and cooperative ties with China. Two of his sons-in-law, including Anna's husband, Helmut Sohmen, were invited by Beijing to sit on the Preparatory Committee, established in early 1996 to oversee the transition.

THERE WAS A PICTURE in my father's study which, for some reason, he always had sitting there. It was of me, aged two, with a couple of plaits, holding a teddy bear, and standing in front of his old Humber car. Every time I see a picture of a similar car I think of that photograph, and memories come flooding back of my early days in Shanghai.

I have fond recollections of my father, dating right back to those formative years. In the evening when the car came home, the driver would honk the horn, and the guards would open the gates. At the sound of the horn, the maids and my nanny would rush me from the kitchen, where I was usually enjoying a lump of ice. That was a special treat: little cubes of ice—not ice-cream—as we didn't have ice-cream in those days. A hand would dig into my mouth, pull out the ice, and then I was quickly bundled upstairs and tucked into bed. I would just be asleep, or probably pretending, when my parents came in to check up on me.

I remember vividly that one complete floor of our house was a ballroom. At that time in Shanghai, ballroom dancing was very fashionable, so it was not uncommon to have a such a room. It seemed a huge room to me then, with a beautifully polished, wooden, parquet floor, and a grand piano. But when my parents held parties at home, I was never allowed to stay up to see all the people arrive.

We came to Hong Kong from Shanghai in 1948, just before the Communists came to power. This caused quite an adjustment to our lives. For a start, we moved from living in a house to an apartment. Life was not too difficult for my mother as she was still able to have a lot of help—our 'wash amah' and my sister's nanny, as well as our driver, all fled with us from Shanghai.

The Shanghainese who arrived in Hong Kong in the late 1940s were very much a clique and kept themselves decidedly separate, mainly because we didn't speak the Cantonese dialect, but there were also cultural differences. We were really rather toffee-nosed. 'We Shanghainese don't eat snake, and eating dog is barbaric. Those sort of habits only belong to the Southerners!' That's what we were told.

There are Chinese rice rolls which in Cantonese are called, 'pig's tripe', pig's intestine. My mother told us, 'Those Cantonese are barbaric eating tripe, we Shanghainese don't eat that.' So she never allowed us to try them. It was not until years later, when I was an adult, that I realized how delicious they were. It's not tripe at all!

Arriving in Hong Kong was quite traumatic for my father who had been a banker in Shanghai. Suddenly he had nothing except a small amount of funds, and he had to start from scratch. We had to live a fairly frugal existence. My father began a small import and export business from a tiny office to which he travelled daily by bus from our Mid-Levels home on Hong Kong Island. We saw very little of him because he was under tremendous pressure, having to support not only his immediate family, but also his parents and his six brothers and sisters. There were sixteen of us in total, all dependent on my father. He wasn't a particularly talkative man at home, but I remember him saying from time to time, 'When you think of the responsibility, you are compelled to keep going.' I didn't quite appreciate then what he meant.

Everything changed during the Korean War in the early 1950s. The import–export trade suffered badly, and my father had to switch the direction of his business. He wanted to go into something which had transportable assets and would not be locked in, should the Communists come to Hong Kong. People in Hong Kong now worry about 1997 and their assets, but my father was always worried about fixed assets, even in those days. He felt that ships were a safe investment then, and it was not until very late in his career that he considered investing in property.

My father had always paid special attention to me since I was the eldest. From when I was still quite young, he tutored me personally, and he was a rather hard taskmaster! From the time that I was about fourteen years old, I had to be the hostess at most of his parties because my mother was too shy. She was one of the old-school 'feminists' and preferred to remain at home. As she grew older, she rarely left the house, except to see old friends from Shanghai.

Around that time I started to travel everywhere with my father, whenever my studies allowed. When I was only fourteen I went on my first business trip with him to Europe. I was left to my own devices during the day, and in the evenings I went out for dinner with my father and his business associates, although I didn't know much about the business he had been doing all day!

The first vessel in his shipping empire was a twenty-eight-year-old coal-fired carrier ship. He was so proud of it that he actually took me on board. It was a rusty old thing that sat in Hong Kong Harbour, and it was difficult to understand his excitement! But, as it transpired, that ship did him very well.

The first new ship my father had built was constructed in northern Japan. It was called *Eastern Sakurah* ('Cherry Blossom'), and he asked me to launch it. I felt extremely honoured. I cut the tow rope with a silver axe, and the ship actually moved off down the slipway into the sea. As it did so, a huge balloon appeared, streamers unfurled, and doves came flying out. It was very moving and so different from launches these days when the ship remains stationary. From then on I formed a strong bond with ships and all that go with them.

As teenagers we saw very little of our father at home. His business preoccupied him and he worked frightfully hard. At that time he was also trying to get a lot of Japanese charters. He had to entertain the Japanese frequently, and sometimes, when the Japanese were drunk, they could behave quite outrageously, breaking out of their usual conforming mould. I found myself struggling with my own national pride, since the Sino-Japanese war was still fresh in the history books. Was this what my father meant by responsibility? Was this what it took to feed sixteen mouths, not to mention all my father's Shanghainese business associates and their families who were also dependent on him?

When I went to the United States to study in 1963, he visited me at university. We went together to watch an American football game. Whenever a goal was scored, the supporters would all throw paper streamers in the air and the cheerleaders would shout, 'Go! Go! Go! Go all the way!' My father, who didn't understand a thing about American football, eventually stood up very excited and started shouting the same thing! Afterwards, I said jokingly to him, 'And where do you think you are going to?' He said quite seriously, 'Charters! Go! Go! Go! All the way!' I believe that football match was a turning point in his career. It seemed to have somehow inspired him to determine his own goals in life. He made up his mind, at that point, to go all the way to building up his shipping empire to be one of the largest in the world.

And that was exactly what he did. The secret of his success was sheer hard work and fortunate timing—the Suez crisis, for example, was a bit of luck. [The closure of the Suez Canal in 1956 led to an increased demand for shipping due to the longer journey times.] There was also the ability to raise the necessary finance. His friendship with the former Chief Manager and Chairman of the Hongkong and Shanghai Bank, Sir John Saunders, helped him enormously. They became life-long friends, and even now when I meet Sir John there is a tear in his eye when he talks about my father: that's how close they were. There was mutual understanding and they saw eye to eye. Sadly, this kind of mutual trust can't be found in the banking world anymore.

It was my father's friendship with Sir John which also proved a great asset later on in the early 1980s, when the Hongkong and Shanghai Bank helped him to purchase the Wharf Company from Hong Kong Land. It was quite an interesting time! I was living with my family in London at the time, and my father was visiting us there. During dinner, he hardly ate and was jumping up and down from the table trying to arrange a flight. He was supposed to be returning a few days later to Hong Kong, but he arranged a last minute flight that night to Hong Kong via Frankfurt. He knew that, while he had been out of town, the Keswicks [the dominant influence at the time in the British *hong*, Jardine Matheson] were trying to manœuvre a hostile takeover of Wharf themselves behind my father's back. In fact the weekend before my father left the UK, he was amassing all the bank support he could muster, and that primarily came from the Hongkong Bank. The circuitous route took my father secretly back to Hong Kong. As soon as he returned, he went straight to the Hilton Hotel and had a swim, and from there he went straight to a board meeting, taking everyone by surprise. Then he stormed the market and purchased enough shares to give him a controlling stake in the Wharf Company. The acquisition in 1979 really marked the diversification of my father's company into the property market. It was amazing really that he had the foresight in the late 1970s to realize that the shipping world had peaked and that it was time to draw back and diversify his interests.

During this period, my father also renewed his contacts with China, having left the country thirty years earlier. I went with him on his first visit in 1978. It was a real eye opener. The sheer poverty, the sheer backwardness of the place, the drab uniforms, and dimly lit factories, all made me imagine nineteenth-century England during the industrial revolution. Later in 1981, I went on a tour with my sisters to Chongqing, the largest city in China, where I was born. I even returned to the hospital where my mother had given birth to me. I was amazed that I had survived and had not become just another infant mortality statistic. The hygiene was just appalling and the place was so run-down. My mother said that of course in those days it hadn't seemed so bad!

My father became an unofficial adviser to the paramount leader, Deng Xiaoping. He met Deng Xiaoping in 1981 and again in 1982. He was advising him on the economy, and persuading him of the importance of opening up China's markets. He told him, 'Can you imagine if each person in China were to buy one biscuit, how many biscuits would be produced and sold?' In terms of consumer goods, and opening up the domestic consumer market, it was mind boggling! The problem was how to boost domestic consumption to fuel economic growth. I think my father saw his contacts with the Chinese leadership, in particular with Deng, as an opportunity to sell his capitalist ideas. But of course, my father had a charming way of putting things across. I marvelled at the great way he had of talking. He had the ability to put ideas into people's minds, without them realizing, with his wonderful charm and his endearing smile.

My father also acted as an intermediary between Britain and
China during the negotiations over
Hong Kong's future. He was really
an ambassador at large between
the two countries. He felt very
strongly about Hong Kong,
and the Territory's future was
important to him. He also felt
very strongly about China.
He knew there would be
many difficulties in actually
bridging the cultural gap
between two very different
philosophies. He had a very
fine, sensitive feeling for both
the Western and Chinese ways of
thinking.

I think if he had been given a choice, my father would not have opted
for the reversion of Hong Kong's sovereignty to China: he would
probably have searched for an alternative solution. He was a pragmatic
person though, and he faced up to the facts, so he always made the best
of a situation. He had fled from the Communists in 1946 and had
rejected early overtures to join the Party.

Strangely enough, that opportunity had come from my uncle. None
of us knew until years later, in 1978, that father's cousin was a
committed Communist and had actually been an undercover
Communist agent since the early 1940s. This uncle was very close to my
father when we were still living in Shanghai in 1945, and he tried to
tempt him to join the Communists, supplying him with Party literature.
My uncle realized that my father was a true, blue capitalist when he
found the books, untouched, under a bed. Nobody, not even my father
guessed my uncle was a Communist agent, though. My father was
shocked when he discovered the truth years later!

Father was also in a position to advise the former British Prime
Minister, Margaret Thatcher. He was a great friend of Mrs Thatcher,

simply because he himself had the same strong beliefs in a market economy. This also brought him together with the former American President, Ronald Reagan. During the negotiations on Hong Kong's future, he gave Mrs Thatcher tips on who best to speak to in the Chinese hierarchy, as it was sometimes very difficult for the British to identify the right person. He was also a messenger, quietly reflecting the Chinese viewpoint on particular issues. He would also advise the British on timing—when not to say something, or when to act.

I have to say though that I would not have liked to have been in Mrs Thatcher's shoes. She had a lot of difficult decisions to make, and that takes courage. She certainly had the personality to take those decisions though!

I believe that Hong Kong can have a great future if we get it right. It depends very much on ourselves. Although a lot of people are looking to China, I don't think we can depend on China to decide our basic policies or how to implement them. We need to act together and prevent the community becoming too polarized. I fear that differences amongst ourselves will only be an invitation for intervention, making it impossible to implement the 'one country, two systems' concept.

We should not consider 1997 as the end of an era, but rather as the beginning of a new one. I am sure that my father, being the pragmatist that he was, would have agreed.

Raymond Wu
Understanding China

The Basic Law, Hong Kong's constitution from 1 July 1997, was drafted by a committee of thirty-six mainland Chinese and twenty- three Hong Kong appointees, mainly businessmen and professional people. One of them was Dr Raymond Wu, a cardiologist from a Shanghainese Catholic family.

Dr Wu had long been involved in Hong Kong medical affairs, having served as an adviser to Government on various committees in his capacity as Vice Chairman of the Medical Association. In 1984 he became President of the Association, a position he held for four years. But it was not until he was invited by Beijing to sit on the Basic Law Drafting Committee in 1985 that he became involved in the Territory's political affairs.

Raymond Wu has been deeply concerned with issues arising from the transition ever since. He was appointed a Hong Kong Affairs adviser to Beijing; and he sat on the two committees set up by Beijing in the 1990s to oversee the transition to Chinese rule: the Preliminary Working Committee and the Preparatory Committee, which superseded the former at the end of 1995. Dr Wu has never considered himself a Communist sympathizer, and has never had particularly leftist leanings. Since he joined the Drafting Committee, however, he has often been identified as a supporter of the 'pro-Beijing' line.

Raymond Wu was born in Ningbo in 1937, the year the Japanese invaded China. That same year his father, a Shanghai silk merchant, decided to transfer his business to Hong Kong, and two years later the whole family moved to the Territory. Raymond Wu was educated in the Territory, and studied at the University of Hong Kong. He then followed the traditional path at that time and went to the UK for post-graduate medical training. He returned to work in Hong Kong in 1969, working in the public sector for ten years before going into private practice.

Dr Wu has witnessed a steady improvement and development in Hong Kong medical facilities over the years and has devoted a great deal of his time to community work. He initiated the idea of a heart foundation that could mobilize community resources to help the Government improve cardiological services. In the early 1970s he organized the first fund-raising campaign for the formation of the Heart Foundation with the first health education exhibition in the City Hall. It is this spirit of community service that drove him to take an active political role in the Territory's future.

I HAVE NEVER had any doubt that Hong Kong should be returned to China; it has just been a question of at what stage this should happen. Even now, I can't tell you whether 1997 is the most appropriate date, or whether the handover should have been earlier or later.

China never stated that Hong Kong should be handed back in 1997. Beijing never recognized the so-called 'unequal treaties' as being valid, so the year 1997 was immaterial in China's eyes. Beijing always maintained that sovereignty over Hong Kong would be regained 'when the time was ripe'. Therefore if Britain had not raised the question of the expiry of the New Territories lease in 1997 with China in the first place, Beijing might not have considered regaining sovereignty over Hong Kong until a later date. On the other hand, China might have decided to take back Hong Kong much earlier. It could have happened any time. Sometimes, if you have the choice and have to decide when something should happen, it is not always easy to know the right answer.

I have always been involved in community work since returning to Hong Kong in the mid-1960s, after completing my medical training in Britain. I had spent some time in a London hospital, and I returned to work in the recently completed Queen Elizabeth Hospital. At that time, there were more than eighty patients in each ward, originally designed for just thirty-one; there was hardly any space between the beds, and camp-beds had to be put up in the corridors. Now it seems ridiculous that it didn't occur to me to query why there should have been such a vast discrepancy in conditions between hospitals in Britain and those in Hong Kong. Cramped hospital wards, limited facilities and manpower were all conditions we in the medical profession had come to accept as a result of Hong Kong's circumstances at the time. Over the years I've witnessed considerable improvements and an upgrading in medical facilities, and, as I became more senior, I tried to help in a small way to initiate new ideas and introduce new services wherever I could, particularly in my field of cardiology.

My first involvement in public affairs came in the early 1980s. The Government consulted the Medical Association on its proposals in 1984 for the further development of representative government. I lobbied hard, in my capacity as Vice President of the Association, for a functional constituency seat [a seat on the legislature representing a particular industry or profession] for the medical profession in the 1985 indirect elections to the Legislative Council. But even though we were successful and were given a seat, I decided not to stand for election. I was already standing as President for the Medical Association, and, in any case, I was never convinced that the legislative system, and the way it was developing, would be a very efficient and effective process. I felt that I could make better use of my time in other aspects of community participation.

When the Joint Declaration was signed in 1984, the medical profession discussed the document in some detail. The conclusion we drew was that Britain and China had not been able to iron out their differences over the future of Hong Kong, and that the Joint Declaration was thus not a happy compromise. I always believe that any agreement that has not been arrived at willingly risks running into trouble at a later stage. The agreement in the end had been rushed through because both sides were keen for an understanding to be reached. The differences which still existed between Britain and China were emphasized by the fact that they both had to make separate statements embodied in the Annexes and the Exchange of Memoranda attached to the main agreement. It was obvious that there were many areas where the two sides had 'agreed to disagree'.

The approach Britain and China had adopted during the negotiations also differed. Britain wanted a clearly worded document. China, on the other hand, knew that it would be the future master, so it cared less about the presentation of the agreement. So, while the two sides thought the Joint Declaration had solved the problem of Hong Kong's future, there were many problems which were left unresolved.

In 1985 I was quite surprised to be appointed to the Basic Law Drafting Committee. I think I was invited in my capacity as the then

President of the Hong Kong Medical Association. But I still ask myself why I was selected. I had never developed a close relationship with China; I didn't have any family members who had become close to Beijing; and I had never shown myself to be very 'patriotic' either openly or privately. So the fact that I was picked made me feel that it was a sincere gesture on China's part to involve Hong Kong people in the drafting process.

I also felt that China had passed my initial test by the mere fact that someone like myself had been asked to join the drafting process. I felt that I wanted then to see for myself how genuine Beijing was about giving Hong Kong the autonomy promised in the Joint Declaration. I had heard so much about 'Communism' from my Shanghainese compatriots who had fled China in 1949. I also had friends who had suffered, or whose relations had suffered, during the Cultural Revolution. Therefore I had some of my own nagging doubts about the future and whether the 'one country, two systems' concept could be achieved in practice.

So for all these reasons I welcomed the invitation to sit on the Basic Law Drafting Committee. I have always felt that I should give the benefit of the doubt, and therefore I thought it was my duty to participate in the drafting process with an impartial and unbiased view, then judge the situation for myself.

There were a number of guiding principles which China applied throughout the Basic Law drafting process. First and foremost, we had to stick to the wording and spirit of the Joint Declaration—that was a rule of thumb given to the law drafters. Secondly, although China repeatedly stipulated that the drafting of the Basic Law was the sole responsibility of China, in reality the British Government, either officially or unofficially, was kept well informed of every discussion and argument held in the drafting committee. As a result, British views played a very important role in the content and wording of the final draft of the Basic Law. In fact, at the very end of the process, we had to idle away a few days in Guangzhou, killing time by discussing peripheral issues, before we were able to endorse the final version of the Basic Law. What we were really doing was waiting for Britain and China to agree finally on the composition of the post-1997 legislature. So the whole time Beijing was looking over its shoulder for approval from

Raymond Wu in 1987 with other members of the drafting committee: Lu Ping (centre), now director of the Hong Kong and Macau Affairs Office, and democracy advocate Szeto Wah (right).

Britain of the contents of the Basic Law. Therefore it would be grossly unfair for anyone to suggest that China ignored Britain's views during the drafting of the Basic Law, or that the Basic Law deviated from the spirit of the Joint Declaration. China clearly hoped that involving Britain at this stage would lead to a cooperative transitional period, but this was not to be.

Over the years that I was involved with the drafting of the Basic Law I felt that China was sincere about the promises contained in the Joint Declaration. The problem has been the finer definitions of some of the terminology in the Sino-British agreement. The prime example has been the definition of election. [This was no more apparent than when the Head of the New China News Agency in Hong Kong, Xu Jiatun, announced in 1985 that 'consultation' was a form of election.] But the differences in interpretation are quite understandable, given China's cultural background. Just look at the election of Deputies to sit on China's National People's Congress! [The process in effect means that the Deputies are appointed.] China has always viewed that as a form of election, but there is clearly no 'election' in a Western sense. It was Britain that insisted on the wording in the Joint Declaration which stated that the legislature would be 'constituted by election', but China claimed subsequently that it was not aware of the serious consequences of the British definition of 'election'. As a result, the Sino-Portugese agreement of the future of Macau made it clear that the future legislature there would only be partially constituted by election.

I had always felt that the development of democracy in Hong Kong should be paced slowly. The ten-year plan for a slow and steady increase in democracy laid out in the Basic Law is acceptable. Unlike many independent countries, Hong Kong cannot afford to make mistakes. If our development of democracy should fail, in the sense that it created any threat to society or to China's stability, China would intervene to protect its own interests, and that could be the end of 'one country, two systems'.

Hong Kong's ultimate goal should be more important than fighting for democracy in Hong Kong: it should be for China to move forward and become democratized. That is not to say that I believe that there should be 'one country, one system'. Both capitalism and socialism are changing the world over, and I think eventually they will evolve into one system with fewer differences. We should be striving to create a new system which will merge the strengths of both existing systems. That should be Hong Kong's goal over the next fifty years.

It has been said that it is China's wish to put in place a system in Hong Kong which it could ultimately control. There have always been those feelings and doubts, and I personally would oppose the imposition by China of a system it could manipulate. But it is a question of degree. Beijing has to look at the situation from a 'risk management' point of view, and consider how Hong Kong presents a risk. Other people may also want to paint a picture of the risks that China will face, but, if that view is exaggerated, Beijing may want to take a stronger hold over Hong Kong, and that would not be entirely China's fault.

Beijing clearly felt that Hong Kong posed a greater threat to its future stability after Tiananmen in 1989. Hong Kong's reaction to the events surrounding 4 June was quite natural and admirable, but it was an emotive response which did not take account of the consequences. That, too, I think was to be expected: the masses are always naïve and often behave just like children; they do not think sensibly or rationally. I do not feel, however, that the events of 4 June 1989 should alter one's views about China. The results of the student movement in Beijing did not come as a surprise to anyone who knew China well. The minor details might vary, but the fundamental approach was within one's expectations. I, for one, was not surprised to see the tanks rolling in on the night of 3 June. The problem was that it happened under the spotlight of the international media, which perhaps amplified the situation. The actual events might not have been as horrifying as they appeared; other incidents in the past have been more horrifying, but were not witnessed by the rest of the world.

I found the British reaction difficult to believe. They made statements along the lines that they never realized China could be such a tyrant! Britain just used Tiananmen as an excuse to try and revoke the Joint Declaration because London had never been happy with the document in the first place. Britain was hoping that the Chinese Government would crumble so it could then declare that it was not in the best interests of Hong Kong to implement the Joint Declaration and hand the Territory back to China. Britain should have understood the Communist system better. However, the action taken in Hong Kong did have an impact on Beijing and resulted in consequences which I think few in Hong Kong probably had thought about at the time.

China started taking a much harder line towards Hong Kong, and this was reflected in the Basic Law drafting process. Beijing felt threatened by the demonstrations that called for political changes in China, and felt it had to take appropriate measures to counter those threats. This was seen in particular with Article 23 of the Basic Law which was inserted into the final draft after Tiananmen. Article 23 allowed for the future Special Administrative Region Government to enact laws to prohibit any act of treason, sedition, or subversion against the Central People's Government.

The cultural differences between Hong Kong and China sparked off numerous conflicts during the drafting of the Basic Law, and these were heightened when China adopted a harder line towards Hong Kong. The media has sensationalized the occasion when I emerged from one of the drafting committee meetings on the future political structure in tears. It was an emotional outburst following the strain and frustration I had experienced during one of our meetings during the later part of the drafting process. It had become clear that the Chinese leadership was trying to bulldoze through our committee a new proposal setting up a bicameral legislature with only 25 per cent of the seats directly elected in 1997. It was such a stupidly conservative proposal which risked paralysing the post-1997 administration of Hong Kong. As committee chairman, I suggested we deliberated the issue further, but because this proposal had received Beijing's blessing, there was no room for further discussion. I felt strongly that the proposal was unreasonable, but it was the total disregard of our viewpoint which upset me most. I realized that even though eighty years had passed since the end of China's imperial era, the culture of the infallibility of the emperor still existed there. I called on the Hong Kong drafters who had been in the meeting to speak out against China's actions at a press conference. Following that, I was the subject of a bitter backlash in the pro-Beijing newspapers in Hong Kong. But by that stage I did not mind if I was blacklisted by China. Eventually we succeeded in amending the proposal.

When the final version of the Basic Law was published in 1990, I felt it was a document I could be proud of and that it truly reflected the spirit and the letter of the Joint Declaration. I think that it will be in Hong Kong's best interests if the Basic Law is implemented faithfully.

I was involved in particular with two areas in the Basic Law drafting process, sitting as I did on the Political and on the Cultural sub-groups, and it is clear that Basic Law provisions reflect the spirit of the Joint Declaration. The Central People's Government has delegated the autonomy of all the decisions in these areas to the Hong Kong SAR Government, and in most matters it will be for the Hong Kong people to make the decisions. There is not one section in the Basic Law which could allow for Chinese interference and which could threaten existing labour rights, religious or cultural freedoms, or our academic and professional freedoms. There is no basis for some of the fears which have existed: recognition of academic qualifications, for example, will be up to the SAR Government, while professional qualifications will be recognized by professional bodies in Hong Kong. There is no mechanism in place which could permit China to dictate what criteria there should be or to jeopardize the freedoms which already exist and which have been promised in the future.

Many of the worries which have existed during the transition have arisen out of fear that the future SAR Government will be under the control of the Central People's Government. That is the crux. It is understandable to have doubts. The main worry is that the SAR Chief Executive will be in effect a Beijing appointee, China's puppet. Only time will be able to tell whether that will be the case or not. However, logically speaking, it would be quite impossible for that to happen! Just imagine being in the position of Chief Executive of Hong Kong! How would that person be able to live with his own conscience if he just listened to what Beijing wanted and went against the wishes of the people of Hong Kong. How long would that person be able to survive in those circumstances? I can't imagine that happening!

My attitude towards China and the future of Hong Kong has to a large extent been dictated by my own Christian beliefs. If one really wants to take a true Christian attitude, one has to be understanding and forgiving. Ideological differences should not be used as reasons for segregation or barriers to communication. Over the years a much greater respect and understanding has developed amongst differing religions the world over, and, since Communism, like religion, is a system of beliefs, that same understanding and positive approach should be adopted towards China.

There is no doubt that attitudes towards China are coloured by the past, but does that mean that China should continue to be cast out like a criminal? Christians should be forgiving and should give people another chance. Condemning a person who has erred and continuing to segregate him is not going to achieve anything. That has been my approach towards China. In addition, I feel that, as a Chinese, China is part of my own family, who unfortunately has made mistakes in the past. Would it be right not to give them another chance and help them with their difficulties?

Zunzi

Art, Politics, and Black Humour

Hong Kong started to shed its image as a 'cultural desert' in the 1970s, when events such as the annual Arts Festival brought international performers and artists to the Territory. It was not until the 1980s, however, that the city began to develop resources and facilities to encourage its own visual and performing artists. Zunzi, a well-known, local political cartoonist, was one of the many who was able to benefit from the boost given to local artists during the decade.

The decade witnessed an increasing cultural awareness and appreciation with the establishment of the Academy for the Performing Arts, the Arts Centre, and the Hong Kong Museum of Art. Many Hong Kong artists who had trained and lived overseas began to return to work in the Territory. The boost to the visual arts, however, did not go far enough. Local artists have complained about the dearth of places for them to exhibit, the lack of training courses, and the general feeling that funding for the visual arts has a low priority. By the mid-1990s, the Chinese University was still the only tertiary institution offering a practical Fine Arts course, and heated debate continued over the funding priorities of the Arts Development Council.

Zunzi was one of the few students to win a place at the Chinese University to study Fine Arts, and was perhaps the first of his generation to consider art, not as an esoteric or frivolous pursuit, but as an occupation with a serious social function. His daring social and political commentary and his talent as a cartoonist have made him famous in Hong Kong, and demand for his work is high—he draws five different cartoons a day for three of the Territory's leading newspapers, in addition to his contributions to a number of magazines each week.

Hong Kong artists, unlike their counterparts in China, have not traditionally been motivated in their work by politics. One could even argue that for them art has been an escape from it. Zunzi has chosen an alternative route. The reaction of the Chinese Government to the student demonstrations in 1989 shocked many Hong Kong artists, encouraging them to take on politics through art to an unprecedented extent.

IT WAS QUITE UNUSUAL for someone from a working-class background like me to go to university to study Fine Arts in the mid-1970s. Before then, most of the people who did so, came from rich families, and studied art for its own sake. They didn't have to worry about making a living, and they didn't see it as a means to exist. I also went to study art for pleasure—it was one of my main interests—but I took a risk as I didn't know whether I would be able to make ends meet after I had finished the course. I would have taken a vocational course in design at a polytechnic if I hadn't been able to go to the Chinese University to study art.

My father was a merchant seaman, who worked as a boatswain in a cargo ship. We lived first of all in Jordan Road near the cargo terminal, and then moved into public housing near the airport. At primary school, my brother and cousins were older and much better artists that me. We used to draw our own comic strips on rough, cheap paper. The subject matter usually centred around fighting or Kung Fu. My artistic skills improved as I got older. I was the second of six children in the family. My parents didn't have time to give me too much attention or put much pressure on me, so I just quietly got on with my drawing.

My father was very left-wing, and, when we were very small, my brother and I used to follow him to union meetings. That's where I learnt a lot of patriotic songs, and first heard of Mao Zedong. The union took great care in looking after the families of its members, so, for example, whenever any of us was sick, we went to the union clinic which paid for any medical treatment we needed. However, my father gradually changed his beliefs after he started his own business as a garment manufacturer.

He became even more disillusioned after the fall of the Gang Of Four, which occurred while I was at university. [The 'Gang of Four'—Mao's wife, Jiang Qing, Zhang Chunqiao, Wang Hongwen, and Yao Wenyuan— were arrested late in 1976, and variously accused of plotting to seize power and persecuting large numbers of officials during the Cultural Revolution. Following a show trial in 1980, they were imprisoned.] My father felt very cheated for a long time, when he found out that Communism in China was not as beautiful as the propaganda had portrayed. I think, though, despite his left-wing background, my father was very liberal at heart. He did not try to dissuade me from studying Fine Arts.

University in the 1970s was a great political debating ground, and many of my classmates did become very involved, and, as a result, gave little time to their academic studies. There was a split between the pro- and anti-China sympathizers, with the pro-Beijing Communists on one side, and, on the other, the socialists, who were anti-Communist, but who were becoming concerned with issues such as corruption and social conditions in Hong Kong.

The fall of the Gang of Four affected me a great deal: that was when I started to think about what was really happening in China. My fellow students and I found it difficult to accept that a country could control news and information to such an extent that so many outside China were duped and didn't have a clue about what was really going on during the Cultural Revolution. I learnt then to become more sceptical when I was listening to arguments, and reading. Now I rarely accept anything at first sight, and perhaps that explains why I shifted to drawing cartoons. It allowed me to become more cynical.

Cartoons certainly suited my temperament. I'm not the sort of person who can draw and paint a picture over a month to express my feelings. There are so many things—thoughts and ideas—inside me that I have to throw them out, express them, as quickly as possible.

We spent a lot of time at university talking about the function of art in society. I believed that art should take a form that served the people, and shouldn't be a medium to escape from society, from reality. I recognize now that there are different types of art, and that each person can choose his or her own means of expression. No one form of art is better than another. However, I still feel that, no matter what your own feelings are, art must have some kind of social responsibility, even if it doesn't have direct social impact.

After I graduated I went to Europe for a short period, and then taught Art and English in a secondary school. I had nothing else to do and I needed a job. [The expansion in schools meant there were more teaching jobs available.] However, I gave that up after a year and became an evening-school teacher, since it gave me more time to draw and paint during the day. It provided an opportunity to read, which I did a great deal of then. I was particularly anxious to learn more about differing political philosophies.

I also began drawing cartoons for a small news magazine produced by some friends of mine. The magazine was critical of Hong Kong society in the early 1980s, and my cartoons reflected that criticism. One issue which I felt very strongly about was the move to shorten the Chinese University courses from four to three years. I drew one picture of the Chinese University Vice Chancellor sitting in a chair and someone had sawn off one of the chair's legs, so it only had three legs instead of four. I was also concerned then about the problem of inflation and the great discrepancy between the rich and poor.

In 1980 I started to work for *Ming Pao* [a leading Hong Kong Chinese daily newspaper] where, initially, I was given general training in all aspects of newspaper production. I also continued drawing and painting for some of the new political magazines. Louis Cha, editor of *Ming Pao*, saw my work, and made some enquiries about the cartoonist. He didn't realize that the artist was already working for him! He then asked me to draw for him, but I didn't start my own regular column until 1983.

My first cartoon about the 1997 issue appeared in 1981 in one of the magazines, and I believe it was the first cartoon in Hong Kong which addressed the question of the Territory's future. It depicted people on a rollercoaster approaching a dark tunnel with '1997' above it. At the tunnel entrance, stood Deng Xiaoping waving to the people as the roller coaster moved towards the tunnel. I was trying to express my view that it was right that Hong Kong should return to China in 1997, despite the uncertainty of such a move—hence the dark tunnel entrance. However, I felt that Deng's economic reforms were sound and gave us hope that China, and therefore Hong Kong, had an optimistic future.

Three years later, when the Sino-British Joint Declaration was signed I wanted to emphasize the frustration Hong Kong people felt about not having had a chance to express their own feelings about the future. I drew Deng Xiaoping and Prime Minister Margaret Thatcher sitting together as parents: Hong Kong was represented by a girl who was going to marry, not a person, but a roll of paper which was held by an anonymous, headless man. The two were standing side by side. To me, Hong Kong's return to China was like a traditional Chinese arranged marriage, and the roll of paper was the Joint Declaration.

I was sceptical that China would stand by the pledges made in the Joint Declaration, and I haven't had much faith that the freedoms and the assurances about Hong Kong's way of life will be able to continue after the transfer of sovereignty. I believe that China will ultimately change into a more open society, but, until then, the political system there will find it difficult to accommodate the spirit, little less the letter, of the Joint Declaration.

During the 1980s, I commented on key issues and personalities, and tried to reflect public perceptions and concerns. This included the problem of the Vietnamese boat people, and the genuine feeling of grief that followed the death of the Governor, Sir Edward Youde. Following the 1987 political review, I characterized Sir David Wilson as a person who wasn't in control of the situation all the time. He was always depicted being beaten or scolded by the Chinese Government and by Zhou Nan, the local head of the New China News Agency. There were many lame ducks in my pictures at that time! [The transitional colonial administration was frequently characterized as a 'lame duck' unable to resist Chinese pressure on Hong Kong issues.] Sometimes the lame duck had a few secret weapons, or was hissing and trying to bite back, usually ineffectively!

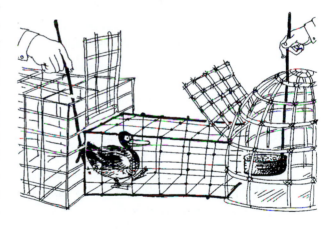

My work during that decade was overshadowed by the impact of the Chinese military suppression of the student movement in 1989. I must have drawn more than 500 cartoons about the Tiananmen Square protests in the months following June 4th.

In the run-up to Tiananmen, I, like so many other people, hoped that the student movement would begin to bring about a change in the political culture of China, and that some political shift might take place. We were all following the events very closely, and, even now, I think that, if the students had had a wiser plan, there could have been some kind of dialogue between them and the Government. A couple of weeks before the protests I began to worry that there had to be some way out other than confrontation. By that time the students were split into two camps—those who wanted to retreat from Tiananmen Square, and those, particularly students from other parts of China, who thought they should stay.

At that stage, my assessment was that the Government would have to do something. I thought they would physically remove the students from Tiananmen Square, and arrest some of them. Never for one moment did I think that they would order the army to open fire on their own people and cause bloodshed on the streets.

That night, the night that the tanks rolled into the square, I cried for the first time in twenty years. A columnist friend of mine called me twice in the middle of the night to tell me what was happening. We talked for a long time and we both started to cry together on the phone. My wife and I stayed up for the rest of the night. I might add that since then my friend has emigrated to Canada to 'escape from the rule of Communist China'.

It was almost impossible for me to control my emotions and I found it very difficult even to draw. Each day, when the time came to pick up my pen, I had to make a real effort to cool myself down before I started sketching any pictures. I tried then to be logical, find out what was happening, and keep as calm as I could, while I tried to portray my feelings in my drawings in the best way possible. Some days, when I couldn't keep my emotions under control, all that materialized was pages of senseless doodles.

I used a lot of black in my cartoons. One showed Li Peng in a bathtub full of blood. Near the tub was a skeleton wearing a PLA uniform, and in its hand was a bucket full of fresh blood. The skeleton was asking Li Peng, 'Is the bath warm enough?'

It has been said that Hong Kong people should not have become so involved in what China views as an 'internal affair', but I disagree. Hong Kong is linked to China. In fact, since Tiananmen, I have begun to think of myself more as a cartoonist of China, than just a cartoonist of Hong Kong. As a result, my cartoons have reflected some of the social problems in China, such as corruption.

The 'one country, two systems' approach doesn't mean that we should just close our eyes to what's happening in China. If Hong Kong people want Hong Kong to be a better place to live, the only way to do so is to make China a better place as well. So I now draw more about China than before, I read more about China than before, and I try to draw what is real, rather than what the Communist party believes is real but isn't.

I also feel my destiny should be tied up with Chinese cartoonists who are still in China. I'm in touch with many artists there. We talk to each other. I know they have a lot of things to say, but no means to express their feelings.

Over the years, I have most enjoyed drawing Deng Xiaoping, and, more recently, Li Peng, whom I always seem to portray as a fool. People ask whether I will continue to draw cartoons like that after 1997, making fun of the Chinese leadership. I argue that it will be good for Hong Kong if I do. If I keep on with my cartoons in the same way after 1997, and China allows them to be published in Hong Kong's local newspapers as they are now, then it will be a good sign. It will show that Hong Kong hasn't changed as a result of the transfer of sovereignty. If I stopped, it would send out the wrong signal.

That is not to say that I don't have fears about artistic freedom after 1997. That is why all of us who are artists in Hong Kong have to work harder to fight for greater freedom and more space, so that if these freedoms are curbed a little bit after 1997, we shall still have a wider territory to draw. By this I mean that Hong Kong artists should be making use of every single avenue possible for their work. They should seek as much international and overseas exposure as possible: this might help protect their freedoms after 1997.

The worst that could happen to me in the future is that I wouldn't be allowed to draw and I'd have to find other means of making a living. In a worst-case scenario, perhaps some excuse might be found to imprison me, and I might be arrested for a petty crime like littering! But I don't think it will come to that.

A lot of Chinese artists who have come out of China to Hong Kong warn me by saying, 'You haven't gone through the Cultural Revolution, you don't know how horrible that was.' People of my own age from China tell me just how bad the Chinese Government might be to people like me. I say, 'Thank you', and carry on. Cartoons are my life.

Sir Piers Jacobs
The Last 'Colonial' Financial Secretary

Financial Secretary for five years from 1986, Sir Piers Jacobs was responsible for the Hong Kong Government's fiscal policies, as well as the management of its HK$60 billion annual budget. His term of office was marked by controversy and more strident criticism of policy than ever before. It was a sign of changing times.

Successor to a distinguished, if somewhat imperious, tradition, Sir Piers found himself increasingly having to argue for and defend his proposals before a legislature which could no longer be counted on for unanimous and automatic support. The progressively contentious situation followed the growth in political awareness among the Territory's legislators, who also began to realize that public finance could be more easily influenced than politically sensitive issues, such as Hong Kong's future relationship with China. The Finance Committee of the Legislative Council assumed a new importance as it discovered its effective influence over a wide area of Government policy: it could simply vote down the administration's expenditure proposals.

Sir Piers Jacobs was criticized for being both too conservative and, almost at the same time, too liberal. Faced with the stock market crisis in 1987 and the decision to close the Stock Exchange following a collapse in share prices worldwide, he was condemned for not acting swiftly to prevent the closure. When he introduced legislation to strengthen regulatory controls, he was condemned for acting too hastily.

Sir Piers also became embroiled in the controversy with China over the Chek Lap Kok airport project. When approval for the HK$127 billion new port and airport plan was announced in October 1989, Beijing saw it as part of the Government's confidence-boosting package in the wake of the Tiananmen Square protests, and refused to endorse the project. Without China's blessing, banks were reluctant to finance the proposals. A Sino-British agreement on the airport, the Memorandum of Understanding, was eventually signed by British Prime Minister John Major in Beijing in 1991, the first visit by a Western leader since Tiananmen.

Sir Piers Jacobs retired from the Government in 1991, after nearly thirty years in the service.

I HAVE SUGGESTED that I was Hong Kong's last 'colonial' Financial Secretary. Let me explain.

During my tenure the whole atmosphere of the administration, its relationship with the Executive Council and, more particularly, with the Legislative Council, was quite different from what it is today. In my con-cluding speech in my first budget debate, everyone who spoke was

addressed by name, and I was busy thanking members for their pro-found comments. You could afford to be gentlemanly and orderly because you knew you were totally in control, and the chances of any-one really upsetting what you were proposing were not great. I remem-ber in my first budget in 1987, someone had the temerity to vote against the Appropriation Bill. I was furious!

A colonial administration expects to govern; it doesn't expect real opposition, and certainly not in the Legislative Council! Incidentally, when I first arrived in Hong Kong and entered the Government in 1962, I was a very junior chap, and the Legislative Council was the Olympian heights. It consisted of the great and the good. I never dreamt that I would sit in such an august body.

As time moved on, one experienced a complete change in the relationships that existed. Contention entered the scene. The Tiananmen Square protests obviously gave a great jolt to the feeling of Hong Kong, but a change in sentiment is inevitable when you face something as fundamental as a change of sovereignty. People were naturally going to become very conscious that sovereignty was a matter of substance, and I think that sense developed progressively from the late 1980s onwards.

When I retired I was asked what advice I would give to my successor, and I replied that he would have to spend much more time on the Legislative Council, which indeed he did. By 1991, the job of Financial Secretary had become different, as indeed had Hong Kong itself from the time of my arrival.

In those early days in the 1960s the high-rise had hardly been invented as far as Hong Kong was concerned. The Peninsula Hotel in Kowloon towered above most of the other buildings there, and the tallest on the island was the old Bank of China building, just a few feet higher than the old Hongkong and Shanghai Bank.

I lived for a time in Kowloon. Each day I drove my battered Morris 1000, and parked near the Star Ferry—not at a meter, just free car parking. I would board the Star Ferry to cross the harbour. A pleasant trip, which seemed quite a distance.

One of the most striking things was the shipping. There were no container ships and all Hong Kong's cargo was shipped on those attractive cargo vessels belonging to the old Glen Line, Blue Funnel, Ben Line, Royal Interocean, and so on. They were lovely vessels, all about twelve to fourteen thousand tons, much smaller than the ships you see today. You used to see them coming back every couple of months or so. Crossing the harbour, you became familiar with shipping lines. You felt far away from the 'home country', and the ships provided a nautical and sentimental link. It was a special feeling.

The civil service was a much more colonial structure then, and one was conscious of the hierarchy. The media didn't seem to take a vast amount of interest in individual civil servants and you had no Policy Branch Secretaries. The only administrators who were public figures in any real sense were the Governor, the Colonial Secretary, the Financial Secretary, and that was really about it.

Of course 1997 was not an issue in those days. I remember I once mentioned the date as a potential problem. I was at a party and I said so to an old British colonial. He roared at me, 'Things will go on. Obviously things will go on. Why should you be worried about 1997?'

That was the old thinking. But even before MacLehose's visit to Beijing in 1979, attitudes had started to change. Frankly, it was becoming apparent that the shortening term of leases held from the Crown could prove to be a problem, and that was what MacLehose sought to address.

However, it was with the sad and untimely death of Edward Youde that the atmosphere really changed. It was seen as the end of an era. Had Youde been Governor for longer, I think we could have had a healthier situation. He was a more experienced and mature man than his successor in many ways. I am not saying that in a derogatory sense where David Wilson is concerned, but I think a few more years of Youde's Governorship would have made a difference.

My own feeling is that, once the decision was made to hand Hong Kong back to China, the best thing really would have been to stretch out our hands rather more enthusiastically than actually happened, even though the Chinese, for historical reasons, might not have understood. Nevertheless, relationships could have developed along more productive lines.

David Wilson undoubtedly came in too early, which was unfortunate for Hong Kong, in that we were not yet ready for a change of Governor. Perhaps it was also unfortunate for David Wilson himself because when you have an untimely or premature appointment, the person who is placed in that position obviously does not carry the same authority as his predecessor.

By the time Wilson arrived in 1987, the Joint Declaration was history, and he was clearly the head of what I would describe as an exiting team. Wilson had an extraordinarily difficult task coming in as he did. On his appointment he did not have the sort of charisma and political weight that might have carried Hong Kong further along the path to a comfortable transition.

When Edward Youde died, we discussed what sort of Governor we should have as a replacement. Some felt that what was needed at that moment in Hong Kong's history was a big man, not necessarily a sinologist, but a big man, someone of weight. Notwithstanding his undoubted qualities, I think it is questionable whether Wilson actually had the right background for this time.

He came in as a sinologist. He was immensely conscientious, and he worked extremely hard. But for all his abilities, he was still relatively junior in the Foreign Office, and, rather more importantly, he was very much a known figure as far as the Chinese were concerned, since he had been one of those from the Foreign Office who had negotiated the Joint Declaration, the Chinese had his measure. That doesn't necessarily work to your advantage when you are in negotiating mode, so to speak. It is as though you have put all your cards on the table face up. One might argue that Youde was also a known quantity, but he had the weight of long tenure in office.

In some ways David Wilson and David Ford, who was Chief Secretary of the Hong Kong Government, were an ill-chosen couple for that time. Having said that, David Wilson felt comfortable with Ford, and I think it is true to say that he allowed Ford to have a lot of the running of the administration. Someone like Youde would probably have run his administration on a tighter reign.

David Ford was a most able administrator, but with an information background; David Wilson also had that inclination. So what you saw during that period was increasing sensitivity to media pressure, and I don't think that was particularly healthy.

Let me illustrate what I have in mind with some anecdotes. When I was first appointed Financial Secretary, I remember that Edward Youde called me up to Government House. 'Congratulations,' he said. 'You are to be Hong Kong's next Financial Secretary.' I made a quick mental note to get rid of my Hong Kong dollars!

Youde made it quite clear to me that he did not expect me to emulate my predecessor, the great and ebullient John Bremridge—not that I could have done so—and that he wanted a change of style. He went on to say, 'Just explain things as you see them, as they are. That's why I have chosen you. You are not there to provide headlines for the *South China Morning Post*. Don't become a media plaything.'

With Wilson and Ford, the administration became much more the creature of the media. I believe that once you start to operate on the basis of how you think things will appear in the press, it begins to distort your view of what is right. Statements become somewhat skewed—not untrue, but just a little skewed towards their public impact.

During the time that we were putting together the new airport proposals, I remember we had to work on the 1988 Governor's speech to the Legislative Council. We were still in the midst of a lot of studies relating to the airport, but the draft speech made it clear that we would be going ahead, which was a decision we had not yet made.

I advised that we could not make such a statement, and I was asked by the Governor what we should say. I replied that we should say something along the lines that the studies were continuing—which was the situation.

David Ford clearly did not care for this approach and asked how it would run in the media. Too negative.

When we eventually announced the decision to go ahead with the new airport, and this was done by the Governor in his October speech in 1989, the announcement came not so long after Tiananmen. The project was therefore seen by many as a confidence-boosting measure. I think that was unfortunate because we had in fact been studying the airport since 1979. It was and is something that Hong Kong needs. It was not done simply to boost confidence at a difficult time.

I remember that when we were looking at the original draft of the Governor's October speech, I was uneasy about including any reference to the price tag and date of completion. Indeed, in the original draft, I recollect that it said the airport would be open for operation by 31 December 1996. I advised the Governor that that date was not possible, and that if he felt he had to say anything about the date of completion at all, he should say that the airport would be completed some time in 1997, and then we could have drifted into 1998 with respectability. There was, however, a feeling that we had to get on with it. That seeming haste to complete under British sovereignty caused some political problems.

Chek Lap Kok has been a real saga. When I took over as Financial Secretary, I suggested to the Governor, Edward Youde, that we should resuscitate the project, which had been shelved earlier for good solid reasons—in particular because of the cost. Youde was somewhat hesitant, but I said to him after a while that what I would like to do was to put together a series of options that we could take to the Executive Council. Youde, the supreme bureaucrat, in the best sense of that term, said, 'Yes, that I like.'

We went to Executive Council at the beginning of 1987, but the options required study because life had moved on since the original concept. So we engaged in a series of studies. They were perfectly genuine, they weren't political studies, and we looked at many, many options. The decision to build at Chek Lap Kok wasn't a snap decision. But it matured, perhaps unfortunately, a few months after Tiananmen.

A question frequently asked both by the media and by bankers was, 'Where does China stand in relation to the airport?' The line we had taken was, 'This is Hong Kong's project', which, of course, is true, but if you think of it technically, if you think of it legally, an airport is a very special piece of infrastructure development. An airport is uniquely dependent on air services agreements. The Joint Declaration and the Basic Law state that the SAR Government is empowered to enter into its own air service agreements under the specific authority of the People's Republic of China. So China has a say in air services agreements under the Joint Declaration and Basic Law.

It was obvious, therefore, that China had to be consulted, involved in some way. There is no doubt that the Chinese were told what we were doing, and they had certainly acquiesced initially. There was no suggestion that the Chinese did not want us to build an airport, and, at various stages, they had said, 'Could you give us some brief information?' We did so, and they then came back and asked for more.

In the end, we advised the Chinese authorities that the best thing for us to do was to hand over the various consultancy reports, and there were many of them. I personally handed over two large cardboard boxes containing all the consultancy reports.

The Chinese seemed to think that we had produced a snow job. So it was decided that we should resolve the matter through so-called 'expert talks', but, by that time of course, the Chinese realized that they had a very valuable political lever in their hands, and, ultimately, in order to reach an agreement for the project to go ahead, they managed to secure John Major's visit to Beijing to sign the Memorandum of Understanding.

In so far as involving the Chinese was concerned, even though I mentioned the matter, I will accept some blame in that I ought to have stressed the importance of involvement at an earlier date. I did not do so because, quite frankly, I thought it was self evident. We ought to have opened up a formal channel for that purpose of involvement, probably choosing on both sides financial people, technical people. Certainly one would like to have seen the Bank of China there at the table.

The new airport was, of course, one of the more interesting projects which I had to deal with during my term in office. Of a very different nature was the Stock Exchange crisis that hit us in October 1987. We were caught up in the worldwide collapse in stock market prices. The consequences in Hong Kong were dramatic in that the committee of the Stock Exchange decided to close the market. The task then was quite simple: to open the market again as soon as possible and in an orderly manner. And that we did.

We spent some frantic days putting together a financial rescue package. The market had closed for four days, so we had that short period of time in which to obtain help from the players in the market, the banks, and, last but not least, the Exchange Fund, of which I was Controller. We were working till all hours of the night, and indeed into the early hours of the morning. I reminded some of my colleagues of how lucky we were to be involved. The world had not seen anything like this since 1929.

The most exciting and constructive time from my point of view was the aftermath of the crisis, when we put together a new regulatory regime, both for the Exchange itself and for the Government. On the advice of Ian Hay Davison [formerly the Chief Executive of the London Stock Exchange], whom we had engaged as our consultant, we established a separate body, the Securities and Futures Commission. What we put in place did much to restore the reputation of the market, which had been tarnished by the abrupt closure in October 1987.

I took a lot of stick at the time of the closure because many seemed to assume that the decision to close the market was that of the Government rather than of the Stock Exchange itself. It was not a decision with which the Government could prudently have interfered without exposing the public purse to unknown financial risk. One of the factors that I had borne in mind in my various public utterances was the need to keep the temperature down as far as possible. Hong Kong can be a jumpy place, and I felt that I needed to calm the situation as much as I could. Whether I was successful or not is another question. We had to remember that the crisis took place after the Joint Declaration in which we had agreed to ensure Hong Kong's prosperity and stability. We needed to take into account views that might be formed in China if matters got out of hand. I think this influenced the attitude that I adopted in relation to both the closure itself and the rescue package.

The China dimension permeated most issues when I was Financial Secretary. Constitutional issues became of greater and greater concern. In the 1987 electoral review, there was much discussion about what would be acceptable in total terms, not only acceptable to the people of Hong Kong, but also acceptable in the context of our relations with China.

With the benefit of hindsight, if we had just gone straight to direct elections immediately after the Joint Declaration, if that had been made abundantly clear to the Chinese, by now the arrangements would have been history and we would have a fairly quiet Legislative Council getting on with its business. It is because elections became over-symbolic of Hong Kong's autonomy that we have all this present turmoil.

I think that too much time was spent in trying to put together a package that we could get away with in the circumstances. We spent far too little time on what I would regard as constitutional principles, such as whether we were edging towards some sort of ministerial system, or whether we were talking about separation of powers, or how we intended to handle some of the things that are coming up today, for example, the relationship between the Executive Council and the legislature. There was debate about that, but far too little. What sort of constitutional model were we working towards? That ought to have been the nub of it. I don't feel that we got our minds adequately around the real problem.

I remember discussion in the Executive Council, sometimes informal discussion, and I recollect one meeting when I said, 'Look, you are moving to the point where the Government will be defeated in the Legislative Council'. Two eminent members of the Executive Council looked at me pityingly, and, laughing, replied, 'Piers, you don't understand Hong Kong.' They thought Government by consensus would continue and carry the day.

Maybe I don't understand everything about Hong Kong—who does?— but I do understand political reality. It is inevitable that when you put together political arrangements in a situation such as we have in Hong Kong with no governing party in the legislature, you get to the point where a Government can be defeated, and we have seen that happen.

So how do you handle this? That is a question you must ask yourself at the very beginning. That's far more important than whether you should have twenty directly elected seats, ten functional constituencies, this, that, and the other. The numbers game is not of such importance. The constitutional relationships are right there at the centre. Maybe opportunities were lost for putting in place something rather special for the long term.

How do I see the future? In the public sector, those local officers who have decided to be part of the future will play a critical role in seeing Hong Kong into the next century. How successful they will be depends entirely on the sort of pressures brought to bear on them. That is something that none of us can foresee. But, if individual officers find themselves under political or family pressure or the pressure of friends, then you have a very difficult situation.

My advice to anyone staying in Hong Kong is, 'Maintain your standards'. If people maintain and even improve their standards, and behave well, then I think they can make an enormous contribution to the future of Hong Kong and indeed to China itself. If they start to waiver and adopt other ways then that is extraordinarily dangerous, and could go right through the fabric of society. Incidentally, I'm not just talking about corruption, I'm talking about how you make decisions.

But with 1997 now upon us, everything depends, frankly, on how China progresses, and, if China progresses well as an economy, as a political entity, then I think Hong Kong is going to be probably one of the better cities, if not the best city in China. If you have a situation in which China is in difficulties, there is no way in which the Joint Declaration is going to insulate Hong Kong from those difficulties. That cannot happen.

So I see a growing emphasis on the 'one country' part of the formula.

A number of things will obviously survive. A number of concepts set forth in the Basic Law. But name me any situation in which something can stand still or follow a closely defined particular course for fifty years? Can you envisage someone in twenty years time waving the Basic Law and saying 'one country, two systems'? It doesn't happen like that, does it?

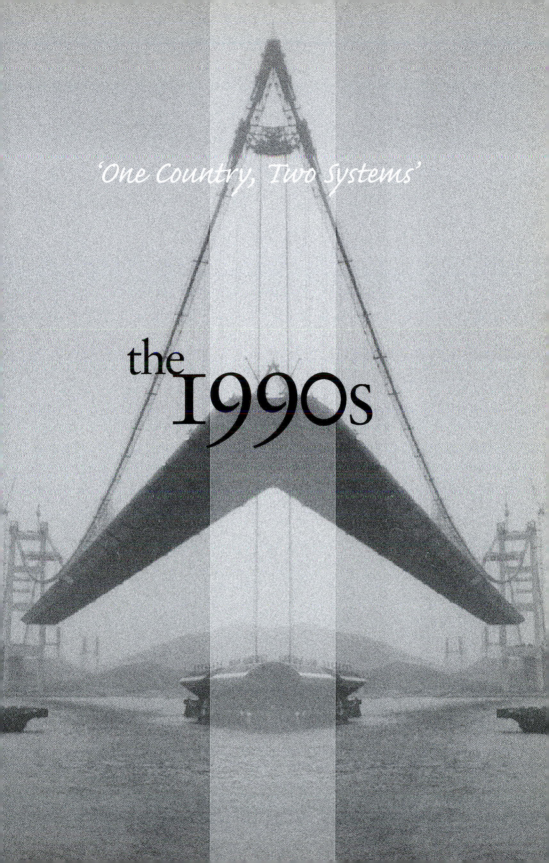

'One Country, Two Systems'

the 1990s

While Tiananmen and the events of 1989 marked a turning point in China's policy towards Hong Kong, 1992 marked a change in course in British policy. This was signalled by the appointment of Hong Kong's last Governor, Chris Patten, a British politician. He represented a break from the line of Foreign Office diplomats with close links with China, who had, for more than twenty years, occupied Government House.

Tiananmen had also brought Hong Kong's future into the international limelight. The one question asked by everyone both inside and outside the Territory was, 'What will happen after 1997?'

In 1990 people still believed in the 'through-train' concept and that there would be minimal change. By the middle of the decade, there was no doubt in anyone's mind that there would be significant changes in 1997, and all the indications were that China intended to run Hong Kong with tighter control than had been previously imagined. An increasing number of people began to feel that there was a question mark over the 'one country, two systems' concept, despite repeated assurances from China that it would still uphold the promises made in the Joint Declaration.

The key question has been: would this have happened regardless of Britain's change of policy towards Hong Kong? It is a question which has polarized the community. On the one hand, business and commercial interests have blamed Chris Patten's lack of understanding of China and the democratic changes he introduced, for derailing the 'through-train' concept, and forcing an enraged China to establish its own institutions. On the other hand, democratic forces initially lauded Patten's courage and initiative as a belated but crucial attempt to bolster fragile democratic institutions which could act as a buffer after 1997 against a potentially oppressive Marxist regime. Many believe that China never had any intention of allowing Hong Kong the 'high degree of autonomy' it had been promised.

In the words of one cynical British diplomat involved in Hong Kong affairs, 'all the Joint Declaration did was give Hong Kong people thirteen years warning to get out'. That may be an exaggerated view, but it was almost inevitable that the differing Sino-British interpretations of the Joint Declaration would come to a head as the date for the transfer of sovereignty drew closer.

The most contentious issue was the question of political reform. Many in Hong Kong felt that Britain neglected the opportunity in 1990 to put in place a political structure which had the full support of all Executive and Legislative Councillors, as well as strong backing from the community as a whole. As a result, conservatives and democrats united in the wake of Tiananmen, and reached a consensus which allowed for 50 per cent of the Legislative Council to be directly elected by 1995. (This became known as the OMELCO Consensus.)

The Basic Law, Hong Kong's future constitution, had not yet been finalized. If Britain had backed the Hong Kong consensus, and taken a unilateral decision, the onus for ensuring the continuation of the 'through-train' concept would have been on China. However, arguing that it was preferable to reach an agreement with China for a system that was sure to last beyond 1997, Britain instead quietly negotiated a compromise deal with Beijing, which was then written into the Basic Law. The agreement laid down how the democratic process in Hong Kong would proceed until the year 2007: only one third of the 1997 Legislative Council (twenty seats out of sixty) would be directly elected. It fell far short of the consensus reached in the community.

The vagueness and ambiguity of the Joint Declaration led both sides to interpret its terms and implications very differently, and many observers believe that this allowed the Basic Law to depart from the 'spirit' of the 1984 accord. The Basic Law was finally promulgated by China in 1990, and Britain whilst making clear, at least in private, to the Chinese that it was unhappy with certain provisions of the Basic Law, has never stated publicly that the post-1997 constitution represented a breach of the Joint Declaration.

The pro-democracy forces, however, did not mince their words. To them, the Basic Law represented a step backwards from the Joint Declaration, an indication of Beijing's hardening line in the wake of Tiananmen. In the post-1997 constitution, the Standing Committee of the National People's Congress was to have the ultimate power of amending and interpreting the Basic Law. It therefore had the power to revoke Hong Kong's laws at any time, if they were deemed contrary to the Basic Law. This was despite assurances in both the Joint Declaration and the Basic Law that the legal and judicial systems would remain unchanged. The future constitution also laid down a series of procedures which, in effect, amounted to China having the final say in the appointment by Beijing of the Chief Executive to replace the Governor and, in turn, to influence the appointment of principal officials in the civil service.

The British Government realized by 1992 that it had very few cards left to play, and was being perceived as a 'lame duck' administration in Hong Kong. Prime Minister John Major was the first Western leader to visit Beijing after the 1989 suppression of the student movement. His trip in 1991 to sign a Memorandum of Understanding on the financing of the airport was viewed as a capitulation. Many saw it as giving China a say in Hong Kong's finances before 1997, and it did not end the disagreements with Beijing over the funding of the project. The 'through-train' concept, which was supposed to ensure a smooth transition, was increasingly being seen as giving Beijing a say in the running of Hong Kong before 1997, and a veto over all major decisions which would straddle the handover.

The British Government calculated that it would be better to change course in its dealings with China over Hong Kong. At the beginning of 1992, it was announced that the Governor, Sir David Wilson, would retire. Chris Patten arrived in July that year with what many have interpreted as a mandate to ensure an honourable British withdrawal.

With just five years to go before the handover, many of the thorny transitional issues had not been tackled. Both Chinese and British diplomats knew privately that reaching agreement on many of these issues would be very difficult, if not impossible.

Chris Patten's room for manœuvre was very limited. He made it clear that he would not go back on what had already been agreed. Instead, with his political reform proposals, he set about exploiting the 'grey areas' in the Basic Law, in a bid to 'make possible the widest democratic participation by the people of Hong Kong in the running of their own affairs, while reinforcing certainty about Hong Kong's future'. His proposals included abolishing all appointed seats to the Municipal Councils and on the District Boards, and significantly broadening the electoral base for the functional constituencies. From China's viewpoint, he added insult to injury by announcing his proposals in Hong Kong in October 1992 before seeking an endorsement from Beijing. This was contrary to past practice when Britain and China had negotiated and taken decisions without involving the people of Hong Kong.

The Chinese reacted angrily to the Patten proposals. Against the background of a disintegrating Soviet Union and the aftermath of Tiananmen, Beijing saw the modest electoral changes as an attempt to destabilize China through the introduction of democratic institutions in an important and visible part of the country. Moreover, the reforms were perceived as concrete proof of Beijing's long-held suspicion that the British would sustain their influence through a political system which they, rather than the Chinese, could better manipulate. China's indignation also reflected the belief that Britain had gone back on 'secret understandings' reached earlier. Britain insisted that there had been no such understandings: China maintained that there had.

The argument that ensued permeated the full range of Sino-British relations. China made it clear that there would be no 'through-train' for the Legislative Council. The Legislature elected in 1995, which saw victory for democratic forces in Hong Kong, would be scrapped two years later and replaced, in effect, by a Beijing-appointed provisional body. The provisional Legislative Council would devise its own methods of electing the next legislature in 1998, which, whilst keeping within the limits of the Basic Law, would probably ensure the limitation of democratic representatives.

Once Chris Patten's reform plans had been put in place, Britain tried to close the door on the disagreement and open a new chapter in its relations with Beijing. This apparent U-turn in British policy was marked by a willingness to compromise over the bill to set up a Court of Final Appeal. China had delayed approving the legislation setting up the Court. Finally approval was given, but on the condition that the Court was not set up until 1 July 1997. This contradicted the earlier Sino-British agreement that the Court would be set up well in advance of 1997. The early establishment of the Court was seen as imperative by both the British and the Hong Kong Governments and the legal profession. It would have enabled the Court to gain experience and international credibility ahead of the handover, and would have maintained international investor-confidence in the future of the legal system.

Ultimately, despite Britain's compromise over the Court of Final Appeal, Beijing continued to withhold its endorsement in other key areas crucial to the transition. China reiterated its vow not only to dismantle the Legislative Council, but to dilute other reforms, such as the Bill of Rights, after 1997.

By 1996, the civil service, with its traditional reluctance to share power, was trying to come to terms with the harsh political reality of the times. There was to be no guarantee that top civil servants could remain in their jobs after the handover. The resulting strain has been considerable, with a number of local officials unsure about whether they should or even would be welcome to continue to serve in Hong Kong after 1997. Those who have wanted their future secured have backed away from Chris Patten, despite their earlier support for his reform proposals.

The commercial sector, however, has long recognized the political realities of the transition and has been critical of Patten's political reforms from the start. The cosy relationship which existed in the past between business and the colonial Government seemed set to continue in the future with the new SAR Government, as business leaders court their new masters in Beijing. For them, Hong Kong's autonomy and democratic reforms were not key issues.

The 1990s have seen the completion of Hong Kong's transition from a manufacturing to an essentially service-driven economy centred on its position as the gateway for investment into, and exports out of, China. Steady annual growth in gross domestic product figures was underpinned by the currency link with the US dollar. Hong Kong's financial institutions were strengthened further, with the formation of the Hong Kong Monetary Authority, which effectively functioned as a central bank.

However, beneath the optimistic economic forecasts, was a growing recognition that China's way of doing business was threatening to replace the Hong Kong way. The importance of political cover, China's determination to take stakes in strategic industries, and, behind all this, the threat of corruption, all combined to threaten and sap the confidence of the business community.

As the 1990s drew to a close, Hong Kong, now a major international financial and trading centre, found itself where it began, on the frontier between East and West and the ideologies which divide them.

Martin Lee

The Fight for Democracy

Of all the Hong Kong politicians in the 1990s, Martin Lee has been the most vocal advocate of democracy and the most renowned within and outside the Territory. The Hong Kong and British Governments have often seen him as a 'thorn in the side', whilst the Chinese Government has viewed him as a subversive. He is sometimes referred to as 'Hong Kong's future martyr'.

Martin Lee does not see himself as a radical agitator, however, but a man of principle, prepared to stand by what he believes is right for Hong Kong. A Legislative Councillor since 1985, he has defended to the hilt the rule of law, the promotion of justice, and human rights.

The first direct elections to the Legislative Council in 1991 brought overwhelming victory for Martin Lee under the banner of the Territory's first political party, the United Democrats of Hong Kong. He also carried the day in the next elections in 1995, as Chairman of the newly formed Democratic Party.

Detractors of Martin Lee and his party have argued that, given the lower voter registration in 1995 and even lower turnout figures on election day, only a very small percentage of the population actually supported the Democrats. This level of support, they point out, hardly amounts to a mandate by the people. But his advocates have interpreted both sets of elections results, in the context of Hong Kong's first tentative step towards democracy, as an overwhelming success for pro-democracy forces. In 1995, the Democrats and their allies captured seventeen out of twenty of the directly elected seats, representing 65 per cent of the popular vote.

The curious fact is that Martin Lee was little heard of before the mid-1980s. He was born in Hong Kong, studied at the University of Hong Kong, and went on to obtain a British legal training, before returning to practise as a barrister in 1956. His rise to political stardom began when, in 1980, he first entered public life as Chairman of the Bar Association, a position he held for three years. During the negotiations on Hong Kong's future, Martin Lee had the ear of influential Chinese officials and believed that quiet discussions achieved much: he persuaded Beijing that the ultimate recourse for legal appeal after 1997 should rest with a Court of Final Appeal in Hong Kong, rather than in Beijing.

Martin Lee twice won the legal community's seat in the Legislative Council elections in the 1980s. In 1985 he was selected by Beijing to sit on the Basic Law Drafting Committee. Four years later, he was removed from that committee for his condemnation of the 1989 suppression of the student democracy movement in China, and for his role in the founding of the Hong Kong Alliance in Support of the Patriotic Democratic Movement in China, an organization branded as subversive by Beijing.

During the final years of the transition, China refused any dialogue with Martin Lee and his allies. The question has been: will Martin Lee be able to maintain his political role in the future?

ON 4 APRIL 1990 when Hong Kong's future constitution, the Basic Law, was promulgated, I was invited to be a panelist on a television programme which was being broadcast live that evening. It was an unusual show because, while the programme was being shown, a survey of the viewers was conducted simultaneously to gauge their views on Hong Kong's future. At the very end of the programme, they announced the results: public confidence at that point was slightly lower than following the June 4th massacre. That result took me by surprise.

When I got home my eight-year-old son, Joey, was already in bed. He is a wonderful character and was a very lively, happy child. But that evening, when I went to kiss him goodnight, he was sobbing his heart out. His mother could not understand what was wrong and could do nothing to console him. We both went in, and I asked him, 'Joey, why are you crying?'

He said, 'Oh, Daddy, I'm worried that I won't ever be able to have a birthday present from you in the future.'

I assured him that he would always have a present, but he replied, 'How can you promise me that after 1997? You've already said you won't leave Hong Kong in 1997, and this evening I watched the television programme. After 1997 they are going to arrest you, they are going to put you in prison. How can you give me a present then?'

The episode made me very sad because, in my fight for democracy and human rights, I knew there would be personal sacrifices, but I only realized then the likely cost to those dearest to me. It was clearly unfair to the boy to be put in such a difficult and emotional position when he was so young, and I felt extremely unhappy about it. However, I was not persuaded to stop my work. If everyone put family considerations first then there would be nobody to stand up for Hong Kong.

I don't think of being imprisoned after 1997, but I cannot exclude that possibility. Where do you find a country in this part of the world, where there haven't been political prisoners at one time or another? And China isn't really a country which tolerates a dissenting voice.

I never envisaged when I was younger that I would be playing the role I am now. My involvement in Hong Kong affairs started back in 1981. All my friends were in the law and were talking about emigration, over lunch, over dinner, whenever we met. Discussion centred on a two-stage process to obtain a Canadian passport, by first acquiring one from the Dominican Republic. For a US$180,000 investment in a piece of land there, you were given a passport, and with that you could travel to Canada and the United States. With one passport in hand, it was possible then to get a better one, but that meant going somewhere else to live. It was a major decision for me whether to join them or not. I thought about it long and hard, and I decided to stay.

By 1981 I was already a Queen's Counsel. I was successful and could live comfortably. I felt it was then time to give something back to Hong Kong. I did not know or believe that I could actually do much for the community, but at least I had to try. That was the basis of my decision to stay.

My involvement in Hong Kong affairs increased in 1984 when the Sino-British Joint Declaration was initialed. I asked for and was given a sneak preview of the accord. As I read the document, I was happy because I could see in it provisions which would make the 'one country, two systems' concept work. I had previously told my Chinese and British friends involved in negotiating the Joint Declaration that, if I could see in the accord a possible future for Hong Kong, I would do my best to help make it work However, if, on the contrary, I saw it was doomed to fail, then I would not have been prepared to lift a finger in support. When I read it, I was thrilled, because it promised that the people of Hong Kong could elect their Chief Executive and legislature and, through them, hold the government accountable to the people. To me that meant democracy.

I had also been working hard behind the scenes to persuade Chinese officials that Hong Kong should maintain its common law system, and that was promised in the Joint Declaration as well. My success in quiet negotiations then led me to believe the best way to deal with the Chinese Government was behind closed doors. Only if there was a major disagreement should the matter be aired in public. At that time, I achieved a lot behind closed doors. Mind you, those were early days when Chinese officials trusted the people of Hong Kong. They trusted me. Therein lies the difference: that trust does not exist any more. Beijing just wants to control Hong Kong, and therefore the best method of dealing with Chinese officials doesn't work any longer. But that doesn't mean that you just give up trying. My philosophy in life is, so long as I'm there fighting, I haven't lost. It is only when I give up that I lose. That's why I've been fighting all these years.

I spent five years on the committee set up by China, in 1985, to draft the Basic Law. When I started off, I was extremely enthusiastic and the mainland Chinese delegates were also very confident. Two of them separately told me that since the Joint Declaration had been warmly welcomed in Hong Kong, the Basic Law would find even greater support; if it didn't, then they would consider that the committee had failed in its duties. I was extremely encouraged by that approach, and, indeed, I remember that, shortly after the Joint Declaration was announced, I was asked by the Chinese side whether they should actually wait until the very end of the transition period before drafting the Basic Law—which, I was told, was the British proposal—or whether they should draft it earlier. I said that there was no doubt in my mind that we should start early and follow through the Joint Declaration with an equally successful, if not better, Basic Law. I thought it would be easier to push for a Basic Law acceptable to Hong Kong if we were to do it early, because the Joint Declaration was good. I believed that if we were to wait for a long period, the leaders of China might change their minds and regret having written so many freedoms into the Joint Declaration. Looking back, I don't know whether I was right or wrong.

When the Basic Law was completed, I was much saddened. I had by then been thrown off the Drafting Committee because of my actions during the Tiananmen Square protests in June 1989. The final draft excluded the two most controversial provisions, which I had spent many months—years—fighting to have written into the constitution. The first was on the development of democracy: I failed because the system set out in the Basic Law was clearly very undemocratic. The second was the power to interpret the Basic Law. Again, I failed completely to persuade China that the final power should rest with the Hong Kong courts. Instead, it rests with Beijing, through the Standing Committee of the National People's Congress, which has the final power to interpret all Chinese laws, including the Basic law.

The failure to have a truly democratic political structure I blame on the British. The future political structure, which was to be spelt out in the Basic Law, was the last sticking point left unresolved up to the last minute before the final draft was completed. The role the British Government played in determining how our elected bodies should be constituted was unforgivable. For years the Chinese Government refused to allow the British to have any active participation in the drafting of the Basic Law, saying it was exclusively a Chinese matter. But the Hong Kong drafters [twenty-three of the fifty-nine members of the Drafting Committee were from Hong Kong] strongly opposed the proposals put forward for the post-1997 political structure. Beijing became embarrassed and turned to Britain for help.

China was in a difficult position because, although Beijing could still rely on its built-in majority on the Drafting Committee, it did not want to be seen to be pushing something through which the majority of Hong Kong drafters opposed. A compromise formula on the composition of the Legislative Council, both before 1997 and beyond, was agreed between Beijing and London through the exchange of seven secret letters. It was incredible: the Basic Law Drafting Committee held a three-day session while waiting for the two governments to reach agreement, before it endorsed the final draft of the Basic Law. [The agreement on the political structure was announced in Hong Kong by the then British Foreign Secretary, Douglas Hurd, following a visit to Beijing in February 1990.] After that, the Drafting Committee just became a rubber stamp and there were no dissenting voices when it came to approving the final version of the Basic Law. It was impossible even for the Hong Kong members to oppose a deal which had been reached by the two governments. It was a clear example of Britain agreeing to do China's dirty work.

The British approach typified the policy of appeasement at the time, perpetuated by the then Foreign Affairs Adviser to the Prime Minister, Sir Percy Cradock. I had two meetings with this man. The first one was in November 1991, shortly after my party's victory in the first direct Legislative Council elections in the September. We chatted for one and a half hours, and, although I did not like what he was saying, he appeared to be genuine—which made it worse!

His philosophy could be summed up as follows: We, the British, had already contracted to leave Hong Kong in 1997, so there wasn't very much that could be done for Hong Kong on controversial matters. The UK could push, but not that much. When the British had pushed until they believed they had reached China's bottom line, London then had to consider whether it was better for Hong Kong to reach an agreement on terms, hoping it could continue beyond 1997, or no agreement, allowing China to do whatever it wanted after 1997.

The British believed then that it was better for Hong Kong to reach an agreement with China—no matter how bad the agreement—than to have no agreement at all. So I asked Sir Percy, 'Why are these important decisions not made by us, who are freely elected by the people of Hong Kong?' He said, 'Because we are the sovereign power'. Then I said, 'How do you know when you have reached China's bottom line?' He said, 'Well now, if they tell us both in public and, more importantly, in private, that we have reached the bottom line, then I know.'

I couldn't believe it! So I asked him a third question: 'Sir Percy, how do you know that your philosophy on China is not known to your counterparts in China, so they will just tell you a certain position is their bottom line?' He had no answer.

Six months later, in May 1992, Sir Percy was passing through Hong Kong on his way to Beijing, in his words, 'to say good-bye to his Chinese friends', before he retired from public office. He asked to meet me alone again. His opening words were, 'Mr Lee, how can the Chinese be so unreasonable?' It was really unbelievable coming from him!

Sir Percy was referring to the Sino-British Memorandum of Understanding on the airport, which had been brokered by him, and signed by the two Prime Ministers, John Major and Li Peng, in September 1991. Eight months later, China was breaking the provisions of that accord. Under the agreement, the Chinese side had only one month to respond to proposals relating to the financing of the airport project. Three months after the proposals had been handed over, Beijing was still sitting on them. Of course, history shows that they sat on them for three years.

Britain was in no position to complain that China was breaching the agreement on the airport. By signing the agreement, London was, in effect, just tearing up the Joint Declaration. I said to Sir Percy, 'You asked for it. In 1984, you made a thoroughly good agreement for us, the Joint Declaration, which promised Hong Kong a high degree of autonomy and control over its own internal affairs. Why did you then see fit to make a second deal on the new airport, whereby you gave up a high degree of Hong Kong's financial autonomy? If you think fit to break the first agreement, by overriding it with a second, you must be a very naïve man to think that China will actually carry out its obligations under the second agreement on the airport.'

Sir Percy responded, 'Mr Lee, what a pity it is that your philosophy on China doesn't agree with mine. We cannot afford the luxury of carrying out two experiments to see which one works out better for Hong Kong. There is only one test tube.'

And I said 'You're damn right, Sir Percy, but you've been holding that test tube all these years, and see what a mess you've got us into.'

His logic meant that there always had to be an agreement: Britain was never prepared to walk away, and China knew it.

This of course changed with the arrival of Chris Patten as Governor in July 1992.

The first time I saw his face was when I went to the Hong Kong Club to watch the live televized results of the UK elections in April 1992. Everybody around him was so happy—except him. He was the Party Chairman, and yet he had lost his seat, while everybody else had won. I thought then that this was an interesting politician. Most people in those circumstances would have put on a brave face and at least pretended to be happy. But apparently this guy couldn't do it. So my first impression of Mr Patten was that he was an honest man.

I think he has viewed me as both an ally and a thorn in his side. I have by and large wanted to give him the benefit of the doubt, but there have been times when the facts have been stacked against him, in particular in the case of the 1995 agreement with China to delay the setting up of the Court of Final Appeal until after the transfer of sovereignty in 1997. Having stood up to China over his electoral proposals, to my mind the Court of Final Appeal agreement represented a U-turn in British policy, with a reversion to appeasement and the line peddled by Sir Percy Cradock.

To me there was no doubt this agreement was related to the visit by the then British Minister for Trade, Michael Heseltine, to Beijing in the spring of that year. Mr Heseltine signed numerous trade agreements between Britain and China, and a few days later there was an announcement on an agreement for the setting up of the Court of Final Appeal. To my mind, it was likely that, in return for the trade agreements, Britain had compromised and given China control over the arrangements for setting up the Court of Final Appeal.

People in Hong Kong were extremely angry. The Legislative Council and the legal fraternity had already rejected the first agreement announced in October 1991 [because it restricted the number of overseas judges who could sit on the Court's bench]. But the whole rationale for compromising with China then was that it ensured that the Court would be set up before 1997. When it came to obtaining China's agreement to the bill setting up the Court in 1995—the so-called 'second agreement'—Britain accepted that it would not be formed until after 30 June 1997. So they even gave that away.

Apart from the handover in June 1997, the most important event of the 1990s has been the elections and the development of Hong Kong's political system. It is clear that the people of Hong Kong want democracy. There's no doubt about that. If Patten has achieved anything, he has at least opened up the legislature, so that the people of Hong Kong are now used to at least a modest degree of democracy. I can see that collectively the legislature has matured over the years.

The 1990s has seen the development of a political culture: just look at the number of political parties since my original party, the United Democrats of Hong Kong, was formed in 1990. Over a dozen have emerged since. It's been a chain reaction.

In 1991, for the first direct elections to the Legislative Council, the United Democrats, my party at the time, was new. It was the best organized party—apart from the Communist Party, which didn't seek open elections under that name. We brought all the liberal-minded democrats together under one party umbrella, so we were the largest political grouping, and clearly had the best candidates. We therefore expected to do well, but the local branch of the New China News Agency [China's de facto embassy in Hong Kong] helped us to do better. They were urging people to vote for those who would not cause division and confrontation with China. Hong Kong people rejected that. It was partly a reaction to the aftermath of June 4th when a million people took to the streets in Hong Kong. The democratic movement in the Soviet Union was also beginning to stir around that time and I think that also helped. I did expect to do well in those elections, but I was still surprised at the extent of our success. [The United Democrats and pro-democracy legislators clinched seventeen out of eighteen of the democratically elected seats, and Martin Lee won 74,000 votes, the highest number of votes cast for any candidate.]

The 1995 elections were four years down the road. Everybody said that the so-called 'Tiananmen Square effect' would have completely worn off, and, as we got closer to 1997, people would be extremely reluctant to support a party seen as confrontational towards China. China again urged voters not to support my party, the Democrats, but to vote for the pro-China candidates who could have dialogue with Beijing. I remember that the opponent in my constituency was a political unknown. But in our first public debate she said, 'Mr Lee, why should people elect you? China won't talk to you, whereas I can go to Beijing any day I want to. You cannot even go over the Lo Wu border crossing from Hong Kong into Shenzhen.'

She was right. I had no answer and I became extremely concerned. The argument that 'it was better to work with China than fight with China' was gaining ground. I knew I was sure of success in my own constituency, but, if the same tactic was used in other debates, I was worried that this would affect the chances of my fellow party members. I spent an entire day thinking about it until I had formulated a party response. We argued that if you looked back at our track record of times when we had spoken up against China, every time it was because China had been violating the Joint Declaration. We said, 'If you are not even brave enough to defend the Joint Declaration, you should have no place in the Legislative Council.' Ultimately, dialogue with China became a minus in the election debate. That was why we did so well, and it was a great deal better than we had ever envisaged.

We thought we would win fifteen seats because we had only twenty-five candidates, and two of them were just last-minute additions put up for tactical reasons. So really there were twenty-three, and we expected to win fifteen. We clinched nineteen. Initially, we had no idea of the extent of our victory. At a press conference after the release of the exit poll results, I was just so happy that we had succeeded in winning nineteen seats, but I thought that, even if you counted all the pro-democracy candidates, we were still in the minority—although a very strong minority.

In the middle of the night my aide rang and said, 'Martin, we've won!'

I said, 'Yes, nineteen seats.'

She said, 'No, no, we've won.'

I said, 'What do you mean?'.

It transpired that we had miscounted. When we examined the results more carefully, we calculated that the pro-democracy forces had won thirty-one out of the sixty seats. We had a working majority! Nobody had even considered that possibility. The most we expected to accumulate was twenty-six seats.

Early the next morning, I woke up in a cold sweat. The reality hit me. I thought, 'We've got thirty-one, so what does it mean?' It meant that we were not just a voice in opposition, a pressure group. With a majority in the Legislative Council, we were really going to have to be responsible for our actions.

I had honestly thought that in 1995, the China factor was going to count against us and that was why I had never set our hopes too high. I thought most people in Hong Kong would be scared and would have bought the Beijing line. They didn't. I was ecstatically happy because the election results exceeded our wildest dreams. In a way I feel ashamed that I didn't have more confidence in my own people. But they stood firm.

I hope that I am not being too optimistic, but I think I am going to be able to preserve that support in the future. I have a feeling that, when 1997 is finally here, you may actually find more unity among the people of Hong Kong who have, for whatever reasons, decided to stay here. I think a 'people in the same boat', sort of mentality may begin to emerge. So ordinary citizens may be prepared to do a little more to preserve their own liberties, rather than sit back and say, 'All right, let the likes of Martin Lee do it for us.'

I'm confident that, ultimately, there will be changes for the better in China. In the meantime nobody knows what will happen. Initially the situation could change for the worse. I don't think even the leaders of China know, which perhaps explains why they have adopted such a hard line policy: they are all trying to protect themselves.

I just don't know what will happen to me. My wife wants us to make plans for the future, but the Chinese have an expression, *gin bo hang bo*: you see one step, you walk that step, you see another step, you walk another step. I don't know what will happen tomorrow. All I do know is that I will stay in Hong Kong.

I say, 'Martin Lee is not my problem, he is their problem, because I'm perfectly happy with Martin Lee the way he is, and I will continue to be in Hong Kong. It's they who don't want me, so it's for them to think of a way to get rid of me.'

Anson Chan

Managing the Civil Service

Despite the many differences between the Chinese and British Governments during the 1990s over the definition of 'the best interests of Hong Kong', there is one point upon which both agreed: maintaining stability in Hong Kong throughout the transition must be a top priority. Hong Kong's future livelihood depends upon the smooth and continued functioning of government. Thus, the 190,000-strong civil service—the backbone of government and the key to the stability of Hong Kong— became the focus of attention.

At the same time, the civil service was beset with apprehension from within. Senior civil servants became concerned over their future after 1997, while the uniformed services worried about what the change of sovereignty would mean for them. A mass exodus of leadership and expertise could spell chaos. The person who has presided over the civil service during this 'age of anxiety' is Anson Chan Fang On Sang.

When Anson Chan was appointed to head the Hong Kong Civil Service, she was not only the first woman to hold the position, she was also the first ethnic Chinese. She has achieved a number of firsts during her rise through the ranks: in 1962 she was the first woman to join the civil service as an Administrative Officer, the first female head of department, and the first woman to reach the rank of policy secretary.

Anson Chan comes from a distinguished Shanghai family that moved to Hong Kong in 1948. Her grandfather fought with the Chinese nationalist forces against the Japanese. Her mother, Fang Zhaoling, is an internationally recognized artist. She, herself, is nobody's 'yes-man', and has earned a great deal of respect for her frankness and straightforward approach to dealing with problems. These qualities are not traditionally rewarded within bureaucracies, but they have served Anson Chan well, and made her the obvious choice for Chief Secretary during a time when Britain was emphasizing 'Hong Kong people ruling Hong Kong'.

Her career has not been without its blemishes, and she has been under fire to step down in the past. As Director of the Social Welfare Department in the early 1980s, she was criticized for her department's sometimes heavy-handed and clumsy approach. In the early 1990s, as Secretary for the Civil Service, Anson Chan also became embroiled in the Government's localization policy and the administration's decision to allow expatriate civil servants to switch to local terms.

Governor Patten's appointment of Anson Chan as Chief Secretary heralded the start of the transition of the civil service, as the top posts were hastily localized ahead of 1997 in line with the Basic Law. The localization process was not an easy task and the speed with which changes have had to be made has created tensions, especially amongst expatriate civil servants, as young and able, but less experienced Hong Kong Chinese civil servants have been promoted before and above them.

Anson Chan's calm and collected leadership has held the public sector together during this uncertain period. Her own future has also been the subject of much speculation ever since she emerged during the transition as one of the contenders for the job of the future Chief Executive.

I NEVER DREAMT of being the Chief Secretary. Early on in my career, I used to think, 'Well, it's really very difficult to try and balance a career with your role as a wife and mother.' I thought I'd be doing very well and I would be very contented if I reached, say, mid-stream in my career. Then that would be it, and I'd be happy to stop. But as you go along, you just take things in your stride and you progress.

I wouldn't describe myself as a very ambitious person. I'm not ambitious in the sense of wanting to succeed, irrespective of who you have to trample on the way. I'm ambitious in the sense that I've always been very conscious that no matter what you do, you have a duty to do it to the best of your ability. You have to do it in a way that is principled and doesn't go against your conscience. I think that's generally what's motivated me.

I've always taken things in my stride, and I reckon that if you have the ability, sooner or later this will be recognized. That is one of the great things about Hong Kong society, the degree of social mobility. Nowhere else, I think, would you find so many people irrespective of how humble their beginnings, able to move very rapidly up the social ladder. Hong Kong is a place, where, if you work hard, have the ability, and are determined to make a success, you can be successful. It has also been a place where, by and large, women probably have had more opportunities to do well than elsewhere.

I wouldn't say we were poor, but certainly when my father died we went through quite a difficult time financially. My sister and I both put ourselves through university, which in those days you had to repay after you had started work.

My younger days were reasonably carefree until my father died in 1950. We had only been in Hong Kong for two years, following our departure from Shanghai, and his death was totally unexpected. It wasn't as if he had been ill for a while. He had been admitted to hospital because he was unwell, and apparently something went wrong with the injection, and he died. I remember it very, very distinctly: we were in bed, and then suddenly there was a great deal of commotion. I heard a lot of crying. Everybody was in a terrible state of shock.

I was only ten years old and I grew up very quickly after that. My mother was left with eight of us, aged from one to eleven, quite a handful! She decided to go the UK, and she took my three brothers with her, which left my twin sister and me as the eldest at home.

We were brought up by my grandmother, who was a very resourceful and resilient woman, even though she was not educated. She didn't know how to read or write, but she had a strong personality and she held us all together. We are, even today, a very closely knit family, and it has been a source of great strength. I take a great deal of pride in that.

I joined the Hong Kong Government totally by chance. I had wanted to be a social worker. As it happened, I was able to realize my ambition of doing social work too, because I did eventually get to be the Head of the Social Welfare Department—much more quickly, I think, than if I had simply enrolled as a social worker! So God has a way of fixing things!

The civil service has changed a great deal over the years since I joined in 1962. Women then were only paid 75 per cent of a man's salary. We didn't get equal pay until 1975, and even then it was without any of the fringe benefits. We were given archaic arguments for not being put on an equal footing with the men. For instance, if we were married we were

not entitled to the housing
allowance: we were told
that it was a husband's
responsibility to provide
a roof over our heads!
After a few more years of
fruitless arguments with
the Government, we
decided to take matters
into our own hands, and a
group of us set up the
Association of Female
Senior Government Officers
to fight for equal fringe benefits. I

was one of the founding members and was Chairman for three
consecutive years. As far as trade unions go, we were reasonably
successful. It took another three years before we won our battle and
achieved everything we wanted. No doubt that was partly due to our
own efforts, but also I think it was very much a reflection of the
changing social attitudes during the late 1970s.

Life in the administrative service was in many ways much simpler in
the sixties and seventies. The Government decided what needed to be
done, and it was able to implement those decisions very quickly. I
believe that, in some ways, it was the absence of adversarial politics that
allowed Hong Kong to prosper economically.

Of course, that system suited that particular point in Hong Kong's
history. What I think any bureaucracy needs to be aware of is the need
to move with the times and reflect the changing aspirations of the
community. I think it's very natural, as Hong Kong has grown and
prospered, that people should wish to have more of a say in the way
government policy is formulated, and the way in which they are
governed. The civil service, generally, has coped extremely well with
this change.

At times some of my colleagues have felt very beleaguered, but I
think it's part of the change with which we have to learn to cope.
Fundamentally, what worries civil servants is that we have a structure
quite unlike any other democracy. We don't have the checks and

balances you find in a true democracy. There is a legislature composed of non-officials, so there is no Government voice in the legislature, and it certainly has no majority. So how does the Government get its business through? In the UK, the Government of the day has a majority in Parliament. Ministers are elected and have a real say in policies, and they defend those policies. Civil servants are just nameless people working behind the scenes to implement ministerial policy.

We don't have that. And I think this is what makes civil servants feel uncomfortable. They're spending more time having to formulate policies, explain those policies to the legislature, convince the legislature of the appropriateness of those policies, and then sell the policies. The civil service has to accept that role, though, if we want to be a more open Government.

Ideally, it would have been preferable if the Government had had more time to adjust to the changes towards greater representation. There were and are some officers, to be fair to them, who have genuinely felt that the pace of democratization has been too fast. But I think that what these people have ignored is that it is, after all, the people of Hong Kong who now want to see representative Government develop more quickly. It is ironic that we only moved further down the road towards a more representative Government in the last decade or so as a result of 1997. I don't suppose anybody could have anticipated the 1984 signing of the Joint Declaration or the Tiananmen Square protests. Of course, if one had known that those things were going to happen, a decision would probably have been taken much earlier to move more quickly down the road towards greater democracy.

I think that, given the situation we have now, civil servants would be far happier if there was more of a cooperative partnership developing with the legislature. Legislators have to accept that, ultimately, the Government is responsible for the good governance of Hong Kong. This doesn't mean, however, that only the Government has the right and the power to put forward policy proposals. We put forward policy proposals after very careful consideration, frequently as a result of extensive consultation exercises, either by publishing a paper, or through other means. We try to reflect, collectively, the wishes of the community, and so we take a broader view.

The greatest problem facing the civil service during the transition has been uncertainty at the personal level, particularly for those in senior posts. First, it's the uncertainty of whether they will have a job at all after 1997. Second, and more important on a more macro level, is the whole uncertainty about whether the civil service will survive intact in its current form after 1997.

What most civil servants value is the impartiality, the political neutrality of the civil service. The maintenance of a level playing field, not allowing political considerations to creep into decision-making or the awarding of contracts and franchises, and the extent to which the Chinese may or may not interfere in the internal workings of the civil service.

Some have said that localization of the civil service should have been stepped up at a much earlier stage and I would agree entirely. I'm sure that if it hadn't been for 1997, there would not have been a local Chief Secretary appointed in the early 1990s. Clearly, if we had moved a bit earlier, people would have had more exposure, more experience. This is not to say, though, that we're now at a stage in which inexperienced people are in positions of responsibility. I happen to believe that we currently have an extremely good, first-class team which is well able to cope with the changes and the challenges post-1997.

Throughout the later stages of the transition I have tried to press this message home to China. I have been so keen for them to appreciate and to understand that the best thing is to have maximum continuity in the civil service. After all it does fulfill the underlying principle of the Joint Declaration and the Basic Law.

My greatest fear for the civil service in the future is corruption, particularly syndicated corruption, creeping back into the service. It's taken us all of twenty years to fight that—and I believe we've fought a very successful battle—and we want to keep the civil service clean. I don't see any dangers at the moment of this happening, but so much has to do with perception. You see, if civil servants perceive that after 1997, it's all right to be corrupt, it will very quickly permeate throughout the entire civil service. So you must really nip that in the bud. The message has to be reinforced constantly. It's extremely worrying that some surveys in the 1990s have shown how many young people are becoming more complacent and are taking a relaxed view over the acceptability of corruption.

The other concern I have for the future is that many government officials may decide to leave the service. It is a concern which is always with us. The extent to which the British Government has been able to reassure civil servants during the transition has decreased as 1997 has drawn nearer. Government officials have looked to the future sovereign power to give that necessary degree of assurance. That's why it has been important for Chinese officials to realize that their every act, their every utterance, has had an impact on civil service morale. One example was the suggestion that civil servants should come out openly and declare their support for the provisional legislature. This was extremely damaging and very unsettling. It reinforced fears, which already existed, over whether China would really allow the civil service to continue to operate impartially, free from political interference.

I have never had any ambition to be the post-1997 Chief Executive. Throughout my career I've always felt that I'll go where I'm wanted, where I feel I can do a reasonable job without undue interference. One of the good things about working in the administrative service, and this has been particularly so under the present Governor, is that you do at least feel that your views are given a fair hearing. You accept that your view doesn't always prevail, but, once a decision is made, all those involved at the senior level must pull together to defend that policy. No organization can survive if, as soon as a decision is made, all the other people involved go out and try to dismantle that decision. It's just not workable.

I would just hope that I am able to serve out the rest of my normal term, because I don't have to retire until the year 2000 when I'm sixty. It has been a particular honour to have been involved at this important and crucial stage of our history.

Jimmy Lai

Freedom and Information

When Governor Chris Patten, during a visit to the United States in 1996, criticized Hong Kong businessmen for fearing to stand up to Beijing and speak up for Hong Kong, he was not referring to Jimmy Lai. The colourful owner of the Chinese newspaper *Apple Daily*, Jimmy Lai is one of the wealthiest, but least conventional businessmen of the 1990s.

Jimmy Lai started life as a street urchin in Southern China and was one of the many penniless refugees who fled to Hong Kong in the 1960s. He made his fortune in clothing, founding one of Territory's biggest retail phenomena, Giordano. Outlets can be found on every other Hong Kong street corner.

One should not expect to see this businessman in a suit: his trademark outfit is jeans with braces, and a casual (probably a Giordano) shirt. At a time when others with big money have 'cosied up' to China to ensure continued economic success, Jimmy Lai has stood by his principles. He has remained a solid defender of democratic freedoms, speaking out against Beijing, even at the cost of his own business interests.

In 1989, he used his clothing company as a platform to support the movement for democracy in China, including printing T-shirts for pro-democracy activists. He became a popular figure, frequently seen at the side of leading democrat Martin Lee, with whom he has formed a close friendship.

Jimmy Lai's foray from the world of textiles into the media, came after the Tiananmen Square protests, when he launched the glossy *Next* magazine. *Next* was an almost instant success, renowned for its daring and spirited stories ranging from triads, sex, and sleaze, to politics. Some of the harsh anti-China rhetoric in *Next* has rankled. Beijing took punitive action against Giordano outlets in China in retaliation after *Next* dared to describe Chinese Premier Li Peng as a 'son of a turtle's egg'—a Chinese euphemism for 'bastard'.

Jimmy Lai founded the independent, Chinese-language *Apple Daily* newspaper in 1995. This was seen as a bold move, in both economic and political terms. Against all odds, however, the paper was able to carve a deep niche in an already extremely competitive market. Hong Kong has one of the largest number of newspapers for the size of its population in the world, with nearly forty Chinese-language dailies covering general news. The climate for journalism, however, has not been as liberal as the numbers would suggest. By 1995 many in the media behaved as if 1997 had already arrived. News executives were exercising self-censorship to such an extent that there were few truly independent voices. Always the exception, Jimmy Lai was not dissuaded.

ONE NIGHT, a while ago, I was reading the Old Testament. I often pick up the Bible, but that evening, as I was reading about Adam and Eve, a thought struck me.

I said to my wife, 'If Eve hadn't bitten the apple, the forbidden fruit, the world would not have news because people would not have any concept of right and wrong, or of evil and gossip. So the origin of news is the bite Eve took in the Garden of Eden.'

It was something of a joke with my wife, but when it came to naming my newspaper, I thought *Apple Daily* would be very appropriate.

To me, the newspaper was not a financial venture. The media business means a great deal more to me than just making money. We sell information, and the better informed people are, the better equipped they are to make informed choices in life. That means greater freedom. Freedom is fundamental to me, and I believe that we should be doing all we can to uphold the freedoms we have.

I feel very passionately about that because I was brought up in an atmosphere of oppression, fear, and chaos. All the adults in my family were sent off to labour camps where they didn't live like human beings. They were reduced to the basics of life, living in desperation with no hope, no aspirations for the future. My family was shattered after the Communists took over, and my own destiny changed dramatically.

I was born into a very wealthy Guangdong family a year before the Communist revolution. My parents had to suffer the humiliation of having once been a prominent and respected family, now being denounced as an enemy of the people and a curse. They spent most of my childhood caught up in the troubles, and I really had nobody to take care of me, except a partially handicapped uncle who taught me how to read. I was left to my own devices, and most of the time I just skipped school and took to the streets to try to make some money. I had four sisters: one of them was my twin and another had polio, so I felt I had to help support them. I was either selling something on the black market or stealing; sometimes I hustled people to help them with their luggage in the hope of a tip. I used to hang around restaurants, waiting until people had finished their dinner, so I could grab the leftovers. I was just trying to survive.

There was one day, when I was eleven years old, when I was extremely depressed. I was just sitting in the street, not really doing anything. A tricycle, carrying a man loaded down with bags and a suitcase, stopped close to where I was sitting. I jumped up wildly and helped the guy off the tricycle and offered to carry his bags. He gave me a bar of something to eat as a tip, instead of money. I took a bite and could not believe it! I had never tasted anything so delicious. I ask the man what it was. He said, 'It's chocolate'. There were quite a few tourists coming to Guangdong in the late fifties, and they often brought goodies which were impossible to obtain in China. I asked the man where he was from and he told me 'Hong Kong'. It sent a chill down my spine: from that moment I wanted to go to Hong Kong, regardless of the risks.

At first my mother thought it was a crazy idea, but, after pestering her for nearly three months, I eventually applied for a permit to go to Macau. From Macau I was smuggled in the bottom of a fishing boat to Hong Kong. I was taken to my relatives who paid HK$370 to the smuggler. The next day I started work in a factory as an odd-job worker. That was in 1961. I was earning HK$60 a month, and I lived in the factory.

The conditions, in hindsight, were dreadful, but, given my past experience, it was just like paradise! I was never hungry. I had enough to eat and HK$60 a month was a lot of money. I could buy things to eat: it was just eat, eat, eat!

However, I treasured most something more basic and fundamental: the freedom I had, the hope I had. I knew then there was a future for me, and I was very happy.

I became general manager of a big factory before I was twenty, and, by the early 1980s, I had my own joint venture company which became the biggest sweater-knitting factory in Hong Kong. In 1981, I launched my clothing company, Giordano.

It hadn't been my ambition to become wealthy, but once I started to make money my ego inflated. Fortune went to my head, and I began to think I could do anything I wanted. I made a real mess of Giordano to start with because I didn't know what to do. The company was ego-driven rather than consumer-driven. I was totally ignorant of the business, and I was not interested in learning. It was doomed to fail. By 1986 I knew I would either have to close the company or restructure it.

Ultimately, I was able to turn the company's fortune around, but it was only through trial and error, and that has dominated my business philosophy ever since. Over the years, I have learnt that few people know, when they first start off, how to run a business or what is right, but you learn by your mistakes. It's only when one makes a mistake that one can learn and move forward. Nowadays I always tell my people that when you come to work for me you have to have the guts to stumble and discover what is right. I've always tried to make them feel comfortable about making mistakes because, through that process, they can derive the information to know what they can and cannot do.

This is not a traditional Chinese way of looking at things. Most people are taught not to make mistakes. When I hire very senior people I talk to them for a couple of hours. They are stunned. They say, 'You are paying a lot of money because I have previous experience as a manager, yet you tell me to forget all I've learnt in the past. If I forget about what I've learnt, you might as well hire someone who has no experience!'

I tell them that success doesn't repeat itself, but mistakes do. What I am paying for is the experience gained from making mistakes and the ability to read the message in every mistake. That way I save a lot of money.

I have also taken advantage of many Western companies' innovations and adapted them to my own business. This contributed to Giordano's success. One of the companies I took the lead from was a fast-food chain. I wanted to find out why it had done so well in Hong Kong, and discovered that it was partly because it had a very limited menu. The simpler the business, the more efficient you are, and the quicker you can respond to market demands.

As a result of looking at that company's operations, we cut Giordano's product line from two hundred to fifty items. However, that gave us another headache: people found our clothing range too dull, and didn't return to the shops very often. I then adapted another company's idea of using colourful products. I began manufacturing garments in thirty different shades instead of just four. It was a successful formula; we extended the range of colours instead of increasing the product range, and it cost us nothing!

In 1992, we opened up into China. I spent a year launching the business there. It is no easy task doing business in China.

The main problem is the lack of trust and the little respect which is given to the law. Law based on objective standards of personal liberty is not a tradition in Chinese society; instead Chinese law is based on one's subjective conscience. This is not law. Chinese society was based on social norms of trust, family loyalty, and community networks, but that has all been destroyed by Communism, and there has been nothing to replace it. Communism has destroyed traditional ethics. This means, for example, that there is no guarantee that contracts will be honoured.

Most companies wanting to do business in China believe that the higher the level of official contacts you have, the more successful your business ventures will be. They believe that these officials will open up avenues and get you a 'good deal'. However, this can restrict your operations in China because your business is then dominated and monopolized by the interests of that particular official. The businesses at the end of the day may be successful, but I question whether it is worth all the heartache of cutting through the red tape, and whether the financial returns are really all that great.

When I planned to launch Giordano in China, I had no openings with high-ranking officials, but believed that working at a lower level, with the men on the ground, would be more successful. Again it was a question of trial and error, but we did a great deal of research finding shops in what we believed were good locations but which were losing money. We went into joint ventures with the owners, in which they were the silent partners, with the guarantee of a fixed income in return for the lease of the shop.

We were successful until political factors came into play. Two years after opening our shops in China, I had to sell my controlling stake in the company because the Chinese authorities were harassing my mainland business and intimidating my employees. This was after a controversial article, criticizing the Chinese Premier Li Peng, had appeared in my magazine, *Next*.

In 1996, I sold my remaining interest in Giordano but, despite that, two months after the sale, the authorities in China closed down more of the company's shops. To me it was a clear message to the Hong Kong investor: don't upset China. Why should the Chinese authorities want to take action against a company which I no longer even owned? I believe that Beijing is trying to isolate me and force the closure of my businesses by frightening off people from investing in any of my companies in the future. This has been sparked by the role I played during Tiananmen and the publishing ventures I subsequently set up.

I was very moved and touched by what the students in China were trying to achieve in 1989, and I admired their courage to stand up and fight for greater freedom. I empathized with the student movement, and I was able to relate to China in a way I had never been able to do before. It was as if China was my mother, but I'd never been able to talk to her until then. I was very excited and I wanted to be part of the change which I thought was about to happen. I did many things in support of the pro-democracy movement in China. I donated money, I used Giordano to display banners and print T-shirts, and I was very outspoken in my views.

It was after the intense media coverage I received at the time that I appreciated the importance of the media. In 1990 I started *Next* magazine, which, despite being a glossy publication, is respected in the market for having the courage to take a stand on issues and to speak out. We have attacked China a great deal, but I have never had any regrets about what we have published as it reflects my true sentiments.

In contrast, I found myself becoming conscious of increasing self-censorship in the media generally as 1997 came closer. Newspaper readership was dropping and I knew that this was illogical. I realized then that

many newspapers were slowly alien-
ating their readers by their kow-
towing stance, and I saw an opportunity for a new independent
voice. There was a vacuum to fill,
and I took up that challenge with
the launch of *Apple Daily* in 1995.

I believe that information may be
a saving grace in the future. If China
tackles something unjustly or wrongly in Hong Kong after 1997 they will
be doing it in the face of world opinion. If China treasures Hong Kong,
and is smart enough, it should react
quickly. This makes me optimistic
about the future because the force of
information is increasing every day.

Information is not just the only key to
Hong Kong's future success; essential will
also be the maintenance of a firm structure of law
and order, and a free market economy. Hong Kong will be finished if
either is diluted or even destroyed.

Business in Hong Kong has traditionally had a very big say in the way
in which Hong Kong has been run under the British colonial
administration. My fear is that the cosy relationship between the
tycoons and the Government will expand after 1997 when the Chinese
take over. This could lead to a great deal more Government interference
in the way business is conducted, and spell the end of non-intervention
in the market. The problems of doing business in China could spill over
into Hong Kong. The way of doing business and the cost of doing
business will be different.

I hope that the Chinese are smart enough to keep the 'Chinese wall'
between Hong Kong and the Mainland, but this might be too idealistic.
If the Chinese interfere here and make changes, Hong Kong is very
likely to melt, because it's so small in comparison with China. It's just
like a small ice-cube next to a big oven: if a lot of heat is induced, Hong

Kong will melt and become part of China. It will be no different, then, from any other part of the Mainland. Hong Kong then wouldn't be any good for China.

I have to face reality. The Chinese, if they want to, can stop my business anytime. What the hell can I do? I have to face the repercussions of my actions. They could strangle me and force the closure of businesses; they could, for example, make it very difficult for me to continue publishing my newspaper [for example, by preventing Chinese companies from advertising in the paper]. In the end, if I have to close *Apple Daily* down, I will close it down. But I won't do so without putting up a fight.

What I'm trying to do is gather resources which will have the strength to stand up to the changes of 1997. Self-censorship or diluting the news achieves nothing. On the other hand, there is no need to be deliberately anti-China. It is better to love what we love, without hating those who oppose it. We have to do that for the sake of Hong Kong.

I don't have a goal in life. The future is always uncertain and you never know what hurdles lie ahead, so it is futile to set yourself a goal. I solve my problems day by day, and, as long as I am moving forward, it does not matter where I arrive eventually. I think this is typical of a survivor. I learnt from a very young age not to look beyond the immediate problems because if those weren't solved I might not even have a meal that night.

Rosa Mok & Isaac Lung

Voices of the Future

S tudents in Hong Kong in the 1990s have been described as radical and
politically apathetic in almost the same breath. It would be fair to say,
however, that the majority are more concerned with their studies than with
political demonstrations. The fervour which led the whole community to
rally in support of the student movement in China in 1989 appeared to
wane several years later. According to student leader Rosa Mok Pui Han,
the sentiments still exist: many are just too afraid to speak out.

Student identity and involvement in political affairs first emerged in the
1960s during the 1967 riots, when 'leftists' spurred on by the Cultural
Revolution in China rose up against the 'oppressive colonial regime' in
Hong Kong. During the 1970s there were a number of movements which
unified the students, in particular the campaign in support of China over
sovereignty of the Diaoyu Islands, to which Japan also laid claim. By the
late 1970s, however, there was little which brought the student movement
together until the 1989 democracy movement in Beijing. Even the talks on
Hong Kong's future had failed until then to agitate a great deal of
passionate debate among students in the universities.

Rosa Mok studied social work at the University of Hong Kong, and by
the mid-1990s she had emerged as one of the more outspoken leaders of the
Hong Kong Federation of Students, the umbrella organization for all the
university student unions in Hong Kong. She has been one of the few
prepared to speak out. She hit the headlines in 1996 with her involvement
in a student protest against plans for a Provisional Legislature, which
Beijing had vowed to set up in 1997, to replace the legislature elected in
1995. The student protests were staged during a highly publicized meeting
between the student leaders and Chinese officials in Hong Kong.

In contrast, Isaac Lung is typical of the vast majority of students who
have little interest in politics, but were compelled nonetheless to take to the
streets to protest in 1989. Like many students, he was rueful but resigned
about the way in which China and Britain negotiated the handover. A
recent graduate of Hong Kong's Lingnan College, he has held to the belief

that politics should be left to the politicians. To him the most important thing to accomplish as a student was to achieve the best results possible through sheer hard work. He concedes that it may be the education system, itself, which has bred political apathy, because there is scant discussion of politics built into primary and secondary school curricula. Hong Kong's few universities, while rarely hopping with radical activism, were fertile ground for political discussion in the 1960s and 1970s when the times demanded it (as Tsang Yok Sing has attested in this book). They have since become more subdued, but will continue to thrive whilst students like Rosa Mok are still fighting.

ROSA MOK

I WAS BORN and brought up in Hong Kong, as were my parents, so I suppose you could say that I am a third generation Hong Kong person. There was nothing particularly special about my family background: I was just a normal student. I was brought up in Kowloon East on a large public housing estate, and I went to school near there as well.

Rosa Mok (centre) commemorating 4 June.

My parents had mixed feelings when I qualified to go to Hong Kong University. On the one hand they were obviously pleased, but on the other, it presented financial problems for us. My father had not been very well, and they were relying on me as the eldest to start earning some money to help support the family. They didn't try and dissuade me from going to university, and I respected them for that. The problem really arose when I decided to change course after my first year at university and study social work. That meant one more year of my studying, and that was when they got upset. I understood how they felt, and I guess I felt bad, but it didn't stop me from changing course, as I realized that was what I really wanted to do.

There hadn't been any political influence on me from my family, yet my involvement in politics started before I went to university. I am not sure what prodded my interest, except when I was a Form 6 student I helped organize a series of civic education programmes in the school. I went to the Civic Education Committee library where they had a collection of newspaper cuttings and some of the Government policy papers. I found it all fascinating reading and I ended up spending the whole day in that library. I didn't think then that I was studying political issues: to me they were just subjects which affected our daily lives, and which I was interested in reading more about.

Politics was quite a taboo subject in schools, never really discussed by anyone. That all changed though in 1989, when I was sixteen years old.

Tiananmen and the suppression of the student movement had an enormous impact on the whole school. None of my classmates nor I attended our lessons. We spent the whole day discussing 'democracy', what it was all about and what it meant. It was really the first time I had thought about what it meant, even though I had heard the word many times. Some of the teachers joined in our discussions and helped to explain some of the concepts to us, and they gave us some historical background and analysis so that we might understand more about China's cultural background and history. After that I was interested to learn more about Chinese culture and the characteristics of its people.

It wasn't just in school that the events in Beijing impacted on my life, it was at home too. My parents had never been politically involved, and yet, for some days before 4 June and the suppression of the student movement, the whole family was glued to the television to find out the latest news from Beijing. We were all following the events as they unfurled, step by step, and were all extremely concerned about what was happening in China. We were living in hope that the student movement would lead to fundamental changes in China, not just politically. I couldn't conceive at that time how I wanted the country to change, just that I wanted it to happen, for the better, of course.

The impact of the student movement in China on my school and family affected me deeply. It may sound silly now, but I felt that I just had to do something.

I started to pour out all my own personal feelings into letters and articles I wrote, which I intended sending to the authorities in Beijing, as well as to ordinary citizens in China. I was simply going to fax them to any number I could get hold of, or send them to any address I could find. In the end, my mother discovered what I was planning, and she stopped me from mailing the letters. It wasn't because she disagreed with what I was doing, but because she was afraid that maybe we might hurt somebody, and get them into trouble for receiving such letters. I hadn't thought of that, but, although I didn't think my mother was right, I still did as she told me, and I have kept everything that I wrote at the time.

After that, I was so frustrated and I felt so helpless. I kept wondering how come the people in Beijing, the students, the ordinary citizens, were willing to sacrifice their lives? What was it that drove them to take up such a challenge—to confront the Chinese Communist Party? These were unending questions for me. They were issues in my heart which I couldn't really comprehend.

I attended one forum at which both Martin Lee and Szeto Wah were speaking. [They were the two leaders of the democracy movement in Hong Kong and founder members of the Hong Kong Alliance in Support of the Patriotic Democratic Movement in China, denounced as 'subversive' by Beijing.] Over the years, many speakers had come to give lectures while I was at school, including Martin Lee and Szeto Wah, but never before had I heard someone give a speech like the one Szeto Wah gave on that day. I was extremely moved. He spoke about Hong Kong's future, and it was then that, as far as I was concerned, political seeds were sown.

However, despite this, I was not particularly active in politics immediately after that. Even during my first year at university, two years later in the early 1990s, I spent time just listening to the debates which were going on around me, but not really participating. I realized though that Hong Kong faced a great many challenges in the future, and the better grasp I had of what was happening in the political arena, the more I wanted to become involved. At the end of my first year at university, I decided to run for President of Hong Kong University's Student Union, and I won.

The main issue I was dealing with that year was the selection of the new Vice Chancellor of the university. I think I learnt more then about what political life was like, and what a dirty world it could really be, than I would have picked up anywhere else!

Our concern was over the selection process. The students were not allowed any voting rights and no involvement in choosing the new Vice Chancellor. It was an issue which was debated long and hard during student union meetings. We felt that students were a major component of the university, but on the selection committee for the new Vice Chancellor, there were four committee members from outside the university, and yet no student representative. The university administrators should have realized that we also had our own ideals and expectations of how the university should develop, but we were just told that we were 'ignorant'.

I remember an incident when I was telephoned by one of the selection committee members one evening. That person told me that I knew nothing. 'You are just a student,' he said, 'You would be better spending your time studying because you are ignorant.' I was crying as he spoke, I felt so insulted by his remarks. In fact, I couldn't believe what I was hearing, and this wasn't even in a meeting.

What upset me even more was that our motives were generally interpreted that we were actually favouring one candidate over another, and that was why we were demanding a say in selection process. But it was really a question of principle.

The whole issue of the selection of the future Vice Chancellor took up all my time as President of the HKU Student Union, and I had had no time to concentrate on what I wanted to be involved with most, the future of Hong Kong and 1997. So in 1995 I joined [the umbrella organization] the Federation of Students.

One interesting thing I have found since I have joined the Federation is that six or seven years after Tiananmen, students generally are just not so interested in politics nor are they really concerned about their future. I think one of the problems is not that they are uninterested, it's more that they are afraid to speak about it.

At the university, for example, every year around 4 June, students are invited to write about their feelings and comments on Tiananmen now.

Some students write a short contribution, but many do not want to have any part in any of the commemorations to mark the event, even though they joined the demonstrations in 1989. They deny that they even took part in any actions then. It is too sensitive a topic for most.

I feel it's quite odd, because those students who do participate in any political activity are automatically labelled 'radicals'. Yet when I speak to students privately, many tell me, 'Yes, I agree with you and I support what you are doing, but I'm not prepared to take action.' I think it's a cultural problem. Hong Kong people are not used to being assertive, and they do not know how to express themselves.

The other point is that while some students are too afraid to speak out, others genuinely are uninterested in political issues, and that goes back to the fact that people here are more interested in making money. I have been very disappointed when I have been invited back to speak at my old school, to advise the older children about their future careers, and which university course to choose. They are generally only interested in the vocational courses. I am always asked about the qualifications needed for accounting, business administration, computer engineering, and the like. I take a long time to try and explain that it doesn't matter how much money they might earn at the end of the course, if they are not interested in their studies, their student lives will be miserable, and they will gain none of the other benefits of a higher education.

I have experienced the same apathetic attitude with other issues the Federation of Students has tackled, not just those associated with Tiananmen. These have included student welfare, the level of tuition fees, and the setting up of the Provisional Legislature in 1997 and the selection of the first post-1997 Chief Executive. Overall only a very small minority of students have participated in any of the activities which we have organized, although again, privately, many have told me that they supported what we were doing, but preferred others to articulate their views for them. They are not prepared to come out themselves. We have tried to stimulate a more academic debate, on the legality of the Provisional Legislature, for example, but most of my classmates have just said to me, 'So what if there's a Provisional Legislature?'

One of my personal concerns has been the future of academic freedom after 1997. I seriously question whether the university Vice Chancellors who sit on the Preparatory Committee would support academic freedom, judging by their performance on the Committee. I just wonder how principled they would be if faced with certain threats in the future, such as a cut in funding. Some question whether I am just being too cynical, but it is a real threat. I attended a lecture course in politics, and, right at the end of the last talk, the lecturer said there were some people who had been sitting at the back of the hall, who had attended that particular lecture, and whom he believed were not students at all. According to him they were from Xinhua [the New China News Agency in Hong Kong]. I have no idea whether he was right or not, but it was a worrying thought and could intimidate academics in the future. Maybe they were just coming to learn? I hope so.

Things have been changing though. A number of lecturers have left Hong Kong in the last few years before the transition—both local and expatriate. Not all of them have been retirement age and that indicates something to me.

The other feature of student life in the 1990s is the way that both democratic and pro-China political parties have been active on the campus, trying to attract new members. As a student union member, I have had no part in their activities, but they have tried to encourage students to distribute leaflets for them, and party members have attended fora organized by the students, not as speakers, but as part of the audience.

My parents have worried a great deal about my involvement in student politics. They think it is extremely dangerous, and they are afraid I might be imprisoned one day! They have never lived in China, so they have no basis for the fears they have. I suppose their views on the Communist regime go back to the Cultural Revolution and the bad impression they had of China at the time, especially as they saw so many refugees fleeing across the border into Hong Kong.

My prime aim for the future at the moment is to concentrate on my social welfare studies and to consolidate my concept of society and community. I have many small pieces, like a puzzle, but I cannot yet complete the picture, so I have no plans to join any political party at the moment.

My own feelings for the future are quite complicated. I have a sense of belonging and I want to do something for Hong Kong, but I don't know what. I feel that if the leading lights in the democracy movement, like Martin Lee and Szeto Wah, are stifled, then the people from my generation will have an important role to play. I am willing to stand up and speak out. If I stepped back, I would not be personally fulfilled. I worry about the future and what we can do about it.

ISAAC LUNG

MANY STUDENTS IN Hong Kong do not have strong feelings or opinions about political issues. This is one of the downsides of living in a colonial system which just focuses people's interest and motivation on business and money rather than on politics.

There was considerable political debate in the universities in the sixties and seventies, but this has cooled down because nowadays students' critical faculties are repressed right from primary school. The school system in Hong Kong replicates the colonial political system. The emphasis is on maintaining the status quo. Even in secondary school the teachers tell students they are too immature to deal with and understand political issues. I suspect it's easier to control them that way. The result is that only a minority of university students are really concerned about broader issues affecting our society.

The whole education system is a failure and needs to be overhauled. Without changes at the macro level, the present authoritarian system can be very easily manipulated by those who want to indoctrinate students. The Government needs to take a lead in this because endless debate will not bring about significant structural change.

There must also be changes at the micro level because the present system cannot even teach me how to master my own mother tongue! The debate is not really about which language or languages should be officially taught in schools, but rather how language skills—and other subjects—ought to be taught. If things continue as at present, the next couple of generations will be illiterate.

Nowadays a lot of students come from China to study in Hong Kong, and such interaction is clearly good for both places. Many of these immigrant students are brilliant and more motivated than their Hong Kong counterparts because of pressure from their parents to work very hard, achieve success, and become outstanding in Hong Kong, or continue their studies in the United States. But they have little or no interest in, or knowledge of, politics and social issues in Hong Kong other than that in 1997 Hong Kong's sovereignty will revert to China.

The 1997 issue was not of much significance to me or my friends when we were at secondary school in the 1980s. But the events of June 4th did have a considerable impact on us all. What happened that month made me grow up.

I spent all of the evening of 3 June watching television with my family. We saw the flares go out and all of Tiananmen Square was very dark with nobody making a noise. We were just lost for words, and I think all of us were stunned.

At the time my feeling was that we were doomed. Although I was only a secondary school student, I had an affinity with those university students in Beijing. I didn't understand very much about their political objectives but, deep in my heart, I knew that what they were fighting for was for the good of China. I did not believe that the Chinese Government would use the army or heavy weapons to attack them. I wondered what hope was there for us if Hong Kong was to be ruled by such people.

Like many other Hong Kong people, I went with some of my friends to protest on the streets. It was very moving. Years later it is important that we continue to remember. We have to keep the pressure up on the Chinese Government to ensure such a sad event never happens again.

I am sure that after 1997 there will be less academic freedom than at present and it will be confined to academic circles. If academics voice their opinions on social or political issues in public and in the media, I think they will definitely experience some pressure to exercise restraint. I'm not as pessimistic as some people are about the future, though we have to realize that the basic principles of the Communist Party will never change. It may appear in another form, but it will never change.

Lo Tak Shing
Political Realism

Most Hong Kong politicians in the 1990s eschew the loaded terms 'pro-British', or 'pro-China', and prefer to be considered 'pro-Hong Kong'. For some, the very definition of patriotism is support for Hong Kong's future with China, and that means support for and cooperation with Beijing before and after the handover on 1 July 1997. Lo Tak Shing takes this view, and has won both friends and enemies for his stance.

Some consider him the man who 'jumped ship' in 1984. An Oxford-educated lawyer, he was decorated as a Commander of the British Empire, and appointed as both a Legislative and an Executive Councillor. He resigned from both bodies after the signing of the Joint Declaration, accusing Britain of selling out Hong Kong. Lo Tak Shing believes that full British citizenship should have been granted to all British passport holders in Hong Kong.

In what many people saw as a complete turnaround, Lo Tak Shing accepted an invitation to serve as an adviser to Beijing, and, since then, has been a leading and outspoken member of the 'pro-China' camp. His name has come up repeatedly in the mid-1990s as a candidate for the post of Chief Executive after 1997. He gave up his British nationality in the early 1990s in favour of a Chinese passport, as a sign of loyalty to the future sovereign power.

In many respects, Lo Tak Shing, who was born into a highly respected Eurasian family, has followed in his father's footsteps. His father Man Kam Lo, also an English-educated lawyer with his own law firm in Hong Kong, was appointed to the Legislative Council in the mid-1930s, and eventually became the Senior Executive Councillor.

Lo Tak Shing was appointed by Governor MacLehose to the Legislative Council in the mid-1970s and to the Executive Council in 1980. After his resignation, he set up his own emigration advisory company, a move which many feel contradicted the faith he later proclaimed to have in Hong Kong's future. His conversion may have been a natural result of his feeling of betrayal by London, but he was not immediately embraced by Beijing. He was passed by for the Basic Law Drafting Committee in 1985 and named instead, as a consolation prize, for the Consultative Committee, a body set up to solicit public opinion on the Basic Law. Since then he has forged good relations with top senior cadres in Beijing. He was appointed to the Preliminary Working Committee, and then the Preparatory Committee, both of which were set up by China to oversee the transition.

Lo Tak Shing was one of the first local people to pay a 'friendly' visit to Beijing following the events of 4 June 1989. In the early 1990s he invested a great deal of money to found the weekly English-language magazine, *Window*, widely seen as a mouthpiece of Beijing. He also established his own political party, the New Hong Kong Alliance, a conservative business group. Whether one calls him 'pro-China', a Hong Kong patriot, or a turncoat, he considers himself simply a practical man.

WE ARE AN OLD Hong Kong family with a long association of doing things for Hong Kong. We have been involved with government and administrative affairs, although not strictly speaking with political matters. My father was an extraordinary person, who came first in his Law Society finals without ever having been to university. He set up his own law firm, and went on to become a member of the Executive and Legislative Councils, before and after the Japanese occupation. I suppose I inherited the family tradition of community service, and in Hong Kong, it's in the blood. I never felt this sense of community responsibility outside Hong Kong, in Britain for instance.

My father told me that one of his most important jobs was rice controller after the war. In those days people were speculating in rice. From time to time, they made use of rumours of shortages to increase the price. People used to get really quite scared, and prices rocketed sky-high. My father was asked to devise a system which would prevent these major price fluctuations, and stabilize the community. What he did was very simple. He licensed rice importers, and made it a condition of the licence that they keep a six-month supply of rice in Hong Kong. Whenever there was a run on rice, the Government simply ordered the importers to sell, which brought down the price immediately. It was a very effective system, and is still more or less in place, although there is no need to keep so much in stock—now we eat bread and hamburgers!

Although my background is Eurasian, I don't think that has affected my role and position in China. China is accustomed to minorities, and, unlike people in smaller countries, the mainland Chinese are not particularly racially conscious.

I'm rather tired of those who suggest that in 1984 I switched from being a member of the British colonial establishment to being an adviser to China. I never changed sides at all. My family has always worked for this community. When Britain and China decided to return Hong Kong to China, it was clear that if one wanted to do anything for Hong Kong one would have to get along with the future sovereign. This was not difficult since naturally the future sovereign's interest coincides exactly with Hong Kong's, whereas the outgoing sovereign's did not. To switch allegiance from British to Chinese sovereignty was, in effect, what the Joint Declaration required of everyone in Hong Kong. It wasn't a question of waiting until 1997 to do this, but in 1984 when the Joint Declaration was signed, it was clear then that the people of Hong Kong had to start working towards the system that would be in place in twelve years time.

I went up to Beijing in 1985 because I had to make up my mind whether or not I wanted to stay in Hong Kong. I met many people and, by the end of my five-day visit, I felt sufficiently relaxed to decide to stay in Hong Kong after 1997. Like everyone else, at first I had fears about the Communist Government, but as far as I was concerned my worries were dispelled following that trip to Beijing.

The people I met persuaded me by their behaviour, by their reaction that they were dedicated people, dedicated to China certainly. And they really did need the support of people who were interested in, who had a feel for, who loved Hong Kong, to give them a helping hand.

I came to those conclusions although I was in a better position than most at the time: I had a British passport. There was no difficulty about my emigrating, but there were very many people who did not have this alternative. So, in line with family tradition, I felt I had to do something. In 1985, not long after the signing of the Joint Declaration, I set up the Freedom Movement Company which helped people get passports and emigrate, if that was what they wanted to do. I don't want to belabour the point, but Britain had frightened everybody here by cutting down the nationality rights of British Hong Kong subjects. They did this by depriving them of their right of abode in Britain. Even though Britain had been doing this gradually since 1961, it was not finally brought home to Hong Kong people until the early 1980s. The company helped many people, frightened by the prospect of change and frightened by Britain closing its doors, to obtain foreign passports. I'm pleased to see that many are now coming back to live happily in Hong Kong.

Since my 1985 trip to Beijing I have readily given advice to China, mostly related to Hong Kong's longer-term future. I advised China against setting up an Airport Authority that was wholly independent of the Government. I wanted to see this operation as very much a part of the Government of Hong Kong. It seemed ludicrous for Hong Kong to have an Airport Authority entirely segregated from the present Government, and the SAR Government. More recently I have been giving advice to China to try and prevent the harbour from being filled in by land reclamation. The harbour is Hong Kong.

For me the events of 1989 were very frightening because of their destabilizing impact on China, and their effect on Hong Kong. At that time, the key thing in my mind, and the minds of the Chinese leaders whom I met, was stability. What we need in Hong Kong is a stable China, and Hong Kong can contribute to China's stability by keeping well out of Beijing's politics. The demonstrations which took place in Hong Kong in 1989 did not send China the right signal that we were distancing ourselves from mainland politics. Indeed, the money which was sent from Hong Kong to [students in] Beijing prior to June 4th induced many people who had already left to go back to Tiananmen Square to get a slice of the pie! No one likes to see bloodshed. Stability in China will surely bring a better life to people there and mainland stability is also what Hong Kong needs.

Tiananmen affected Hong Kong in other ways. It ultimately led to a change in British policy which saw the arrival of Chris Patten as Governor.

I think it was very unfortunate that the possibility of having a 'through-train' [by which the constitutional systems in place before 1997 would remain after the transfer of sovereignty] was derailed as a result of the policies implemented by Chris Patten. I wasn't involved in the actual negotiations, and I don't know precisely what Mr Patten did or didn't do. I have no idea whether it was due to ill will on his part, or that he was merely pig-headed, or that he was complying strictly with British Government policy. In any case it seemed so childish and nobody gained—not Hong Kong, not Mr Patten's own personal ambitions, not Britain, and not China. It was a no-win result all round.

The Basic Law is very clear that for a 'through-train' to work an agreement on what it should involve had to be reached between China and Britain. It's not a question of whether Mr Patten's proposals were or were not in breach of the Basic Law.

In any case, the final interpretation of the Basic Law does not rest in Hong Kong or in Westminster, but in Beijing. Even if there are a million interpretations, there's only one interpretation that's going to count. And that's only right because Hong Kong is Chinese territory. I grasped that simple point soon after the signing of the Joint Declaration; but some of us have still not faced up to that reality.

As far as the Chinese Government has been concerned, all Hong Kong's internal affairs will be autonomous, will be managed here, will be decided here. Interpretation of the laws of Hong Kong has been delegated to the Hong Kong courts and the Court of Final Appeal. In turn, what does Hong Kong being a part of China entail? It means not doing anything in Hong Kong that might have the effect of overturning the Government of China, or that might make any part of China—Hong Kong, Taiwan, or Guangdong—become independent. These things are not acceptable. This is the *quid pro quo* for Hong Kong's high degree of autonomy. This is something that people have to get used to; this is China.

There have been fears that China will not allow Hong Kong the autonomy that has been promised and that Beijing will put in place stooges to run Hong Kong who will reflect China's own wishes. I certainly hope they will put this place in the hands of the people they can trust, but also people who will command the support of the public. But the Chinese Government is not going to send its own cadres here. They will not want to waste anyone expert in public administration in Hong Kong. China is a big country and its needs are great. They don't want to send PRC cadres to Hong Kong to administer a different system for which they are not even trained.

I think the situation in Hong Kong is going to be a lot better than in the past. The SAR Government will be very different from a colonial government: for one thing the SAR Government will have a lot more independence from its sovereign.

Some people have suggested that the business community will have a pre-emptive say in running the SAR Government as opposed to grass-roots interests. Whilst Hong Kong will still be a commercial place, a place for business, for it to prosper all sections of the community will have to be taken care of. I certainly envisage that in the future more people from the grass-roots will be elected to the Legislative Council. They will be balanced by appointments to the Executive Council and by the indirect, functional constituency elections. People in Hong Kong have to remember that although the Territory is part of China, their political activities should be limited to the Hong Kong SAR, and they will have to comply with the law here. The laws will be pretty liberal and will allow demonstrations and all kinds of political activities. There will be a lot of freedom.

I don't believe that the future relationship between the civil service and a fully elected Legislative Council will be difficult. It's important not to mix up the role of Legislative Council members and civil servants. At present it is confused because many Government policies are in fact being formulated by legislators. The pre-1997 rules were entirely decided by the Governor, but Article 73 of the Basic Law clearly provides that the Legislative Council will have no role in formulating government policies in the future. The role and duty of the Legislative Council will be to examine, to criticize, and to check Government policies, but not to formulate or execute them.

I believe that after 1997 the Legislative Council will in fact have greater powers than it has now. On the face of it legislators have had an enhanced role under British rule, but, in effect, they have had no real power because any authority is merely delegated to them by the largesse of the Governor who has been able to take away that role at any time. After 1997 their powers will be defined and constitutionalized. There is not even a theoretical possibility that, in the future, the Chief

Executive could say, 'Look here. I've had enough of this. You can't do this anymore.' I think that after 1997 real democracy will begin in Hong Kong. And it will be democracy Chinese-style because Hong Kong is not a Western city, but a Special Administrative Region of China.

My vision for Hong Kong is that we will grow better and better. People will realize that they are not second-class nationals. That is one big thing to look forward to when we return to Chinese sovereignty.

The 'one country, two systems' arrangement enshrined in the Joint Declaration and the Basic Law is a sound model which has been used before elsewhere. It's an arrangement whereby, for protection purposes, you keep the one country, but for economic and perhaps cultural and other matters, you are going to have a little bit more room to develop and to grow separately.

Let me give you an example of where this system has worked elsewhere. Britain is one country, but at the same time the system in Scotland is different in many ways. There are different legal systems, a different church, and a different education system. Banking and financial systems are different as well. People are comfortable with these arrangements which have worked well for nearly four hundred years.

The 'one country, two systems' concept ensures that we don't all have to develop at the same pace. Its a sensible, civilized way of having the protection of the Government without actually having to comply with the mainstream. In China there are many aspects, different layers of society in different areas. 'One country, two systems' overcomes the dangers of separation, and provides stability for the whole. The common man, who doesn't really want too much involvement with politics, can get on with his life.

I don't accept that Chinese officials have been saying things which might shake investor confidence in Hong

Kong either before or after 1997. They might have been saying things which people in the West might not have wanted to hear, but business people have always known where their money can be made. I think they are betting that Hong Kong will continue to have a level playing field, and the maintenance of law and order. They calculate the risk factor and the advantage, and they will follow the money.

I guarantee that, no matter what anybody says, there will be a massive boost of confidence after 1997. Nothing untoward is going to rain from the heavens as long as the key essentials which have made Hong Kong successful remain: a sound economic system, and law and order. That is what I want to strive for in Hong Kong.

Christopher Patten

The Last Governor

Chris Patten's appointment as Hong Kong's twenty-eighth and last British Governor signalled a change in British policy towards Hong Kong. Unlike his recent predecessors, who were drawn from the Colonial and Diplomatic Services, he was a leading British politician who was appointed Governor shortly after losing his parliamentary seat in the 1992 General Election.

Chris Patten brought to his new role considerable political experience, and a close personal friendship with and access to the British Prime Minister, John Major. However, he had little direct knowledge of the dynamics of Hong Kong society or of Chinese sensitivities to the transfer of sovereignty in 1997.

Chris Patten's tenure as Governor has been controversial, and his policies have polarized the community. His advocates have maintained that he ended the British policy of accepting the blame for implementing before 1997 policies which China wanted in place after the handover. They argued that Patten stripped away the camouflage, and refused to be drawn into covering up Beijing's attempts to reinterpret the Joint Declaration.

His detractors have affirmed that Chris Patten's lack of knowledge of China, and insensitivity to Beijing's view ended the period of cooperation between Britain and China over Hong Kong, jeopardizing the future stability of the Territory.

What Chris Patten did do was to stick rigidly to the terms of the Joint Declaration. He refused to be knocked off course in implementing policies which he viewed to be consistent with the Sino-British accord. No more clearly was this demonstrated than in his political reform package. But what incurred Beijing's wrath was the way he exploited grey areas in the Basic Law to widen the democratic base.

Chris Patten has argued that his 'modest reforms' met an increasing demand by a better educated and more prosperous community for greater involvement in the policies which governed their lives. He refused to compromise with China on any proposals which were viewed as an attempt by Beijing to rig the elections and dilute the representation of democrats. China has maintained that the reforms breached all previous agreements with Britain, including the Joint Declaration.

The question has been: how much public support has Chris Patten enjoyed? The verbal backlash from Beijing to his policies was more virulent than he had anticipated, but the Governor vowed on his arrival to be 'no braver' than the community wanted him to be. He has therefore tried to stay in step with local opinion. He was unable to sustain the support of the business community and, as he was seen to be speaking out of turn against China, opinion polls saw his support slowly waning. For a British Governor, he has, however, enjoyed an unusually high popularity rate among Hong Kong Chinese people.

Despite firm denials, Chris Patten has found it difficult to escape from doubts that he has been more concerned with his own honourable withdrawal. But, whatever his critics say, he has persuaded Britain to put at risk its wider relationship with China and to provide Hong Kong with a modicum of democracy.

SHORTLY AFTER I arrived in Hong Kong, I went for a meal at a well-known restaurant in Sai Kung in the New Territories. I'd gone with my family, and, after getting our table, we wandered around to the front of the restaurant to choose the fish we would eat. A great crowd built up around us and people were pushing their children forward. One little girl came up to me, and I started chatting with her father who was standing behind. 'Where does your daughter go to school?' I asked, fully expecting him to reply that it was one of the local schools. He replied, 'Wycombe Abbey'. So much for the poor Sai Kung fishermen!

I didn't have the feeling when I arrived that I was viewed as an 'oppressive colonial tyrant'. I have, in fact, been overwhelmed by the friendliness of Hong Kong people. I don't just mean out on formal district visits, which I do every week, but going shopping, going to the cinema, driving around in a car. I could literally count on the fingers of one hand the number of times I've had anything but a cheerful, thumbs up, enthusiastic reception. Now I have to tell you that was not entirely my experience of British politics during the previous thirteen years!

My appointment as Governor of Hong Kong in 1992 affected me at a number of levels. Clearly the disruption to my life, and to my family's life, was a concern. At a practical and political level, I was excited and a little daunted by the size of the challenge, particularly since many people took the view that the job was inherently impossible. Others suggested that the choices one would have to make would be pretty bleak. But I knew it was going to be a job where there would be plenty of scope for taking decisions and for trying to move things along. That's the thing which has always most attracted me about politics. I hadn't been bored before, and I haven't been bored in Hong Kong.

At a historic level I was fascinated by the episode of history in which I was to take part. I don't say, deliberately, over which I was to preside, because I think that would be extraordinarily presumptuous. But this is the end of an empire, or will be so regarded by international opinion and, I guess, by historians. It's an end, different in nature from other places. Elsewhere we have a settled way of doing these things: we transfer sovereignty to the people of the dependent territory itself, in a way which, I think, benignly and good-naturedly attempts to transfer some of our own value system. In the case of Hong Kong that has neither been on offer, nor been an option, but it doesn't make the job any less difficult, indeed rather the reverse. It makes it a bigger challenge, and one is trying to rise to that challenge in an extraordinary city which stands at the frontier between East and West, between the new economy and the older successful economies, and between, in a literal sense, Leninism and freedom.

My remit was to give Hong Kong the best chance of surviving as that free society as described in the Joint Declaration. I've always believed that the closer we came to achieving that objective, the more honourable the exit would be. It doesn't seem to me unreasonable to have that as one's aim.

What I did, which perhaps gave me a different view on these matters from others, was to re-read the Joint Declaration. It was the first piece of briefing I undertook. I also read what accompanied the Joint Declaration—the debates in the Houses of Parliament when it was signed, and the promises made to people at the time. I assumed, and still assume, that we at no time resiled from all that. With the agreement of ministers, and having taken soundings in Hong Kong, I then set my course.

I felt it was important when I arrived that I set out very clearly what my agenda was for the final five-year period. It's of passing interest, but when I was in Singapore and had two meetings with Lee Kwan Yew [Singapore's Senior Minister], he made the point very strongly that it was important for me to lay out my stall when I arrived, and tell people exactly what I intended to achieve in five years. At least in style, if not in substance, there was that endorsement, replete with Asian values.

The last five years of the transition were destined to be an extremely tricky period. As I set about detailing the course I would take, however, I was surprised to find on my arrival that there were so many areas in which the 'doctrine of unripe times' seemed to have been pursued. The argument that it is not quite the right moment to take on this or that issue is always seductive. But it did mean that there were an awful lot of thorny issues which needed to be grasped, which hadn't been.

A key issue was localization in the civil service. I'm not sure whether it was intended before that we should localize as rapidly as we did; I'm not sure whether it was intended that the next Chief Secretary and the next Financial Secretary should be local: but it seemed to me inconceivable that however good and public spirited the expatriate individuals were, however deeply they might have sunk their roots into the community, it would be inconceivable not to move very rapidly indeed towards localizing the senior positions. I now run a Chinese administration. With one exception, every senior colleague of mine is Chinese. We could perhaps have managed the localization exercise with fewer bruises, with fewer legitimately damaged aspirations and expectations, if it had been implemented over a slightly longer period, at a rather gentler trot.

On another issue, it would have been marvellous if the question of the electoral arrangements had been resolved by the time I became Governor, but it wasn't. I'm certain that one day a lot of people will write the history of 1984 to 1997, and they will dwell, I'm sure long and lovingly, on issues such as the OMELCO Consensus in 1989. I've occasionally had to pinch myself when I've read what people used to say in '87, '88, '89, and so on, about elections in Hong Kong, and what the same people are saying in the 1990s.

Some of those issues hadn't been tackled, and I don't say that critically: there were a lot of other issues that had to be tackled. I guess I've never had to deal with events as momentous to the community as my four predecessors: I've never had to deal with anything to touch the turbulence of the Cultural Revolution riots; I've never had to deal with anything like the police protests against the ICAC; like the early discussions about the post-1997 future of Hong Kong; like the negotiations on the Joint Declaration; like the impact on Hong Kong of Tiananmen. All I've had to deal with is the New China News Agency being vulgar.

However, there were a lot of difficult issues crowding in, as it were, at the end of our innings, and I am relieved that the final five years of the transition haven't been more tricky. We could have spent three or four years in a long-running, snarling fight with pro-democracy politicians. We could have found ourselves dealing with criticisms of moral turpitude in the media in Britain and the rest of the world. This has not happened. I'm pleased that Hong Kong is still manifestly governable, and manifestly well governed.

Against this background, there were a number of things about which I felt very strongly when I arrived.

I felt I should try to work with the grain of what was happening in Hong Kong and what is happening in Taiwan, in Korea, and what has started to happen in Thailand. A better-educated, better-off, better-travelled public, with professionals, public servants, and the middle class, in particular, developing a taste for being involved in determining their own destiny and their own future. I thought that whether one was talking about one's own accountability, speaking at public meetings, answering questions from the Legislative Council, or talking about electoral arrangements, that was a very important ingredient. It would ensure that Hong Kong, and the importance of Hong Kong, would continue to be matters which were observed around the world.

A key consideration for me was that the Joint Declaration had to be implemented in the way it was written, rather than in ways in which it might be re-interpreted. There is sometimes a tendency to think that you can draft your way around points of difference, points of substance, points of principle. I don't think you can at all. Do you mean elections, people going into the polling station and casting ballots in a fair way, or do you mean fixing things? Although the Basic Law tried to reflect the spirit of the Joint Declaration, it's a Chinese document, and it's for them to deal with any questions when there may be differences between one and the other. If you take the issue of freedom of speech, which has come up frequently, the Basic Law in Article 27 is absolutely clear and incorporates what the Joint Declaration says on the same subject. The mystery begins when Chinese officials start to say what they think that means.

There was another point, which only became really clear during the course of my first couple of months when I was considering my policy address. It did seem to me that Hong Kong had a first-world economy, but pretty third-world social and community services. Without in any way wrecking our economy or introducing (as though it would be high on my agenda) 'socialism', I sensed that Hong Kong did have to improve the provision for those in need, because otherwise the tensions between the 'haves' and 'have-nots' would create, themselves, problems of political and social balance. I think we have demonstrated that in a society with an economy as successful as Hong Kong's we are able to run a socially responsible public policy without breaking the bank.

I do not believe, despite remarks which have been made to the contrary, that it would have been easier to take forward electoral and other changes if I'd been more aware of Chinese sensitivities: the argument is not really about style, or whether you understand the full subtleties of the minds of Communist cadres in Beijing. The issue is whether anyone, in dealing with China, ever has a bottom line.

There is a sort of political correctness which enters into the argument here, with many people thinking it's somehow wrong to have a principled position if you're dealing with China. I'm afraid I simply don't believe that. I would have been a lunatic not to have taken the advice of the Foreign Office sinologists who were in Hong Kong when I arrived, and the views of the sinologists in London. I would have been crazy not to have listened to senior members of the administration in forming my views. Above all I would have been criminal not to have talked to and taken the advice of political groups in Hong Kong.

What I also had my eye on was what the real options were. As I've said a thousand times, the choice wasn't between having an argument with China or having a quiet life. If we hadn't been involved unfortunately in arguments with China, we would have been involved in an argument with every representative of decency in Hong Kong, plus international opinion, plus, doubtless, the opposition parties at Westminster.

What is quite extraordinary is the way that 'convergence' has come to be defined as us doing before 1997 whatever China thought was appropriate after 1997, rather than convergence being the Chinese fitting into the way Hong Kong had developed over the years before 1997. But we declined to oblige, and refused to connive at arrangements which would have made a mockery of the Bill of Rights, which would have fixed the elections, and so on.

So I don't think the difference between me and some of my critics is that they have a more sinuous, sophisticated view of how to deal with a wily negotiator on the other side of the table. I think the difference is whether you think that Britain's responsibility is to stand up to what it promised Hong Kong, albeit at the cost of the occasional row.

If anybody could ever say that what we were trying to do was clearly out of line with local political opinion, we'd be in some difficulty. But that has never been a credibly argued case. I think we have managed, to an extraordinary degree, to find that point of balance in the community.

The problem the Government has, in this particular phase of our constitutional development, is that there is no governing party in the Legislative Council. Those who used to be, as it were, the establishment, and who have been rendered by democratic development something less than that, deeply resent the Governor and Government whom they blame for the change in their fortunes. At the same time, those who are democrats and who have thrived with 60 or 70 per cent of public support, don't want to be seen as the stooges of the outgoing colonial power merely because they happen to share our core values. I've always been in the position in which I've gone further than some would have wanted, and less far than others believe is essential. And that's not necessarily very credible or very comfortable. It may be one of the reasons why, as I said earlier, there were those who said the Governor's job is inherently impossible! But I think one has to carry on and try to find a consensus in the community and continue trying to reflect it.

One of the problems we've faced, and I don't say this critically, is that many Chinese officials find it difficult to comprehend the nature of a free society and the relationship between, if you like, our software and our hardware—the relationship between the rule of law and the values of an open society on the one hand, and our economic success on the other. Nor, are they helped to understand by some of those who advise them from Hong Kong. Does it help them to comprehend those relationships if there are people from Hong Kong telling them 'Don't worry about any of that: a lot of political guff. So long as Hong Kong can go on making money, everything will be all right!' I think that is unfair to China, but it's also unfair to Hong Kong. After all, the Joint Declaration is, in a sense, a testimony to what you can achieve when you don't do that. Chinese officials had wanted the treaty with Britain to be a minimalist document, they wanted to say as little as possible. But leaders of the community in Hong Kong stamped their feet and said, 'No you have to spell out exactly what it is that makes Hong Kong tick, and exactly what it is that is going to be maintained.' Hence the Joint Declaration comes out as a textbook description of a free society—so it can be done.

Something which has concerned me is the extent to which some people believe they can apply double standards. Those who say one thing to your face, and something completely different as soon as you are out of earshot. I think that Hong Kong has been let down by some of those who made their fortunes here and should have been, whatever they thought of me, a little more assertive in standing up for the things which have helped to create a society in which they became so prosperous: the rule of law and Hong Kong running its own affairs, to take two rather obvious examples. But they have, at least in most cases, managed to ensure that, if things go wrong, they have a free society to which to retreat.

What I don't think those people understand is that most of those who invest in Hong Kong from outside, trade with Hong Kong from outside, get their views of what's happening in our city from their own newspapers: most of those places are free societies. The kaleidoscope of impressions they get are sometimes negative and sometimes positive. You can't say that all the negative impressions are exaggerations that bear no relation to reality. In the lead-up to 1997 there have been too many negative impressions created. Are you more credible in addressing those worries, if you sound as though you didn't know they existed, or if you simply dismissed them out of hand. I think it is more credible if you admit there are challenges and problems, but then set out why, on balance, you come down on the side of optimism, which is what my position is. Would I be a convincing advocate of Hong Kong's interests in America, if I said when there, as some people do, 'Don't worry, nobody in Hong Kong is worried about human rights. Don't worry, nobody in Hong Kong is remotely concerned about the rule of law or the onset of corruption.' People abroad would simply think it was about as useful as talking to a 'speak your weight' machine.

What I consistently say is that we do have problems in those areas of the Joint Declaration, in those areas of our life, which scratch away at Chinese political sensitivities, and there is no point in pretending that life is other than that. But there is an economic momentum in Hong Kong, which is irreversible, at least for the foreseeable future. I believe there is sufficient commitment to Hong Kong's institutions—to civil society, professions, churches, non-governmental organizations, the civil service, independent judiciary, an accountable government—there is sufficient attachment to those things for them to survive.

Most of the things that have been said about Hong Kong, most of the things written about Hong Kong (and that includes things that are said and written by some Chinese officials) seem to be based on the assumption that nobody's here! I mean this extraordinary place has been made by six million people, the majority of them refugees. They've coped with all sorts of astonishing adversity in the last thirty or forty years, and I think they are going to manage the next stage in our history pretty competently. Hong Kong values represent the values of the future in Asia, as everywhere else.

   Hong Kong is a more open, free, and boisterous society than it was, even when I first came here, and I think it is helpful to Hong Kong to have the continuing manifestations of freedom, not for people to feel suppressed, that they can't speak out. It's taken for granted now that the Government has to explain itself when there is a problem, and that the Government's actions are going to be subjected to closer scrutiny. There are all sorts of things which happened in the past in a more closed society which I would have found great difficulty in defending. But that's all behind us, it's not behind us as part of some outrageous British plot, it's behind us because Hong Kong has been growing up, and will go on growing up. This is a great city, it's a city in its prime, and it's not going to be snuffed out.